Chilton's
HARLEY-DAVIDSON
Repair and Tune-up Guide

OCee Ritch

ILLUSTRATED

CHILTON BOOK COMPANY

Philadelphia   New York   London

Copyright © 1968 by OCee Ritch. Published in Philadelphia by Chilton Book Company, and in Ontario, Canada, by Thomas Nelson & Sons, Ltd. All rights reserved. Manufactured in the United States of America.

ISBN 0-8019-5246-8

Library of Congress Catalog Card No. 68-13313

Second Printing, April 1970
Third Printing, January 1971
Fourth Printing, May 1971

Contents

1. Engine Troubleshooting

Starting procedures 1
Engine won't start 1
Engine is hard to start—
 or runs erratically 4
Engine dies when throttle is opened 4
Misfires on acceleration 4
Misfires under load 5
Misfires at high RPM 6
Poor low speed performance 7
Poor high speed performance 7
Poor general performance 8
Overheating 8
Vibration 9
Noises 9

2. The Top End

Glide models 10
Sportster models 16

3. The Bottom End

Glide models 19
Sportster models 31

4. Clutch and Transmission

Clutch 39
Transmission 46
Starter assembly 55

5. Electrical Systems

Generator 59
Alternator 61

Voltage regulator 61
Battery 65
Starter 65
Disassembly and reassembly 71

6. Carburetion

Model M 81
Model HD 85
HD carburetor troubleshooting 87
Model DC 89

7. Frame and Running Gear

Wheels and tires 92
Front brake adjustment 95
Rear brake adjustment 96
Brake shoe replacement 97
Front forks 99

8. Maintenance and Tuning

Engine lubrication 105
Chain adjustment 112
Front chain oiling 114
Rear chain oiling 115
Battery 116
Tuning 116
Ignition timing 117
Magneto 119
Spark plugs 121
Carburetor adjustments 121
Setting valve lash 123

9. Specifications

Many illustrations courtesy Harley-Davidson.

CHAPTER 1

Engine Troubleshooting

The most common complaint or trouble encountered by the motorcyclist is that the machine will not start. The reason can be extremely simple or it can be more complicated, but the basic procedure for finding *what* the cause of non-starting is and *how* it can be corrected should be followed in order to save time and to cover all the possibilities. By following an outline, the troubleshooter can also mentally or visually eliminate some steps and begin his trouble search at any point in the sequence, knowing that he will not have to back-track.

Non-starting is extremely frustrating because it is generally accompanied by hard work. Pumping a kick-start lever on a big-displacement bike adds to the rider's indignation, and the most common reaction is to guess hurriedly at the cause of malfunction—which usually leads to more and unnecessary work. The first rule is to go stcp-by-step and methodically eliminate possible causes.

The Four-Stroke Engine

STARTING PROCEDURES

Engine cold

① Engage neutral between first and second gear.
② Turn the fuel tap on.
③ Operate the clutch lever and depress the kick-starter two or three times to separate the clutch plates.
④ In cold weather it may be necessary to close the choke.
⑤ Partly retard the ignition by turning the control lever (if fitted) away from the closed position (clockwise).
⑥ Flood the carburetor by depressing the tickler on the float bowl until the base of the carburetor is just wet. Do not continue until fuel streams out, for this will cause difficult starting.
⑦ Turn the engine over until compression can be felt on one cylinder. Reposition the kick-starter pedal to almost the horizontal position by freeing the clutch.
⑧ On the models so equipped, switch the ignition key to the "IGN" position.
⑨ Open the twist-grip about ⅛ turn and then depress the kick-starter pedal smartly, or operate the electric starter.
⑩ When the engine starts, the choke lever can be fully opened as it warms up. Do this as soon as possible; otherwise, the mixture strength may be too rich and the oil on the cylinder walls will be washed off.
⑪ Do not allow the engine to idle when cold. The throttle should be adjusted to a fast tickover in order to warm the oil rapidly. This precaution will reduce cylinder wear.

THE ENGINE WON'T START

Assuming that repeated attempts to start the engine resulted in nothing but sweat on your brow, it is time to look for malfunctions. Check the choke and throttle controls first.

Is the ignition really on? Twiddle the switch a bit. Be sure the indicator lights are on or try the horn to see if electrical current is present somewhere in the system.

If there is obviously a supply of electricity: recheck the fuel supply. If there is a smell of raw gas or visual evidence of flooding, open the throttle wide and kick the starter pedal vigorously a few times.

If indicator lights or other accessories do not function: suspect bad connections or bad battery. Check all electrical connections for cleanliness and tightness, particularly the battery ground. This is highly critical.

On any model with an ammeter, a loose connection can cause mysterious malfunctions.

If fuse and connections seem in order, check the battery. The following advice will scandalize battery makers, and it is admittedly not good practice, but you can satisfy yourself that there is juice or not by striking a quick arc across the battery terminals with a piece of wire or the handles of a pair of pliers. Do this very briefly —just enough to get a flash.

If the battery is strong and a good spark results, examine the terminals, removing, cleaning and replacing if in doubt as to their ability to pass electricity.

If the battery responds weakly or not at all to the direct-short technique, either have it charged or use a jumper cable to a good battery.

Caution: If you have the battery charged, read the MAINTENANCE CHAPTER in this

Engine Troubleshooting

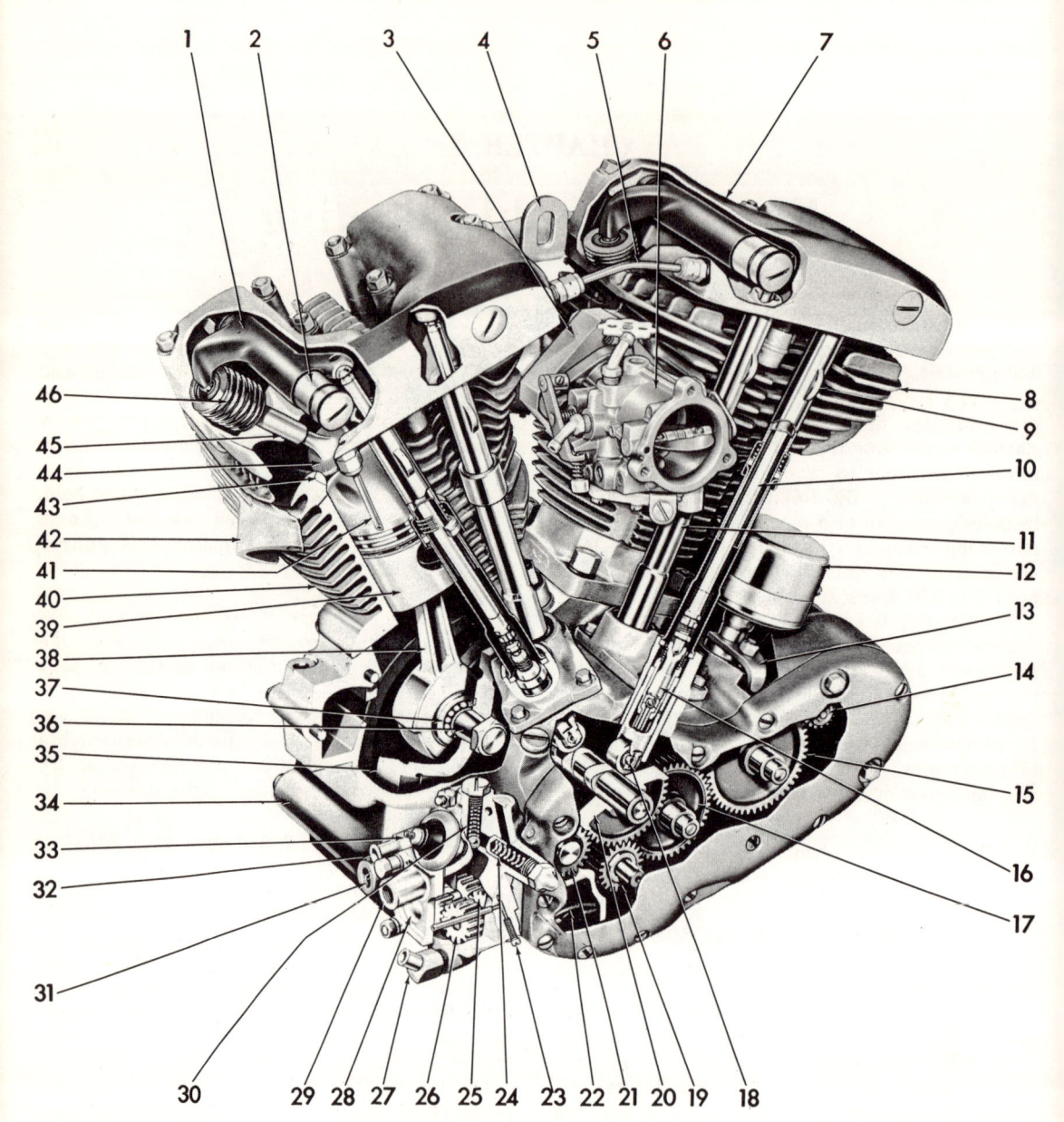

Engine cutaway (1967 Glide model shown).

1. Rocker arm
2. Rocker arm shaft
3. Carburetor insulator
4. Engine mounting bracket
5. Oil line
6. Carburetor
7. Rocker arm cover
8. Cylinder head
9. Push rod cover keeper
10. Push rod
11. Push rod cover
12. Circuit breaker (timer)
13. Clamp
14. Generator drive gear
15. Idler gear
16. Hydraulic lifter
17. Intermediate gear
18. Tappet and roller assembly
19. Pinion gear
20. Cam gear
21. Breather gear
22. Breather screen
23. Chain oiler screw
24. By-pass valve
25. Oil feed pump drive gears
26. Oil scavenger drive gears
27. Oil feed nipple
28. Oil pump cover
29. Oil return nipple
30. Check valve
31. Breather outlet
32. Chain oil return
33. Oil pressure switch
34. Crankcase
35. Flywheel
36. Crankpin
37. Connecting rod roller bearing
38. Connecting rod
39. Piston
40. Cylinder
41. Overhead oil line
42. Exhaust port
43. Exhaust valve seat
44. Exhaust valve
45. Exhaust valve guide
46. Valve spring

The Engine Won't Start

book before rushing down to the nearest service station.

If after taking this precaution the engine still won't catch, it is time to check for a spark at the plugs.

Remove a plug and examine the tip. If it is wet or clogged with carbon deposits, this can be the problem. Replace it with the spare you always carry in the toolkit. Second choice is to clean it.

If the plug appears to be good, leave it connected and place it on the head, making sure it is grounded; then kick the starter briskly. A fat, blue spark should leap between the electrodes. If the spark is a bit weak, check the gap against specifications, since it may be too wide.

Here is a trick which will often get the machine running until you can get new plugs: close the gap right up to .010" or so and re-install. A weak plug may be breaking down under pressure in the cylinder and the smaller gap will permit it to function temporarily.

If you don't have a feeler gauge, an ordinary paper matchbook cover is just under .010" thick. Make the electrode gap a slip fit for a matchbook cover, and it will be close enough to work.

If there is no spark at the electrodes and the high-tension lead (plug wire) is firmly connected at each end, you've got ignition troubles. Now, this may be a bad coil or other problems which are better covered in the ELECTRICAL SYSTEMS section of this book. Just to satisfy yourself whether the system is functioning or not, grasp the plug in one hand and push the starter lever down gently. Don't jump on it or you will get an unpleasant shock. You'll feel a tingle if the ignition system is developing output. If you get no indication of electrical energy, you've isolated the problem.

If the spark plug is good and you get a blue spark, there is a bare possibility that the timing is so far off the bike won't start. But, chances are the trouble is somewhere in the fuel system. Check the timing as a precaution, then turn the fuel tap off and remove the fuel line from the tank. Then, holding a rag or a container under the opening, turn the tap back on and observe the fuel flow, if any. You can also observe whether you really have gas in the tank or some other liquid, such as water. Also, if the bike has been in storage for some time, the gas can have decomposed to such an extent that it won't burn. The highly volatile elements that make for quick starting in a fuel blend vaporize readily. This makes old gas bad gas. It generally has a strong, pungent odor as opposed to the keen, light smell of fresh fuel.

Water, of course, balls up in little droplets on the rag, while the gas soaks right through. Water also sinks to the bottom in a container. How does water get into fuel? Condensation can account for some. Who knows how the large quantities we sometimes find can be accounted for?

If fuel flows freely, or if it is obviously dirty, rusty or full of sediment, there will be trouble farther along the line at the carburetor. You may have to clean the jets. See CARBURETION chapter.

At this point, if there is fuel at the carburetor and the plug is good and not wet, try heavy choking. Make sure the choke is really working.

You have proven that there is spark at the plug and fuel at the carburetor. So, the only reason the engine won't fire must be mechanical.

Before we go farther, and before you put the plug back in the hole, take a pencil, pen or other long, slender object and push it in the spark plug opening until it rests on the piston. Then push the kick-start lever down slowly and observe the movement of the pencil. It should move up and down. If not, the clutch is slipping and all of your kicking is for nothing.

With the plug removed, it is an opportune time to take a compression check. (If you don't have a compression gauge, you are at a point where a visit to your friendly motorcycle shop is required.)

① Remove the spark plug from the second cylinder, to prevent accidental runaway at full power.

② Open throttle *fully* against the stop.

③ Depress starter vigorously three or four times while holding compression gauge firmly in the plug bore.

If compression is low, suspect a bent or burned valve or poor valve seating. If it is nil, or extremely low, a holed piston is probably the cause of your trouble. "Low" is a relative term, to be sure, but the average four-stroke engine should operate after a fashion on 80 psi compression.

For verification, remove the rocker box cover or gain access to the valve clearance adjusting position as required, and check the clearance. A very loose valve is probably bent; a very tight valve is probably burned.

Before you panic, adjust the valves to proper clearances and try to get the engine to run. Poor adjustment *can* prevent an engine from starting. (See MAINTENANCE AND TUNING chapter.) If compression is quite low and you want to be sure that things are as bad as they seem before you pull the cylinder, you can use a small bayonet bulb, such as those fitted as instrument or indicator lights, to help out. Take the bulb, solder a wire to the tip, another to the brass base and connect the two wires to a battery. This light is small enough to slip through the spark plug hole to illuminate the interior of the cylinder—something no other light will do.

If you want to take a closer look at the piston,

Engine Troubleshooting

turn the engine over by putting the transmission in top gear and rotating the rear wheel. Don't kick it over with the starter lever.

All of this can bring you to one of two conclusions:

1. Somewhere along the line electrical or ignition problems beyond the scope of this chapter are present.
2. The engine is generally in bad shape.

THE ENGINE IS HARD TO START— OR RUNS ERRATICALLY

We assume that the bike is in normally good operating condition and that:

1. It either becomes hard to start and runs erratically suddenly, or,
2. The condition has been getting progressively worse for some time.

In either case,

① Check the electrical system—paying particular attention to the battery, if it is a part of the system. All connections, it must be stressed, have to be clean and tight. It is easy to leave the ignition or lights on, and the battery is quickly discharged to a low state.

② Check the spark plugs for type and condition. Perhaps the wrong heat range is being used, or another engine condition can be diagnosed by examining a plug. See MAINTENANCE AND TUNING chapter for details on plug type and analysis.

③ Check the carburetor idle mixture screw. This can often become maladjusted.

④ Check ignition timing and correct if wrong. This cause of hard starting and erratic running is gradual in its onset, rather than sudden, because it is due to the wear of the cam fiber which causes a variation in point gap. So, if sudden hard starting is the case, a more likely suspect is the capacitor. Replace it if points are burned and discolored, which is a good sign of a faulty condenser.

⑤ This brings us to bad points: worn, dirty, pitted or oily. Dress them or replace (preferable) with a new set. If the breaker point area is oily, somewhere there is a bad oil seal in the drive. Replace it. Clean the slip ring on the magneto, if fitted.

⑥ If the engine kicks back on starting, chances are the automatic advance mechanism in the distributor is not working properly.

⑦ Check the air filter. Remove and clean it. If it is ancient and excessively dirty, get a new one.

⑧ If the machine has been stored and has been put into use without proper attention to preparation, the carburetor idle jet can be clogged with varnish or gum residue. The main jet can also be plugged with this substance. Acetone is a good solvent, or regular carburetor cleaner such as that used in motorcycle shops can be used.

ENGINE DIES WHEN THROTTLE IS OPENED

This condition appears to cause some concern to beginning riders, and, while it can be due to engine problems, the most common reason for such performance is that the throttle is opened too widely too suddenly.

But, assuming that you are not being overly quick with the twist-grip, this sort of cut-out or slump of the engine can be attributed almost wholly to carburetion.

1. Make sure that the choke lever is actually operating and opens the choke fully when it is supposed to.
2. Is the idling speed set high enough to accommodate a sudden increase in venturi area? If you have the engine ticking over at 300 rpm, it just can't induce enough pressure drop at the jet to suck up enough fuel.
3. How about the idle jet? Is it clogged?
4. The whole carburetion system can be too rich.
5. This isn't likely, but it can happen: an air leak at the carburetor flange which has been compensated for by jetting and lets the engine run, but reduces the vacuum. Squirt gas from an oil can around the attaching point and note whether the engine speeds up. This is a kind of last-resort suspect for this condition, but it is not uncommon in event of the following:

MISFIRES ON ACCELERATION

A. From low speed

If the engine is dropping shots under acceleration, just off the line, but running satisfactorily otherwise, the odds are that carburetion is the villain.

The first thing to examine is the idle mixture.

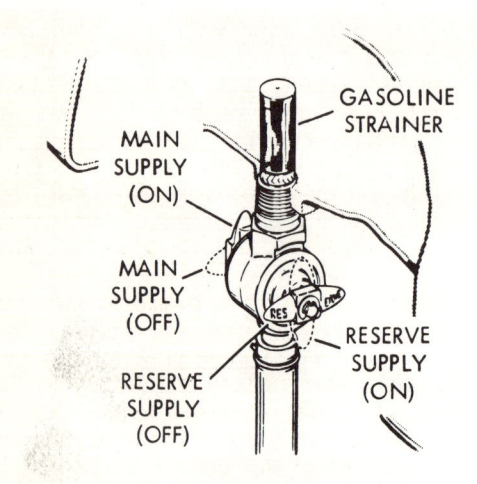

Diaphragm type fuel supply valve and strainer, Glide and Sportster models.

The classic symptom of too-rich low speed mixture is misfiring on application of throttle. This is accompanied by a lumpy idle. Be sure the enriching for low speed is not overdone. Check the exhaust for black smoke, etc.

Don't overlook the possibility of water in the carburetor float bowl which is sucked up at the start before the fuel can be replaced.

A clogged air cleaner can cause misfiring, but it will generally also show up as poor performance throughout the range, too.

A bad spark plug, where the ceramic portion is dirty and causing flash-over, can also be responsible for this occurrence. Where high voltage is being fed into a system, it chooses the easiest way to go, and a dirty plug is an open invitation to a direct-to-ground short.

B. At a given rpm in any gear

If the misfiring occurs at a given rpm, no matter what gear you are using and no matter what the throttle opening, suspect the automatic spark advance mechanism. This can be going out of phase at certain rpm. Over-richness can also be causing "eight cycling."

C. At a given throttle opening, regardless of rpm

If the dropping occurs at a certain point in the throttle sector regardless of the revolutions being turned by the engine, this is poor carburetor tuning.

D. At no consistent throttle opening or rpm

Inconsistent misfiring is ordinarily due to malfunctioning in the electrical system. Go over the bike from stem to stern, sparing nothing from examination. Plugs, points, connections, high tension lead to the spark plug, capacitor, magneto, battery—the whole works can be individually or collectively responsible. The important point is to overlook nothing.

MISFIRES UNDER LOAD

This heading is meant to describe a condition something like this: you are riding along and approach a hill. You open the throttle, and as you mount the slope with the engine working at its best, it begins to drop a few beats. Gearing down or returning to level road clears up the misfiring.

First diagnosis of this condition is that the plug is breaking down from overheating. The wrong plug is being used, or the gap is wrong.

Too large a main jet, with insufficient pressure drop at wide throttle opening and relatively low speed, results in improper mixture. Other possibilities are noted under item #4 in CARBURETOR TROUBLESHOOTING, Chapter 6.

Poor fuel can play a big role in this sort of performance. Premium fuel, as recommended by

Checking Sportster fuel tap.

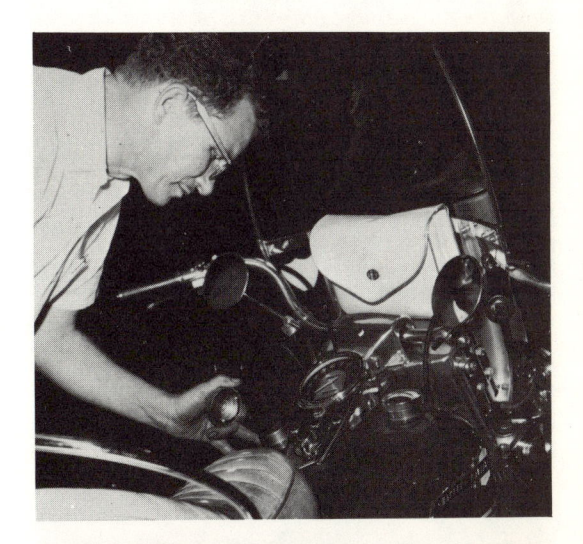

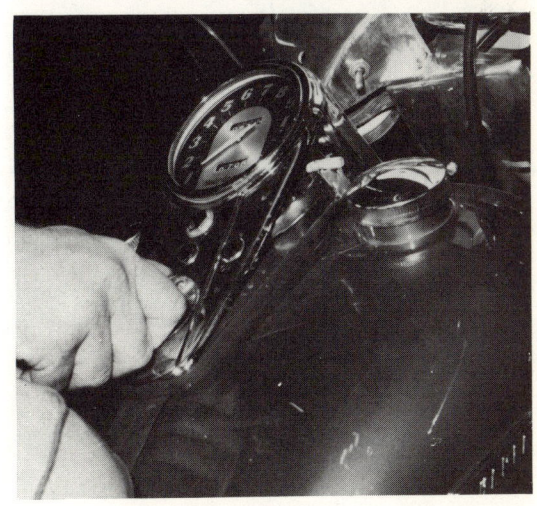

Make a visual inspection of fuel level.

Engine Troubleshooting

Sportster choke lever.

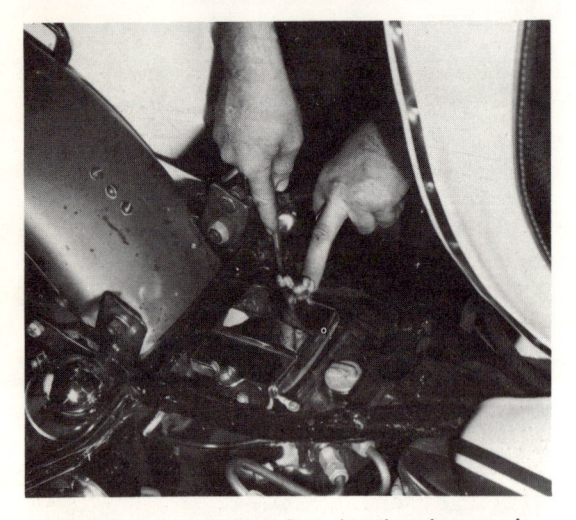

Check battery connections first when there is no spark.

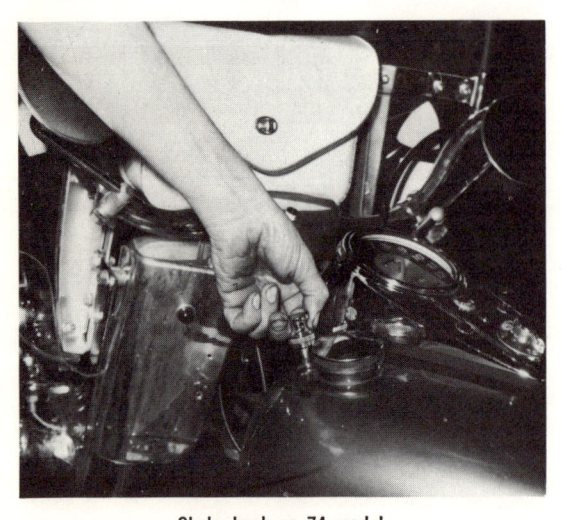

Choke knob on 74 model.

the manufacturer, should be used at all times. "Cheap" gas is poor economy.

Improper timing would be about the last item in line to be considered. Spark timing becomes more critical as the load increases.

MISFIRES AT HIGH RPM

Dropping at high revolutions is sometimes mystifying because so many facets of engine tuning are involved. Before going into them, it is first wise to establish that valve float is not responsible. Some riders twist their engines right up past the red line and never realize that the valves are crashing. The modern engine is so sturdy that it can take a certain amount without disintegrating, so these people never learn—until too late. At over-rev peaks, valves are hurled off their seats at such acceleration rates that the return springs cannot control them, and they stay open too long, then crash down after the cam has turned past the ramp. The prolonged opening period destroys critical valve timing and causes a dilution of the fuel charge and thus the misfiring.

If this isn't the cause, then you have a wide choice of other possible causes:

1. The high speed circuit, jet, needle, economizer valve, and other functions of the carburetor are responsible for mixture control at high speed, and should be looked into first. See carburetion chapter and adjust according to tuning information supplied in other parts of this book.

2. Improper float level is a common cause of high speed misfire. Set too low, the float does not permit sufficient fuel to accumulate in the bowl to serve the needs of the carburetor, or float needle valve and seat can be fouled up.

3. Spark plug—dirty, wrong heat range, improper gap, faulty. Any or all of these plug faults can be responsible. High pressure breakdown of a seemingly good plug can also be the trouble. Heat range is pretty critical in air-cooled engines. If the plug is too cold, it shorts out; if too hot, it welds. If the gap is too great, the cylinder pressure prevents the arc from forming across the expanse between the electrodes.

5. Bad capacitor—a poor capacitor can perform satisfactorily at low speeds yet fail to prevent point arcing at higher revolutions. Have it checked or substitute a new one if everything else is right.

6. Coil—same situation as with capacitor.

7. High tension leads may be leaking. Be sure the plug wire is not touching metal, which would invite a direct ground. Rev engine up and run your fingers along the plug wire. You'll feel a tingle if there is leakage.

8. An air leak in the exhaust system where the pipe joins the head will cause high speed

Poor High Speed Performance

dropping. This is also accompanied by unusual muffler noises.

9. Air leaks at the carburetor are another possibility. Follow recommendations at 5 (above) under ENGINE DIES WHEN THROTTLE IS OPENED.

10. Slightly burned or bent valve, or improper valve clearance. These two items can cause high speed misfire, but they would also make their presence felt in other ways.

11. Clogged or restricted exhaust should always be suspected if the bike is old or has had poor maintenance.

12. In case it has been overlooked somehow, check the choke. Be sure it isn't being put into operation.

POOR LOW SPEED PERFORMANCE

This symptom is presumed to be apparent as stumbling or lack of power at low revolutions which clears out in the upper range of the engine. This is not to be mistaken, of course, for the loading-up which occurs at prolonged idle and which disappears as soon as excess fuel and carbon are blown out, but rather a consistent lack of performance in the bottom half of the power curve.

Number one cause of trouble in this situation is improper carburetion: wrong idle adjustment, wrong needle setting, etc. Tuning is the answer.

Second, and not too far behind in frequency, is improper spark advance. Between these two, you'll find the trouble in most cases.

POOR HIGH SPEED PERFORMANCE

Complaints here are a lack of power at what should be the peak torque of the engine, reduced top speed and the need to shift down more frequently. Actually, in most cases, the rider just doesn't notice it, but there is a general lack of power throughout the range of the engine. It is only that it becomes more noticeable when more is asked of the engine. However, if it clearly is only the top end:

1. Again, wrong carburetion adjustment is the prime suspect.

2. Dirty, clogged or bad air cleaner. This condition can be borderline, permitting enough air flow to take care of low speed operation but causing an over-rich condition at full demand.

3. Ignition timing and cleanliness of ignition system play a big part in top end performance.

4. Spark plug and wiring. See MISFIRES AT HIGH RPM (above) for more details. The engine can drop off in power yet apparently be hitting on every power stroke.

5. How is the battery? Don't overlook this link in the system.

6. Weak valve springs. On an older cycle, this condition can prevail with this result, usually accompanied by some misfiring.

This coil wire is easy to loosen and can cause intermittent running problems.

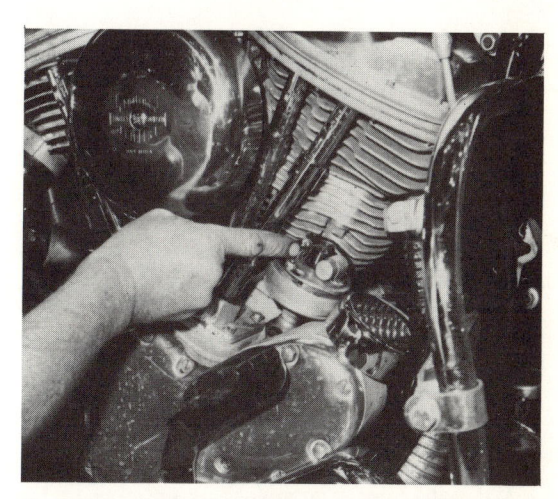

Check at the points by snapping open to determine if current is available.

Use a proper wrench on spark plugs to avoid damage.

7. Lack of compression. Poor mechanical condition with worn rings, valves in need of grinding and so on shows up first as lack of top end performance.

8. Is it a slipping clutch? Could be. See CLUTCH AND TRANSMISSION chapter.

9. Check tire pressure. Low tires cause increased rolling resistance.

10. Partially plugged tank vent.

POOR GENERAL PERFORMANCE

Under this heading, naturally, can be lumped any single cause or combination of causes conceivably connected with the engine . . . and for that matter, other portions of the bike. But let's run through the most common causes, in order of their frequency.

1. First suspicion should fall on the ignition timing. If it is off, performance is just hopeless.

2. Spark plug. Improper type, fouled, dirty, etc.

3. Poor carburetion. Symptoms of over-richness or too-lean mixture are easy to detect by examination of the plug and exhaust pipe.

4. Is the bike running free? Check the rear wheel as the machine sits on the stand. Does it turn over easily? Is the brake dragging? Are the wheel bearings bad? Is the chain too tight? Any of these items can slow the bike so much that the tendency is to suspect a poor-performing engine.

5. Slipping clutch. This should be an obvious condition even to a novice rider, but a surprising number of people don't notice it.

6. Improper valve adjustment, burnt or bent valves can reduce horsepower. Check these items out as directed under **THE ENGINE WON'T START** in this chapter.

7. Tired. Poor compression is the clue to the mechanically-ailing engine. Without good compression, you can't have good performance.

8. Is the sump loaded with oil, by any chance? Too much oil in the crankcase will slow an engine down considerably.

OVERHEATING

The air-cooled engine is designed to be cooled by a *moving* stream of air. This means that the machine must be moving. Your motor will sit there and bang away without complaint for several minutes, but it isn't a good idea to prolong the idling, or to operate while the bike is at a standstill. If this is the "overheating" complaint, all that's needed is a change of habit.

However, if the engine overheats under normal riding conditions—that is, begins to lose power, misfires or starts to seize up, then you must assume that there is a malfunction or a poor operating condition.

1. Too lean a mixture is the most common **reason** for overheating on the road.

2. Next most common reason is improper ignition timing. Insufficient advance is the problem.

3. Wrong heat range spark plug can also produce this condition.

4. Air leak between carburetor and head—resulting in an excessively lean mixture, and **most** noticeable under load. This may not be enough to cause misfiring, but that could be a clue.

5. Not free-running. See No. 4 under **POOR GENERAL PERFORMANCE**.

6. Low oil level. The air-cooled engine is also cooled by oil. A full supply should be carried as recommended by the manufacturer.

7. Improper oil viscosity. A higher viscosity oil is required for hot weather. Do you have the proper grade in the sump?

8. Is the bike's capacity being exceeded? Overloading immediately produces overheating.

9. Is the engine dirty? Cooling fins, particularly, and the rest of the motor casting generally, must dissipate the heat generated by combustion and friction. If there is a film of dirt and oil on the surface, dissipation is retarded. Clean it away. Remember: a clean bike runs better.

OTHER ENGINE PROBLEMS

Excess oil consumption

All engines use oil, even four-strokers, so expect the consumption of a certain amount of lubricant. The greater the clearances in the engine, the more oil will be used. Even if the **high-miler** is clean externally, it will absorb oil. The leaky bike runs through even more, naturally. But there is a limit, and if consumption exceeds the norm, by all means look into the problem.

What is normal? It is impossible to say. The use of oil varies so much with model, displacement and condition that any given figure would be unreliable. However, the clues to excessive oil burning are plain if you examine the spark plug and the exhaust pipe. A wet, black plug is indicative of oil burning. A gray smoke from the exhaust (as opposed to a black smoke, which comes from over-rich fuel mixture) is another sign. An exhaust pipe coated with heavy, sooty deposits is another indicator.

If all these signs are present and accounted for, there may be one of several things wrong:

1. Are you using the right grade of oil? If the oil is too light for conditions (either service or engine wear), a lot of it can blow right out the exhaust pipe. Go up a grade and see if it helps. Drain and re-fill, of course.

2. How is the compression? Worn rings permit the passage of crankcase vapors, which are heavy with oil, into the combustion chamber where they are burned. A compression check will disclose this condition.

3. Bad valve guides, with excessive clearance

between valve stem and guide bore, are responsible for a certain amount of oil burning. If compression checks out well, but other symptoms are present, measure stem-to-guide clearance by applying side-to-side pressure on valve stem with spring removed. It should not rock.

Lack of oil pressure

You should make a check on oil pressure as described in lubrication section of MAINTENANCE AND TUNING chapter. If there isn't a sufficient amount, excessive working clearances may be responsible.

Reference to the engine lubrication schematics will make the oil flow path clear.

VIBRATION

Excess vibration is usually directly traceable to loose, broken or worn motor mounts, and all mounting points should be inspected carefully.

Incorrect clutch assembly, poor timing, bad flywheels are other possibilities, but they are fairly easy to trace, since the onset would either be gradual or following some tinkering. If the bike is new to you, a thorough inspection of all these possible causes should be carried out, since vibration is usually the beginning of some sort of failure.

NOISES

Noises from an engine can be both annoying and meaningful. Each engine has its own particular set of normal noises, and the rider should get used to them. Then when there is a variation, no matter how slight, he is alerted. Some small noises have little significance other than to denote ordinary wear and changing of clearances . . . valve clearance, etc., but loud, heavy or sudden noises generally come suddenly and warn of trouble.

Pinging

This is a high-pitched, upper cylinder rattle at one-half engine speed and is caused by pre-ignition (detonation) of the fuel charge. It occurs most noticeably on acceleration or under load and is brought on by one of several causes. Principal cause is low-test fuel. Using a poor grade (low octane rating) gasoline in a high compression engine is an open invitation to this symptom. It is more than annoying; detonation is harmful to bearings and pistons. Switch to high-test (premium) gasoline.

If you are using high-test gasoline and get the same sound, chances are, first, that the ignition timing is too advanced.

Another possibility is incorrect spark plug heat range, wherein the tip is overheating and acting like a glow plug in a model aircraft engine.

Still another cause can be excess carbon in the combustion chamber; or, if the engine has been recently overhauled, a bit of metal may have been left around the spark plug hole in the form of a broken thread which is heating and glowing. The latter three possibilities should be considered if the pinging occurs only after the engine is hot.

Clatter

This is generally the description applied to excessively loose valve/rocker clearances. It is more noticeable when the engine is cold than when it has warmed up and is clearly in the upper part of the engine. There is a certain amount of valve noise in an air-cooled engine, but if tappet clearance is even all the way through, no one valve stands out as being noisier than the others. A short length of rubber tubing can be used to listen to each rocker arm in turn to isolate the noisy one. A long screwdriver with handle held to the ear and tip against the rocker box can serve the same purpose.

Clank or slap

Piston slap in the air-cooled engine takes on a more metallic ringing sound than it does in the water-cooled engine. So, if you hear a half-speed clank, like bringing a piston and a cylinder barrel smartly together, chances are it is piston slap caused by excessive piston-to-wall clearance.

Slight noise, one that disappears after the engine is warmed up, can be tolerated, but one that hangs on should be investigated. To verify the cause, first determine if it is common to both cylinders, by removing a plug wire from each cylinder in turn. The non-firing cylinder should not make a distinct noise. Ride the machine at low speeds under load and see if the sound intensity increases as throttle is opened.

Rap

Descriptive of excess clearance in connecting rod bearings in most engines, this noise is most noticeable when the engine is running under a light load decelerating. It should also increase in loudness with speed.

Knock

This is a heavier sound than any described so far and comes from the bottom region of the engine, indicating that it is a main-bearing or crankshaft problem. Most easily detected when under acceleration or when starting.

Screech or whine

If this isn't a chain noise, it is bad roller bearings.

Double knock

Symptomatic of excessive piston/pin clearance. This is most noticeable with the engine idling and is a sharp, quick double-rap.

CHAPTER 2

The Top End

On anything but a very high-mileage Harley-Davidson or one which has been abused, top end service (valves, valve train, head, pistons and rings) is about all the rider will be called upon to attend to. For this reason, our engine section is divided into two chapters. This one deals with any service above the crankcase and will be sectioned to allow for quick reference to each model. Inasmuch as valve grinding, decarbonizing, inspection, ring installation, etc., are procedures common to all four-stroke models, explicit directions will not be repeated. Refer to appropriate heading under GLIDE MODELS.

The top end can be repaired with the engine in the frame. The bottom end cannot. So, removing the engine is covered in Chapter 3. However, it is necessary to strip the bike partially in each instance to gain access to the components. By following details of the instructions, a minimum amount of time and labor will be required.

In all cases, the machine should first be thoroughly cleaned with Gunk and dried off.

Glide Models

Preliminary steps

① Remove instrument cover screw from center of base.

② Pry off cover side plate (located at odometer trip reset screw).

③ Pull seat clevis pin and tip seat forward.

④ Disconnect fuel lines.

⑤ Remove upper and lower bolts at the front and the two stud nuts between the gasoline tanks at the rear.

⑥ Remove tanks.

⑦ If so equipped, remove shift lever bottom bolts so shift lever can be removed with left tank.

⑧ Remove cylinder head bracket. (Note number of washers between bracket and frame lug. Use same washers when bracket is reassembled.)

⑨ Remove spark plugs.

⑩ Disconnect ground wire at battery.

⑪ On 1964 and earlier models, turn out center screw to remove horn power pack cover; dis-

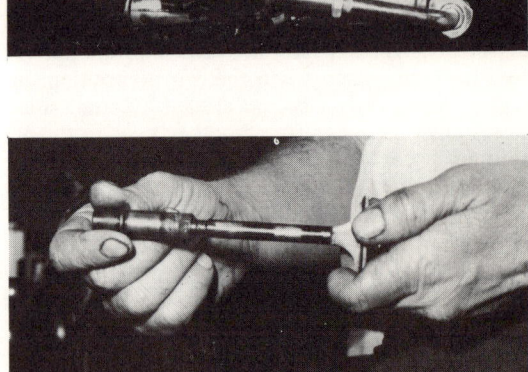

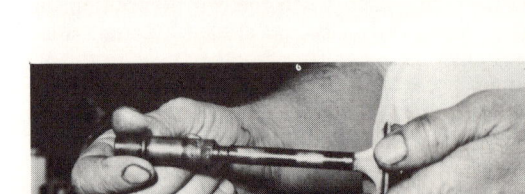

Galled valve and tappet caused by poor lubrication.

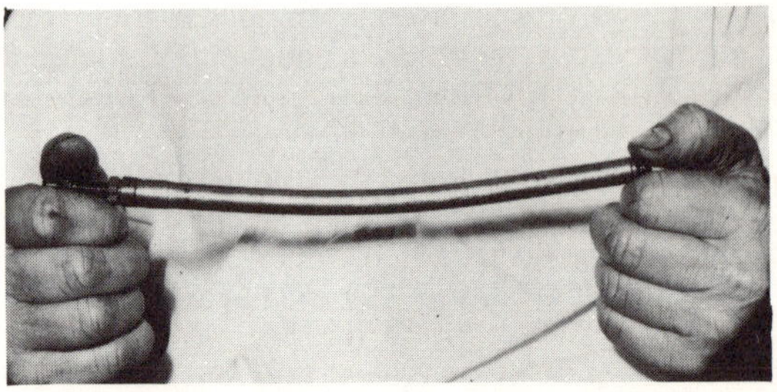

Bent pushrod caused by sticking valve.

Head Assembly

connect two wires from horn power pack; remove two bolts mounting horn power pack to bracket; loosen horn trumpet nut and turn horn power pack off trumpet.

⑫ Remove carburetor intake manifold clamps.
⑬ Remove air cleaner assembly.
⑭ Disconnect throttle and choke controls from carburetor.
⑮ Disconnect fuel and vent lines.
⑯ Disconnect carburetor support bracket and remove carburetor.
⑰ On 1964 and earlier models, remove horn trumpet mounting bolt and horn trumpet.
⑱ Disconnect exhaust pipes from cylinder head ports.
⑲ Remove regulator mounting screws and move regulator out of the way. It is not necessary to disconnect the wires from the regulator.
⑳ Disconnect oil lines at head fittings.

HEAD ASSEMBLY

Removal and replacement

① Pry down on pushrod cover tube cap with a screwdriver wedged between it and the fins, and take out cap retainer.
② Remove five head bolts and washers from each head.
③ Lift cylinder head enough to slip out pushrods and covers.
④ Remove cylinder head.
⑤ Mark pushrods so that they will be reassembled in same position to save time in valve clearance adjustment.

Before replacing, wipe head and cylinder faces clean with a rag. Use new head gaskets.

① Install rear cylinder head.
② Start cylinder head bolts.
③ Turn engine until front cylinder exhaust tappet is just starting upward.
④ Install rear cylinder exhaust pushrod and cover. Make certain both pushrod ends are properly seated in rocker arm and tappet.
⑤ Rotate engine until front cylinder intake tappet is just starting upward.
⑥ Install rear cylinder intake pushrod in same manner as exhaust pushrod.
⑦ Tighten head bolts evenly to insure a proper seal (65 lb./ft. torque).
⑧ Repeat procedure to install front cylinder head.

Disassembly (1965 and earlier)

① Remove the 12 cover reinforcing screws and lift off reinforcing ring, rocker arm cover and cover gasket. The cover pad is cemented and needs no attention if in serviceable condition.
② Back off the eight rocker arm bearing stud nuts and lift intake valve oiler off studs.
③ Remove rocker arm bearing halves with rocker arms.
④ Remove exhaust valve stem pads (if used).
⑤ Compress valve springs to remove valve key halves.
⑥ Remove upper valve spring collar, outer valve spring and inner valve spring and lower spring collar.
⑦ Slip valves out of valve guides.

Note: It is best not to interchange valves, rocker arms or rocker arm bearing halves. Either process parts separately or mark them in some manner so they may be returned to their respective positions.

Disassembly (1966 and later)

① Remove stud nuts and rocker cover.
② Before further disassembly, carefully check the rocker arm pads and ball sockets for pitting and excessive wear. Also, check the rocker arm shaft for appreciable end play.
③ Remove rocker arm shaft screw and "O" ring, acorn nut and washer.
④ Discard shaft screw "O" ring.
⑤ Tap rocker arm shaft from cover and remove rocker arm and spacer. Mark rocker arm shaft and arm in some manner so all parts may be returned to their respective locations during reassembly. Rocker arms are not interchangeable.

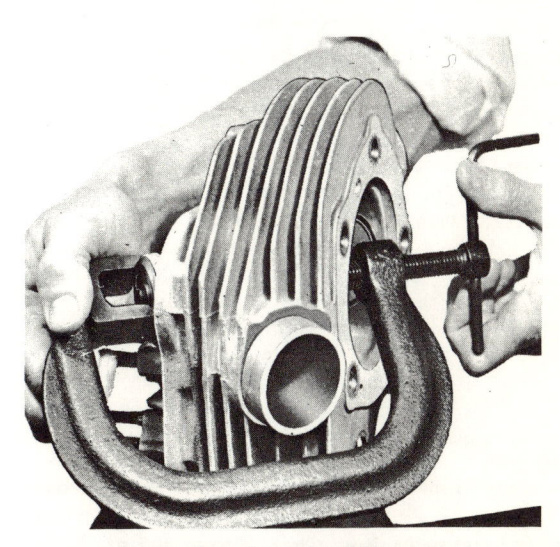

Compressing valve spring, Glide models.

⑥ Compress valve springs and remove valve keys from ends of valve stems. Mark keys to identify them with their respective valves.
⑦ Remove valve spring collars, springs and valves. Mark them in some manner to identify them with front and rear cylinder head.

Inspection and decarbonizing

Factory recommendations for decarbonizing and cleaning the head include the following after valves have been removed:

① Clean outside of cylinder head with a wire brush.
② Scrape carbon from head, top of cylinder, top of bore above ring path, and inlet and exhaust valve ports. When scraping carbon, be careful to avoid scratching or nicking cylinder head and cylinder joint faces or bore.
③ Blow off loosened carbon or dirt with compressed air.
④ Wash all parts in Gunk Hydro-Seal.
⑤ Blow out oil passages in head. Be sure they are free of sludge and carbon particles.
⑥ Remove loosened carbon from valve head and stem with a wire wheel. Never use a file or other hardened tool that will scratch or nick valve.
⑦ Polish valve stem with very fine emery cloth or steel wool.
⑧ Check valve stem for excessive wear.
⑨ Valve heads should have a seating surface about 1/16" wide and be free of pit marks and burn spots. Exhaust valves should contain carbon that is black or dark brown. White or light buff carbon indicates excessive heat and burning.

Note: Standard intake and exhaust valves are made of different materials and must not be interchanged on 1965 and earlier models. Intake valves are marked "IN" on head; exhaust valves are marked "EX." The 1966 models have larger intake valves and cannot be interchanged.

⑩ Valve seats are also subject to wear, pitting and burning. They should be resurfaced whenever valves are refinished.
⑪ Clean valve guides with the Harley-Davidson valve guide reamer, part No. 94830-47, and check for wear and valve stem clearance.
⑫ Inspect valve springs for broken or discolored coils. Check free length or check tension of each spring. If a spring is more than 1/8" shorter than a new spring, or tension shows spring to be below low limit tension of a new spring, replace it with a new spring. Check valve spring compression with valve spring tester against tolerances shown in SPECIFICATIONS.
⑬ Examine pushrods, particularly the ball ends. Replace any rods that are bent, worn, discolored or broken. Check cup at end of rocker arm to make certain that no chips are broken out.
⑭ Blow out oil passages in rocker arms, rocker arm bearings and rocker arm covers.
⑮ If the rocker arm pads show uneven wear or pitting, dress on a grinder, maintaining original curve. If possible, compare a new unit during this operation to insure a correctly contoured surface.
⑯ Carefully check the rocker arm and shaft for wear. Replace rocker arm bushings if shaft is over .002" loose in bushings.

Valve grinding

If valve faces are too deeply pitted to clean up without leaving the edge thin and sharp, it is best to install a new valve. Otherwise, either reface on a commercial machine or lap in with compound if just a touch-up is needed.

Note: Replacing valve guides, if necessary, must be done before valve seat and face are ground since the valve stem hole in the valve guide is the basis from which all face and seat grinding is done. Valve stem-valve guide clearance is as follows: Exhaust valves: .004" to .006" loose; intake valves: .002" to .004" loose. If valve stems and/or guides are worn to exceed the maximum tolerances by more than .002", new parts must be installed. (See below.)

Valve face angle is 45° for both intake and exhaust valves, and the valve refacing grinder must be adjusted to this angle. It is important not to remove any more metal than is necessary to clean up and true valve face. If the end of a valve stem shows uneven wear, true it on a valve refacing grinder equipped with a suitable attachment.

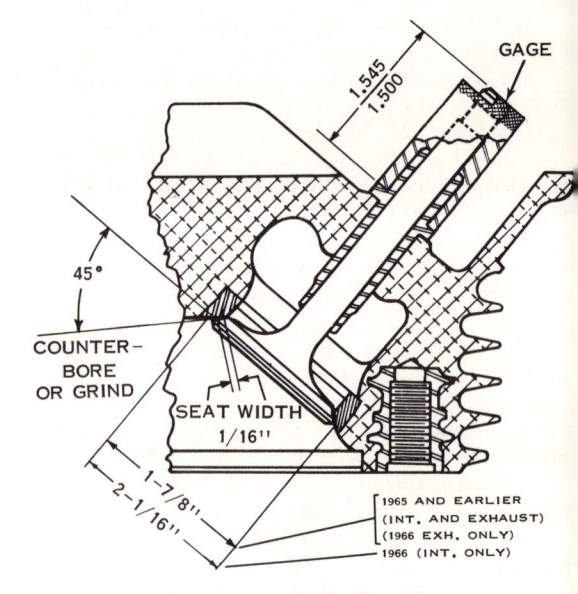

Valve seat tolerances, 74 cu. in.

Refer to drawing for dimensions. To lap valves on their seats:

① Apply a light coat of fine lapping compound to the valve face.
② Insert valve in guide and give it a few oscillations with a valve grinding tool.
③ Lift valve and rotate it about 1/3 turn.
④ Repeat lapping procedure.
⑤ After full turn, remove valve, wash valve face and seat, and dry with cloth that is immediately discarded so grinding compound cannot be transferred to engine parts.

Pistons and Cylinders

⑥ If inspection shows an unbroken lapped finish of uniform width around both valve and seat, valve is well seated. If lapped finish is not complete, further lapping, or grinding and lapping, is necessary.

Replacing guides

Tap out valve guides with a shouldered drift pin (from chamber side) and insert replacement guide with an arbor press. Be particularly careful to press the replacement guide squarely into the hole.

New valve guides are factory reamed to correct size. However, when guides are pressed into heads, they may close up slightly; also, the ends may be burred. Therefore, after new guides are in place, they should be sized and cleaned with valve guide reamer, part No. 94830-47.

It is of prime importance that guides fit tightly, or valves may not seat properly. If original guide or new standard guide is not a tight press fit, an oversize guide must be installed. Oversize guides can be obtained .001" to .006" oversize.

Replacing seats

After installing valve guides, valve seats must be refaced to true them with guides.

If valves have been reseated several times, valve seats may have become too wide and/or the valve may be pocketed (seating itself too deeply in the head). When the seat becomes wider than $1/16''$, a relief must be counterbored or ground to reduce the seat to $1/16''$. Counterbore dimensions are shown in the drawing. Tools for this purpose are available commercially.

To determine if the valve is seating itself too deeply in the head, measure the distance from the shoulder of the valve guide to the end of the valve stem. When the valve stem extends through the guide in excess of maximum shown in the drawing, valve seat inserts must be replaced.

A special gauge to measure this dimension is available under part No. 96490-59.

1966 and later inserts are pressed-in and the cylinder heads may be returned to the factory for installation of new inserts.

1965 and earlier cylinder heads, having cast-in inserts, may be returned to the factory through authorized Harley-Davidson dealers for valve seat insert replacement. Heads are bored out to remove old seats, and new seats are pressed into place.

A $5/32''$ oversize service valve, part No. 18082-60, is available for replacement of standard size, 1965 and earlier, intake and exhaust valves which are seating too deeply. A new valve seat must be cut in the old valve seat insert with boring or grinding tools according to instructions that come with the valve.

Head reassembly

① Replace valve and valve spring assemblies, using a valve spring compressor.

② Position valve keys so spaces between key halves are equal. Spaces between key halves must face front and rear of engine on intake valves.

③ Replace rocker arm assemblies. On 1965 and earlier models, use new intake valve oiler, making sure that intake valve oiler is in place on intake rocker bearing, with oiler tube $3/32''$ from rocker arm. Rocker arms must be free or hydraulic lifters will not fill with oil.

④ Use a new cover gasket.

⑤ Replace rocker arm cover and reinforcing ring. Pull down cover reinforcing screws evenly to obtain a tight seal.

Note: On 1966 models, be sure to see that rocker arm ends do not jam against valve stems, since the rocker box is installed on the head studs. Use a screwdriver to raise the valve end of the arm when cover assembly is installed. Use aluminum paint on cover faces.

PISTONS AND CYLINDERS

With head removed as previously described,

① Remove all cylinder base stud nuts and washers, except one on rear cylinder, using cylinder base nut wrench, part No. 94585-30.

② Raise front cylinder and piston enough to permit placing a cloth over crankcase opening. This will prevent dirt or pieces of a broken ring from falling into the crankcase.

③ With piston at bottom of stroke, remove cylinder.

④ Remove remaining stud nut from rear cylinder.

⑤ Remove rear cylinder in same manner.

⑥ Discard cylinder-to-crankcase gasket.

⑦ Pry right piston pin lock ring off piston pin. Right end of piston pin has slots for this purpose.

⑧ Tap out piston pin and lift off rod. Since rings are inexpensive, it is always wise to replace them. Spring the old rings out until they clear the grooves and take them off.

Scrape hard carbon deposits off pistons with putty knife, then clean pistons, pins and barrels with Harley-Davidson Gunk Hydro-Seal.

Wash all parts in solvent and blow dry with compressed air. Force air through feed and return oil passages in cylinder. Clean piston ring grooves with a piece of compression ring ground to a chisel shape.

Examine piston pins to see that they are not pitted or scored. Check the pin bushings to see that they are not loose in connecting rods, grooved, pitted or scored. A piston pin, properly fitted, is a light push fit in piston and has .001" clearance in connecting rod upper bearing. If

The Top End

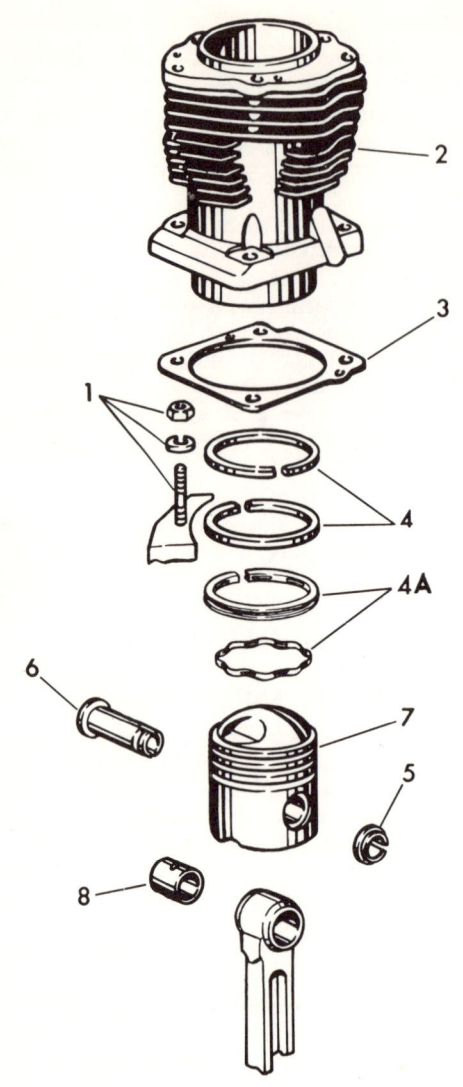

Cylinder, exploded view, Glide models.

1. Cylinder base stud nut and washer (4)
2. Cylinder
3. Cylinder base gasket
4. Piston rings (2 compression)
4A. Oil control piston ring and expander spring
5. Piston pin lock ring (2)
6. Piston pin
7. Piston
8. Piston pin bushing

Figure following name of part indicates quantity necessary for one complete assembly.

Removing piston pin lock ring, Glide models.

pin-to-bushing free fit exceeds .002", replace worn parts. If the piston pin is to be used again, examine the lock ring on unslotted end of pin. If ring is tight in its groove, it is not necessary to remove it. When a new lock ring is required, clean the groove and install ring before pin is installed in piston. The piston pin included with new piston assembly will have the lock ring already installed on unslotted end.

Examine piston and cylinder for cracks, burrs, burned spots, grooves and gouges.

Check rod for clearance on big-end bearings. When up and down play is detected and either rod has more than 3/32" side shake at extreme upper end, rod bearing should be replaced. This requires removing and disassembling crankcase (see Chapter 3).

Rings

The two compression rings are fitted in the upper piston ring grooves with the stamped word "TOP" or a dot up. These rings must have proper side clearance in the grooves. New, this is .004". Maximum side clearance is .008". Compression ring end gap is .010" to .020".

To check end gap, place a piston in the bore about ½" from top of cylinder. Place the ring in the cylinder bore squarely against the piston and check gap with thickness gauge.

If gap is less than .010", ring ends may butt under expansion, and be scored or broken. Compression ring gap may be increased by filing with a fine cut file.

Use only standard size rings and piston in standard bore, and only matching oversize rings and piston in the same oversize bore. However, .005" oversize rings may be used on standard piston in standard bore if ring gap with standard ring exceeds .020" maximum.

U-Flex oil control rings should have 11/32"

Pistons and Cylinders

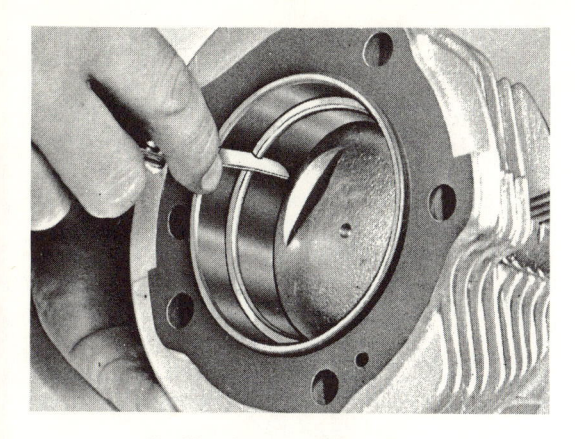

Checking ring gap, Glide models.

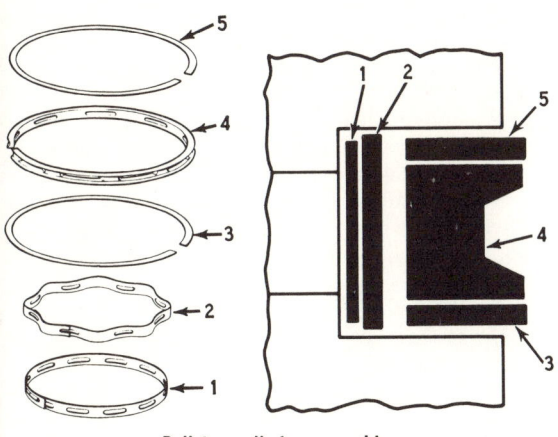

Rail type oil ring assembly.

(install in order shown)

1. Shim (if used)
2. Expander spring
3. Rail
4. Spacer
5. Rail

overlap when placed free in cylinder bore. Replace ring when worn to 7/32" or less overlap.

During 1959, the U-Flex oil control ring was replaced by a rail type oil control ring. This ring consists of two steel rails, one spacer and one expander, which are placed in the lowest piston ring groove. In .040", .050", .060" and .070" oversize pistons, a shim is added under the expander.

During the 1966 season, the rail type oil ring was replaced by a full-width slotted oil control ring using a spring expander.

Reboring

After cleaning, measure the pistons and cylinders to see if they are worn to the point where cylinders must be rebored and oversize pistons installed. Inside and outside micrometers used for piston-to-cylinder fitting should be checked together to be sure they are adjusted to read exactly the same. Subtract piston measurement from bore measurement to obtain clearance. Bore measurement of a cylinder should be taken in the ring path, starting about ½" from the top of the cylinder, measuring front to rear, then side to side. Repeat procedure at the center and at the bottom of ring travel. This process will determine if cylinder is out of round or "egged" and will also show any cylinder taper or bulge.

Pistons are measured front to rear at base of piston skirt. Pistons are cam ground to an egged or oval shape so only front and rear surfaces are touching cylinder wall.

If cylinders are not scuffed, scored and are worn less than .002", it is not necessary to rebore oversize at time of cylinder repair. It may be done at time of next complete engine overhaul. If desired, a new piston may be installed to reduce clearance for more quiet operation.

If cylinders show more than .002" wear, they should be rebored and/or honed to next standard oversize and refitted with corresponding pistons and rings.

Pistons are regularly supplied in the following oversizes: .005", .010", .020", .030", .040", .050", .060" and .070". Oversize pistons have their oversize stamped on head: 10, 20, etc.

Exact final size of the cylinder bore is determined by size of the piston to be used. Measure piston diameter accurately as described previously, then add desired piston clearance in cylinder. This will equal the exact final size to which cylinder bore should be refinished.

Example: the .020" oversize piston to be used measures 3.4575". Adding .001" (desired clearance) equals 3.4585" (finish-honed size). When cylinders require reboring to beyond .070" oversize to clean up, they must be replaced.

When cylinders are worn less than the .002" maximum, and reboring is unnecessary, unless they are scuffed or grooved, the same pistons may be used with the replacement of rings and the roughing of cylinder walls to facilitate ring seating. Use No. 150 carborundum emery cloth to rough the walls.

Reassembly

① Attach piston to rod with a piston pin.
② Position piston so lug on piston pin boss inside piston skirt is to right side of engine.
③ Clean the lock ring groove and install lock ring on end of pin that is not slotted, if it was removed.
④ Start slotted end of pin into piston boss from the left side and drive through in the same manner in which pin was removed. (If the piston is heated in boiling water, the pin may be

The Top End

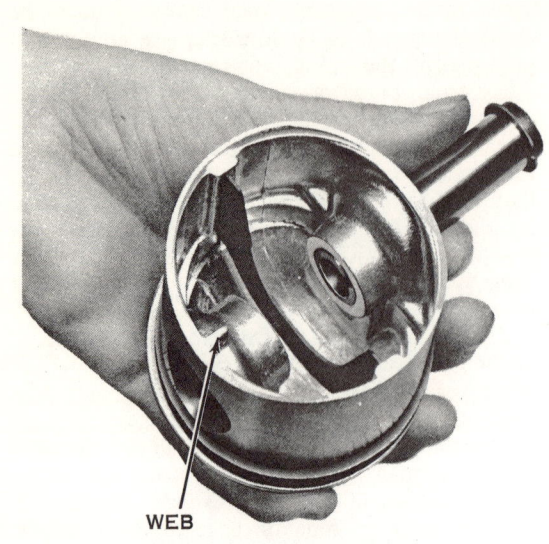

WEB
Piston with web on right side.

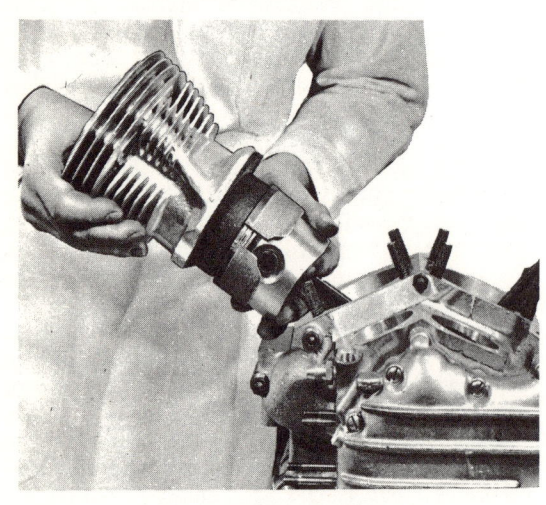

Slipping cylinder over piston.

inserted into the piston as a slip fit.)

⑤ Clean lock ring groove and install the other lock ring. *Note:* It is important that special tool No. 96780-32A be used for installing the lock rings. Other means of installing may over-expand the ring and possibly crack it. Make sure the ring groove is clean and that the ring seats firmly in groove. A lock ring incorrectly installed will soon loosen in service and finally come off pin, resulting in both piston and cylinder being damaged beyond repair. Never install a used lock ring or a new one that has been installed and then removed.

⑥ Lubricate cylinder walls, pistons, pins and rod bushings with engine oil.

⑦ Rotate rings until gaps are around rear piston.

⑧ Turn the engine until crankpin is at bottom center.

⑨ Install a new cylinder base gasket.

⑩ Use a ring compresser, part No. 96333-51, on rear piston and slip rear cylinder down over the piston.

⑪ Install lock washers and nuts and pull them down evenly.

⑫ Repeat process to assemble front cylinder.

Sportster Models

Preliminary steps

① Drain fuel tank.
② Drain oil tank.
③ Remove seat.
④ Disconnect fuel lines.
⑤ Remove fuel tank.
⑥ Take off air cleaner.
⑦ Disconnect throttle and choke cables.
⑧ Remove top motor mount bolt. (Note the number of washers between bracket and frame. These are alignment washers and must be replaced exactly as removed.)
⑨ Loosen clamps and remove exhaust pipes.
⑩ Remove generator and horn mounting screw on 1964 and earlier XLH.
⑪ On same models, remove horn cover and disconnect wiring. Then take horn off bracket and loosen the trumpet securing nut so parts can be separated.
⑫ Remove spark plugs.
⑬ Disconnect XLH battery ground strap at battery terminal.
⑭ On early XLCH and all later models, disconnect horn wires, remove horn from bracket and remove bracket.
⑮ Disconnect throttle cable and bracket from carburetor.
⑯ Pull cable out of way to front of frame.
⑰ Loosen manifold clamps and carburetor support nut.
⑱ Remove carburetor.
⑲ Loosen oil line nuts (see exploded view of head assembly).

HEAD ASSEMBLY

Removal

It is necessary to remove the rear head and rocker cover in one unit. The front rocker cover can be removed separately by taking out the screws.

① Open pushrod covers and press pushrod cover spring retainers down.
② Remove pushrod cover keepers.
③ Telescope lower pushrod cover over upper pushrod cover.
④ Rotate engine until both valves are closed in cylinder head.
⑤ Remove cylinder head bolts.

Head Assembly

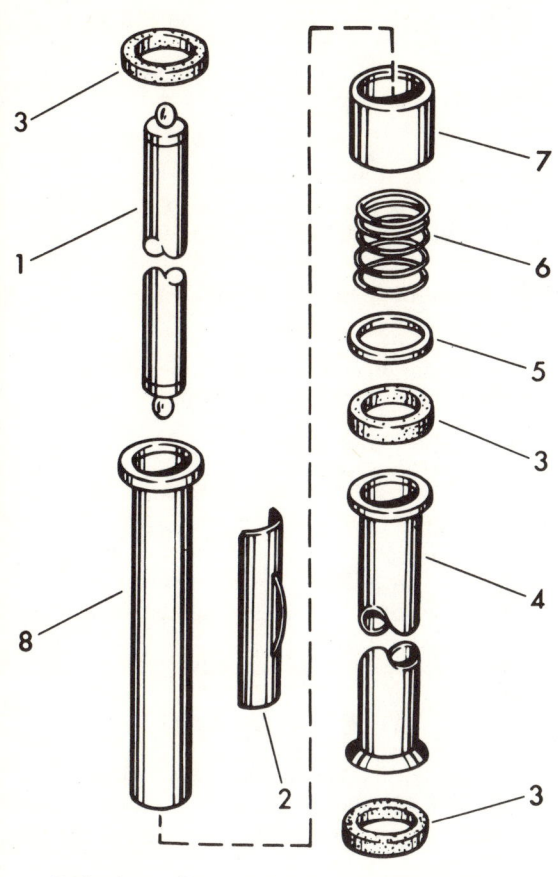

Pushrod assembly, exploded view, Sportster models.

1. Push rod
2. Cover spring keeper
3. Cover cork washer (3)
4. Lower cover
5. Cover screw washer
6. Cover spring
7. Spring retainer
8. Upper cover

⑥ Take head off (from left side), also pushrods, pushrod covers and oil lines in one operation. Mark pushrods to identify them as to cylinder head and valve from which they were taken so a minimum amount of valve adjusting will be necessary. If the cylinder head does not come loose on removal of the head bolts, tap lightly with plastic mallet. Never try to pry head off.

Replacement

Before replacing, clean top of cylinder and head faces with a clean rag.

① Apply a light coat of engine oil or grease to both sides of a new gasket and position gasket on cylinder face.
② Turn engine over so cylinder tappets are at their lowest position.
③ Install head, pushrods and pushrod covers in one operation. Install pushrods in their original position in cylinder head. Be sure pushrods register in tappet screw sockets at bottom end and in pushrod sockets at upper end.
④ Register oil line in head and crankcase connection.
⑤ Install head bolts with flat washers under head of each bolt. Bolts must be tightened evenly to attain a tight joint. First turn bolts snug, then tighten each of them ⅛ or ¼ turn at a time with a torque wrench until all are tightened to 65 lb./ft.
⑥ Make sure rubber sleeves are in place and tighten oil line nuts.
⑦ Replace intake manifold rubber "O" rings.
⑧ Assemble "O" rings on manifold and then slip carburetor assembly into position, aligning the hole in the carburetor support bracket with top center crankcase stud.
⑨ Just snug up the stud nut.
⑩ Carefully square manifold face with cylinder head intake port face and slip rubber "O" ring onto its seat.
⑪ Insert and tighten two manifold clamps.
⑫ Tighten crankcase stud nut securely.

Factory Note: There are likely to be air leaks around manifold-cylinder head joints, unless the manifold is perfectly aligned with the cylinder head intake port face, rubber "O" rings are in good condition, and manifold clamps securely tightened. Air leakage will affect carburetion, particularly at low speeds. If all necessary steps have been taken and air continues to leak around manifold-cylinder head joints, it may be necessary to loosen the cylinder base nuts to allow final shifting and alignment of cylinders and manifold. Be sure to tighten base nuts after alignment.

⑬ Check tappet adjustment and reassemble remaining parts.

Disassembly

① Remove rocker covers.
② Check the rocker arm pads and ball sockets for pitting and excessive wear.
③ Check the rocker arm shaft for appreciable play in the rocker arm bushings. If rocker arm assembly is noticeably worn, disassemble unit for further inspection and replacement of parts.
④ Remove rocker arm shaft screw, "O" ring, acorn nut and washer. (Discard "O" ring.)
⑤ Tap rocker arm shaft from cover and remove the spring, rocker arm and spacer.
⑥ Mark the rocker shaft and arm so they may be returned to their respective locations during reassembly. The arms are not interchangeable. (Exhaust rocker arms have an extra oil hole.)
⑦ Compress the valve springs and remove valve keys from ends of valve stems.
⑧ Mark keys to identify them with their respective valves.

The Top End

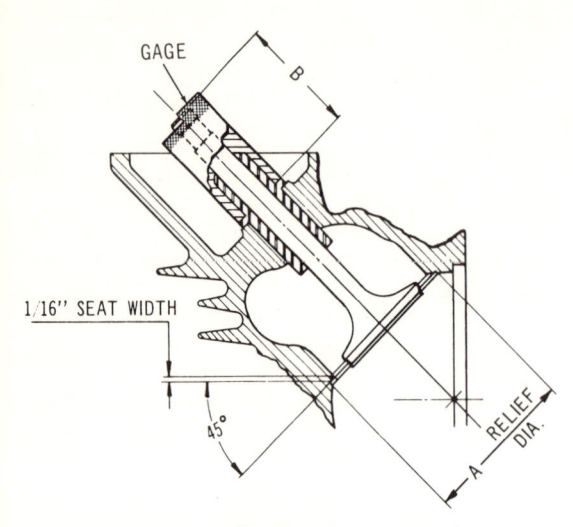

Valve seat specifications, Sportster models.

Model	Valve	Relief Dia. A	B Max.	B Min.
XL	Int.	1.75	1.420 (all)	1.375 (all)
	Exh.	1.62		
XLH	Int.	1.87		
	Exh.	1.62		

Lapping valve face and seat, Sportster models.

⑨ Remove valve spring collars, springs and valves.

⑩ Mark them to identify them with the front and rear cylinder heads.

To replace worn rocker arm bushings, press or drive them out. If difficult to remove, insert a tap (5/8-11 thread) into bushing. From the opposite side of rocker arm, drift out the bushing and tap. Press or drive replacement bushing into rocker arm, flush with arm end, oil hole correctly aligned and split portion of bushing toward the top of the arm. New bushings should be line reamed, using reamer, part No. 94804-57.

If the rocker arm pads show uneven wear or pitting, dress on a grinder, maintaining original curve. If possible, compare with a new unit during this operation to insure a correctly contoured surface.

Inspection and decarbonizing

Refer to this heading under GLIDE MODELS for general information. You can carefully clean up intake valve guides with a 5/16" reamer and exhaust valve guides with an 11/32" reamer.

Valve grinding

See Glide section heading, referring to accompanying drawing for correct dimensions.

Valve guides and seats

See GLIDE MODELS headings.

Reassembly

① Apply a light coat of engine oil to the valve seats and stems.

② Be careful to insert marked valves in their respective guides.

③ Carefully seat lower valve spring collar over valve guide.

④ Install springs and upper collar.

⑤ Compress valve springs.

⑥ Position the keys in valve key groove, using grease to hold them in place, and slowly release compresser tool until keys are correctly locked in groove.

⑦ Position spacer in countersunk hole in rocker arm cover.

⑧ Install marked rocker arms in their respective cover locations.

⑨ Compress spring and position spring between rocker arm and washer.

⑩ Apply a light film of oil to the rocker arm shaft and insert in cover assembly.

⑪ Examine spring ends to be sure they are square with washer and rocker arm.

⑫ Install and securely tighten acorn nut and washer, shaft screw and new "O" ring.

⑬ Check rocker arm action to make sure it is not binding.

PISTONS AND CYLINDERS

Follow recommendations for GLIDE MODELS. Note that U-Flex oil rings in the Sportster engine have 1/4" overlap when inserted free in bore. If overlap is 5/32" or less, replace the ring.

Rail type rings replaced the U-Flex in 1961 and a full-width slotted ring with an expander has been fitted since 1966.

CHAPTER 3

The Bottom End

If connecting rod or mainshaft bearings require attention, it is necessary to remove the engine from the frame. Other bottom end repairs, such as to oil pump, cams and gears, do not require removal from frame. Unlike top end service, several special Harley-Davidson tools are required when working on this portion of the engine. Inasmuch as these tools represent a considerable investment, it is suggested that the average rider refer such major problems as replacement of cam-gear bearings and bronze bushings, tappet guides, pinion gear bushings, aligning flywheels, etc., to his authorized Harley-Davidson dealer.

Since it is of interest to the rider to know how these repairs are made, factory-recommended procedures are outlined under appropriate headings for each model. It is, of course, possible that you will want to do the work yourself.

Glide Models

TAPPETS, CAMS AND GEAR TRAIN

The roller tappets are topped by hydraulic units that get oil from the sump. Nearly all problems center around noisy tappets caused by failure to pump up sufficient oil that is uncontaminated by sludge, engine varnish, or dirt. Late models have an oil filter screen in the sump which helps reduce such complaints.

The factory says that it is normal for tappets to click when the engine is started after standing for some time. Hydraulic units have a check valve which permits the oil in the hydraulic unit cylinder to escape. This is necessary to allow units to compensate for various expansion conditions of parts and still maintain no-clearance operation. Pushrod assemblies are functioning properly if they become quiet before or as engine reaches full operating temperature.

Tappet removal and service
① Remove pushrod cover.
② Back adjusting screw off until pushrod can be removed.
③ Back tappet guide screws off.
④ Lift out hydraulic units.

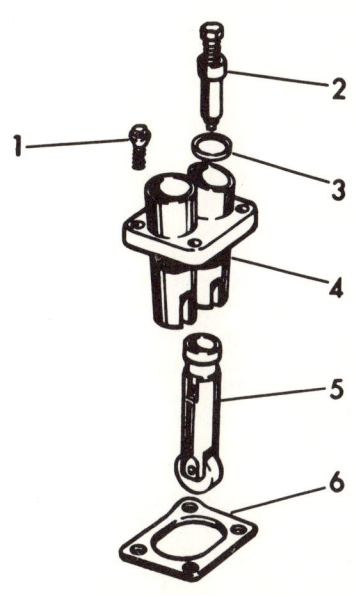

Tappet assembly, exploded view, Glide models.

1. Tappet guide screw (4)
2. Push rod hydraulic unit (2)
3. Push rod cover cork washer (2)
4. Tappet guide
5. Tappet and roller assembly (2)
6. Tappet guide gasket

Figure following name of part indicates quantity necessary for one complete assembly.

⑤ Loosen tappet guides by tapping gently with soft hammer.
⑥ Insert thumb and forefinger into pushrod opening in tappet guide and press tops of tappets against side of guides.
⑦ Remove tappet and guide assembly. Be careful to avoid dropping a tappet through guide mounting hole into gearcase.
⑧ Take pushrod cover cork washers out of top of guide.
⑨ Pull tappet and roller out of bottom of guide and remove gasket.

Note: Hydraulic units are selectively fitted and must not be interchanged. Twist and pull the hydraulic piston and spring from one cylinder, wash parts in solvent and set aside on **a**

19

clean rag as a unit. Repeat with others. Then clean passages in tappets, guides and hydraulic units with compressed air. Insert wire into the openings in the guides to make sure passages are open. Air-dry all parts.

Examine cams through tappet guide holes in gearcase for nicked, grooved or chipped condition. Examine tappet-guide matching surfaces for scuffing or grooving.

If a tappet can be rocked in the guide, there is excessive clearance, and it should be replaced.

After cleaning, hydraulic units should be checked as follows:

① Hold in an upright position and press piston down until spring touches cylinder, without covering hole in bottom of cylinder.

② Hold for count of 6 and release. If piston bounces back, the unit is serviceable.

③ If piston does not bounce back, cover the hole in bottom of cylinder and repeat. If piston does not bounce back, ball is not seating, and the unit should be replaced.

④ Before replacing hydraulic units, check the possibility of plugged or partially plugged screen under the large cap screw located near the rear tappet guide. Remove the screen as described in Timing Gear Disassembly, and operate the engine without the screen and cork washers long enough to compare results.

In reassembling the tappets, be sure that they are installed so that flat surfaces on tappets are toward center of guide. Otherwise, engine oil will not feed across and one hydraulic unit cannot fill with oil.

① Assemble guide gasket dry and insert assembly in place on gearcase, holding tappets in place with thumb and forefinger.

② Assemble pushrod cover cork washers, pushrod hydraulic units and tappet guide screws.

③ Assemble remainder of pushrod assembly in same order as disassembled.

④ Adjust tappet clearance as described in MAINTENANCE AND TUNING chapter.

Timing gear disassembly and reassembly

The timing gear and accessory train is housed in the lower right side of the engine. To gain access to it, proceed as follows.

① Remove pushrods and tappets as previously described.

② Remove oil screen cap, gasket, screen body, or spring screen, and screen seal, depending on model.

③ Remove screen from housing by rotating until notch in screen lines up with key in housing.

④ Remove 12 gearcase cover screws, oil passage screw with washer, and two long generator fastening screws.

⑤ Remove generator.

⑥ Remove two distributor bolts and lift distributor assembly out of gearcase.

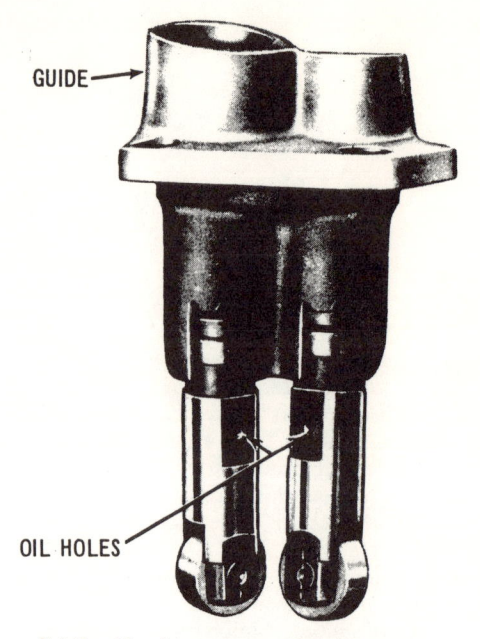

Relationship of tappets to guide, Glide models.

⑦ Tap cover with plastic mallet to loosen, and remove it.

⑧ Remove cover gasket.

⑨ Remove idler gear spacer, distributor drive and intermediate gear spacer. (Make a mark on one of the spacers to insure its assembly to the same gear. The spacers look identical, but one may be thicker than the other.)

⑩ Remove breather valve washer.

⑪ Remove cam gear, spacing washer and thrust washer.

⑫ Remove breather gear, intermediate gear and idler gear.

⑬ Remove left-hand threaded gear shaft nut. If necessary to pull pinion gear, use pinion gear puller and installer, part No. 96830-51 (tool has left-hand threads).

⑭ Remove key, spring, gearshaft pinion spacer, oil pump pinion shaft gear and key.

⑮ Take breather screen and separator out of pocket in gearcase.

⑯ Remove oiler drive gear shaft spring ring, gear and gear key.

⑰ If necessary, remove oil pump stud nuts and washers, and oil pump.

Reinstallation of the gear train is essentially a reversal of the above process, but it is necessary to determine correct end play in the sump breather valve gear and cam gear before proceeding with final assembly.

① Put spacer washer (use the same washer unless it is known to give incorrect spacing) on end of breather gear.

② Place a straightedge across gearcase at spacer.

Tappets, Cams and Gear Train

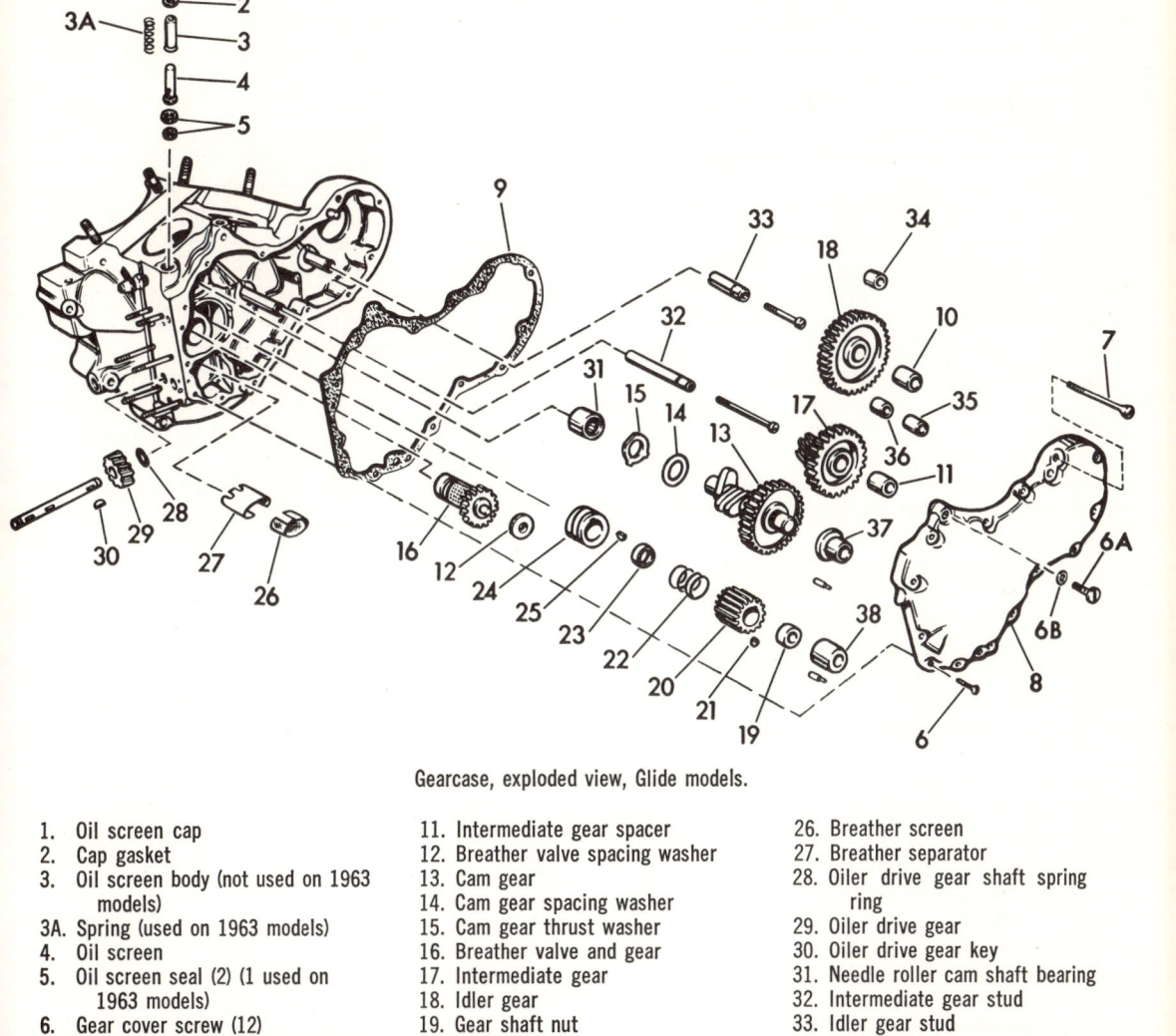

Gearcase, exploded view, Glide models.

1. Oil screen cap
2. Cap gasket
3. Oil screen body (not used on 1963 models)
3A. Spring (used on 1963 models)
4. Oil screen
5. Oil screen seal (2) (1 used on 1963 models)
6. Gear cover screw (12)
6A. Gear cover oil passage screw (1963)
6B. Screw brass washer (1963)
7. Generator fastening screw (2)
8. Gear cover
9. Gear cover gasket
10. Idler gear spacer
11. Intermediate gear spacer
12. Breather valve spacing washer
13. Cam gear
14. Cam gear spacing washer
15. Cam gear thrust washer
16. Breather valve and gear
17. Intermediate gear
18. Idler gear
19. Gear shaft nut
20. Pinion gear
21. Pinion gear key
22. Pinion gear spring
23. Gear shaft pinion spacer
24. Oil pump pinion shaft gear
25. Oil pump pinion shaft gear key
26. Breather screen
27. Breather separator
28. Oiler drive gear shaft spring ring
29. Oiler drive gear
30. Oiler drive gear key
31. Needle roller cam shaft bearing
32. Intermediate gear stud
33. Idler gear stud
34. Idler gear bushing
35. Intermediate gear bushing (2)
36. See item 35
37. Gearcase cover cam shaft bushing
38. Gearcase cover pinion gear bushing

Figure following name of part indicates quantity necessary for one complete assembly.

③ With depth gauge, measure distance between straightedge and spacer.

④ Subtract .006″ (amount gasket will compress) from this figure to determine gear end play. An end play tolerance of .001″ to .005″ is correct.

⑤ If end play exceeds maximum, insert thicker spacer. Spacer washers are available in .115″, .120″ and .125″ thicknesses.

⑥ Install thrust washer, spacing washer and cam bearing.

⑦ Position cover gasket and secure cover with at least four screws.

⑧ Measure cam shaft end play between cam gear and cover bushing with depth gauge through tappet guide hole in gearcase.

⑨ End play should be from .001″ to .005″. If measurement is under or over tolerance, remove cover and replace spacing washer with one that will give suitable clearance. Cam gear spacing washers .050″, .055″, .060″, .065″, and .070″ thick are available.

⑩ Note position of timing marks on pinion, cam, distributor drive and breather valve gear in the accompanying drawing. These must be matched when installing the gears.

The Bottom End

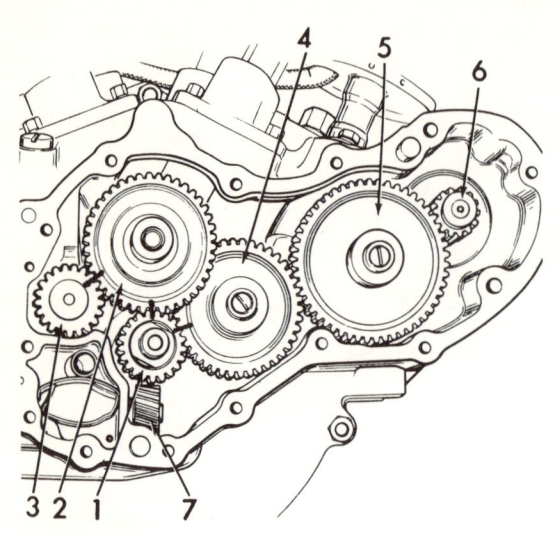

Timing gears with timing marks aligned, Glide models.

1. Pinion gear
2. Cam gear
3. Breather gear
4. Circuit breaker drive gear
5. Intermediate gear (not marked)
6. Generator drive gear (not marked)
7. Oil pump drive gear (not marked); secured on end of pump drive shaft with key and spring ring

⑪ After installing gears, take a small paint brush and coat the gears well with lubricating oil.
⑫ Apply non-hardening gasket compound to case and cover mating surfaces.
⑬ Use a new gasket.
⑭ Install cover with all screws evenly tightened.

Parts inspection

① Wash all parts in solvent and blow dry with compressed air.
② Wash the gear case carefully, using a small paint brush and solvent. Be sure not to get solvent into crankcase. Blow dry with compressed air.
③ Inspect the oil screen to make sure mesh is open. Replace plugged or partially plugged screen.
④ Probe oil screen hole in gearcase with a length of wire formed to a short hook to determine if there are any additional oil screen seal gaskets in hole. More than the prescribed number will block off oil feed channel when screening unit is assembled.
⑤ Inspect breather screen. It must be clean and unobstructed.
⑥ Inspect gear bushings in gearcase cover for pitting, scuffing and grooving.
⑦ Determine the amount of wear in cover bushings. If it exceeds maximum tolerance shown in SPECIFICATIONS by .001″, new bushings are required.
⑧ Attach a dial indicator to the gearcase cover mounting screw hole and determine the amount of piston shaft play in the right main roller bearing. When tolerance in SPECIFICATIONS is exceeded by .001″, bearings should be replaced.
⑨ Inspect needle bearing for wear, broken or gouged bearings.
⑩ If the end of the camshaft shows any appreciable wear (.003″ or more), needle bearing is probably worn to a point where replacement of bearing and camshaft is advisable.
⑪ The needle bearing can be removed and installed in the case without disassembling by using tool, part No. 97270-60 (shown in illustration) to press the bearing into the crankcase. Press the heavier end that bears the manufacturer's name only. Pressing from the opposite end will crush roller race and bind rollers. Push new bearing into crankcase from gearcase side. The pinion shaft main roller bearing may be replaced only when the crankcase is disassembled (see Crankcase Disassembly section).

If cover bushings are worn sufficiently to call for replacement, they must be extracted with

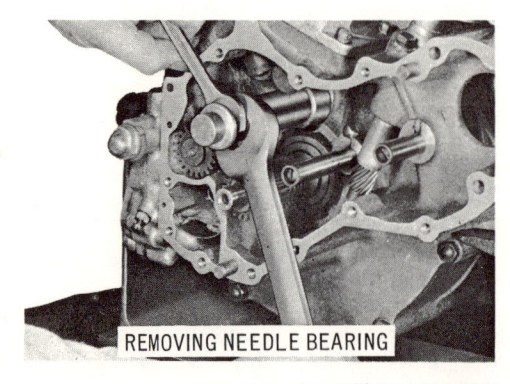

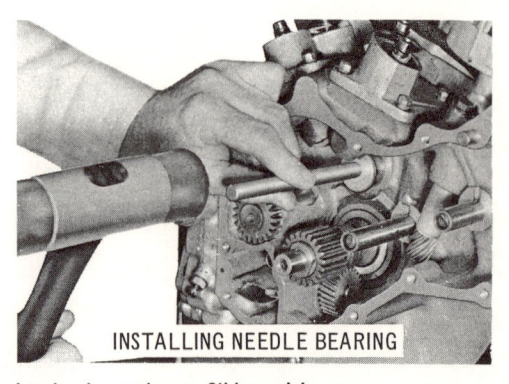

REMOVING NEEDLE BEARING

INSTALLING NEEDLE BEARING

Removing and installing cam gear needle bearing in crankcase, Glide models.

Oil Pump

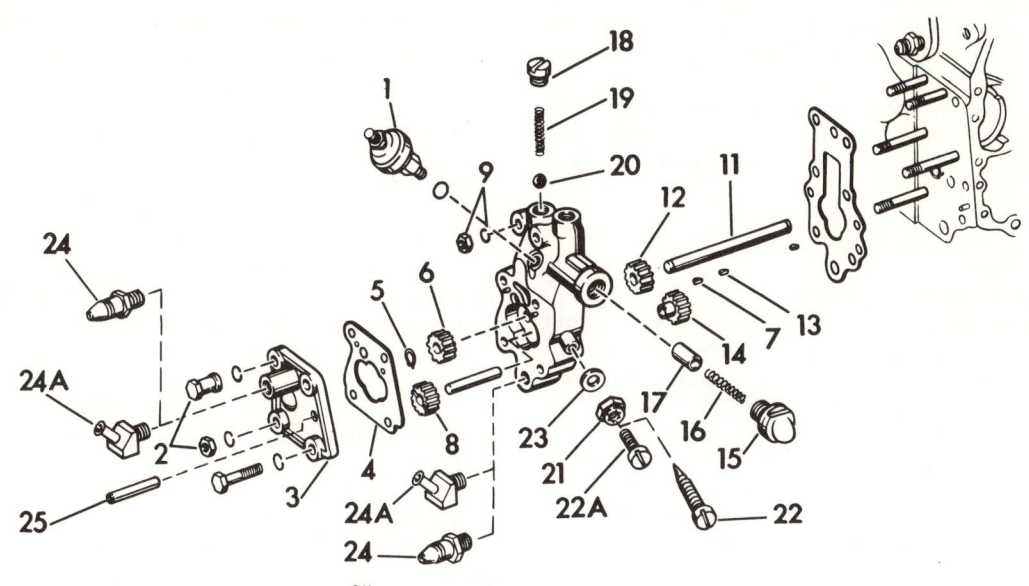

Oil pump, exploded view, Glide models.

1. Oil pressure switch
2. Cover stud nut and washer
3. Oil pump cover
4. Cover gasket
5. Lock ring
6. Scavenger pump drive gear
7. Gear key
8. Scavenger pump idler gear
9. Oil pump body mounting stud nuts and washers (2)
10. Oil pump body
11. Oil pump gear drive shaft
12. Feed pump drive gear
13. Feed pump gear key
14. Feed pump idler gear
15. By-pass valve plug
16. By-pass valve spring
17. By-pass valve
18. Check valve spring cover screw
19. Check valve spring
20. Check valve ball
21. Chain oiler adjusting screw lock nut (1964 and earlier)
22. Chain oiler adjusting screw (1964 and earlier)
22A. Chain oiler screw (1965)
23. Chain oiler adjusting screw washer (1965)
24. Oil line nipple (2) (1964 and earlier)
24A. Oil line nipple (2) (1965)
25. Chain oiler pipe (1965)

Figure following name of part indicates quantity necessary for one complete assembly.

Harley-Davidson tools, new ones pressed in and line-reamed. This is a job for the well-equipped shop.

OIL PUMP

The dry sump system is supported by a two-unit pump in a single housing. The scavenge pump returns oil to the tank; the pressure pump forces oil from the tank to various parts of the engine. (See engine oil flow diagram in MAINTENANCE AND TUNING chapter.)

The pump is a comparatively trouble-free unit. The most common trouble occurs when a metal or hard carbon chip gets between the gear teeth. It is possible for either of these to shear a key, fracture a gear or break off a gear tooth.

If oil fails to return to the tank, check the scavenger pump gear drive shaft key. When the engine receives no lubrication (oil remains in the tank), the drive shaft key on the feed pump drive gear may be sheared. Both of these conditions could be caused by shearing of the oil pump drive gear key. In cold weather, slush ice formed from moisture condensation in oil may block oil passages and cause any of the above troubles.

The pump is located on the rear of the gearcase. It may be removed as a unit only if the engine is removed from the frame. However, the pump may be disassembled without removing the gearcase cover.

① Disconnect oil lines and oil pressure switch from pump.

② Remove four nuts and washers that hold the oil pump cover in place and remove cover with gasket.

③ Remove lock ring, scavenger pump drive gear, gear key and scavenger pump idler gear.

④ Remove two oil pump body mounting stud nuts.

⑤ Pull pump body off studs and gear drive shaft.

⑥ Remove oil feed pump drive gear, key and idler gear.

⑦ Screw relief valve plug out of pump body and remove relief valve spring and valve.

⑧ Remove check valve spring cover screw, valve spring and ball.

⑨ On 1964 and earlier models, loosen the lock nut of the chain oiler adjusting screw and turn in adjusting screw. Count the turns necessary to bottom the screw and then remove it. (Bottom and turn out same number of turns when reassembling.) On 1965 models this is not necessary, since there is no chain oiler adjustment required.

⑩ Oil pump nipples may be removed from pump cover to facilitate cleaning.

Cleaning and inspection

Clean all parts in solvent and blow pump body passages clear with compressed air. Inspect valves and valve seats for pitting and wear. Replace pump having worn or damaged valve seat. Inspect keys and keyways. Inspect scavenger and feed pump gear teeth for gouging or cracking caused by foreign materials going through pump. Pump shafts and bushings normally last the lifetime of the engine.

The pump is assembled in reverse order of disassembly. Note that scavenger pump gears are thicker than the feed pump gears. Also notice that feed pump gear key is smaller than the scavenger gear key. Oil pump gaskets should always be replaced. Wet new gasket with water before reassembling. Use only Harley-Davidson factory-made gaskets. Lock rings are often damaged when removing them. It is advisable to install a new lock ring when reassembling the pump. Make sure the ring is engaged and seated in retaining groove.

On late models, oil hose connections have one-piece band type clamps and must be replaced each time hoses are connected. Use hose clamp tool, part No. 97087-65 to squeeze clamps tight as shown in drawing.

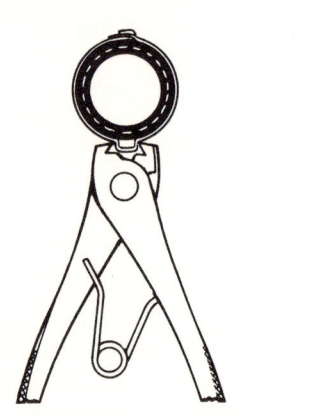

Hose clamp connection.

CRANKCASE ASSEMBLY

To work on this portion of the engine, it is necessary to remove it from the frame. Every Harley-Davidson specialist has his own method of stripping the bike for an engine removal, but for the first-timer, the factory's procedure is best to follow because it eliminates doubling back.

Preliminary steps

Remove heads and cylinders as described in TOP END chapter. Then go ahead as follows:

① Remove left footrest and chain guard cover.

② If motorcycle is equipped with compensating sprocket, use compensating sprocket shaft nut wrench, part No. 94557-55. If not, use 1 3/8" socket or box wrench to remove nut. Loosen nut by striking wrench handle several sharp blows with a hammer.

③ On 1965 and later models, remove chain adjuster mounting bolt and large brass starter shaft thrust washer.

④ Remove pushrod adjusting screw lock nut.

⑤ Put a washer about 1 3/4" in diameter with a 3/8" hole over pushrod adjusting screw and replace the lock nut.

⑥ Remove three spring tension adjusting nuts and pull clutch outer disc and spring collar assembly off clutch drive hub pins.

⑦ Pull clutch sprocket and motor sprocket out and remove from shafts.

⑧ Remove three bolts that attach the chain cover at the engine sprocket shaft.

⑨ On 1965 and later models, loosen the five transmission base mounting nuts.

⑩ Remove the four inner chain guard-to-transmission attaching bolts.

⑪ Remove clutch hub, using clutch hub nut wrench, part No. 94645-41, and clutch hub puller, part No. 95960-41A.

⑫ Remove shaft key.

⑬ Remove the two inner chain guard stud nuts which attach to the starter housing.

⑭ Remove the wire from solenoid.

⑮ Pull inner chain guard from mainshaft, using puller, part No. 95960-41A, which has four screws to fit tapped holes in chain housing.

⑯ Remove chain oiler hose at oil pump.

⑰ Remove other hoses from connections at back of chain housing.

⑱ Disconnect high tension wire at coil.

⑲ Disconnect wires from generator.

⑳ Disconnect wire from oil pressure breather pipe.

㉑ Drain the oil tank and remove oil lines from oil pump.

㉒ On 1965 and later models, remove crankcase breather pipe.

㉓ Remove footboard rear stud nut from inside of frame member and front footboard mounting stud bolts from brake master cylinder by removing nut and lock washer on back side.

㉔ Remove brake master cylinder attaching stud bolt which passes through master cylinder and frame and has a lock washer and nut on

Crankcase Assembly

back side of frame member.

㉕ Remove brake master cylinder sideplate bolt located behind master cylinder plunger boot.

㉖ Master cylinder and sideplate assembly is free to swing down away from engine crankcase.

㉗ Remove exhaust system.

㉘ On 1964 and earlier models, remove spark advance control wire at distributor.

㉙ Remove two rear screws from horn trumpet bracket and slip out spark advance control wire.

㉚ Remove two front and two rear engine mounting bolts.

With the assistance of a helper, the engine can now be removed from the right side of the frame.

With the engine on the bench, first check the end play in the mainshaft.

① Remove gearcase cover.

② Mount dial indicator on crankcase so that indicator lever can touch end of pinion shaft.

③ Rotate shaft and work all end play to right side (pinion end).

④ Set dial indicator to zero.

⑤ Rotate shaft and work all end play to sprocket end.

⑥ Read indicator and check against specifications for sprocket shaft bearing end play in SPECIFICATIONS section. If greater than tolerance shown for your particular engine series, the bearing set must be replaced.

Crankcase disassembly and reassembly

① Remove two crankcase bolts (⅜").

② Remove nuts from crankcase studs, working across the case in an "X" pattern (rather than around it). Loosen each one a little at a time.

③ Turn crankcase with right side up and tap with soft mallet to loosen top half.

④ Lift right crankcase half off.

⑤ Remove spiral lock ring from pinion shaft. Take bearing washers, bearings and retainers off pinion shaft.

⑥ Remove sprocket shaft spacer.

⑦ Install pinion shaft end of flywheels in soft vise jaws and remove left-hand thread sprocket shaft bearing nut. (Use sprocket shaft bearing nut wrench, part No. 97235-55A.)

⑧ Support the left hand case on the table of an arbor press and press the mainshaft with flywheels and rods out of the sprocket side main bearing.

⑨ Pry flywheel side outer race snap ring from groove in case with screwdriver and knife blade.

Sprocket shaft bearing nut wrench.

1. Crankcase stud bolt, ⅜ x 3¼ in. (2)
2. Crankcase stud, 5⁄16 x 5 in. (right center)
3. Crankcase breather stud and chain oiler (1963 and earlier)
3A. Crankcase breather stud and chain oiler (1964)
4. Crankcase stud, 5⁄16 x 6 in. (left center)
5. Crankcase stud, 5⁄16 x 5 7⁄16 in. (2) (top and top right)
6. Crankcase stud, 11⁄32 x 5 13⁄16 in. (2) (left and right bottom)

Figure following name of part indicates quantity necessary for one complete assembly. Locations are as viewed from left side of engine.

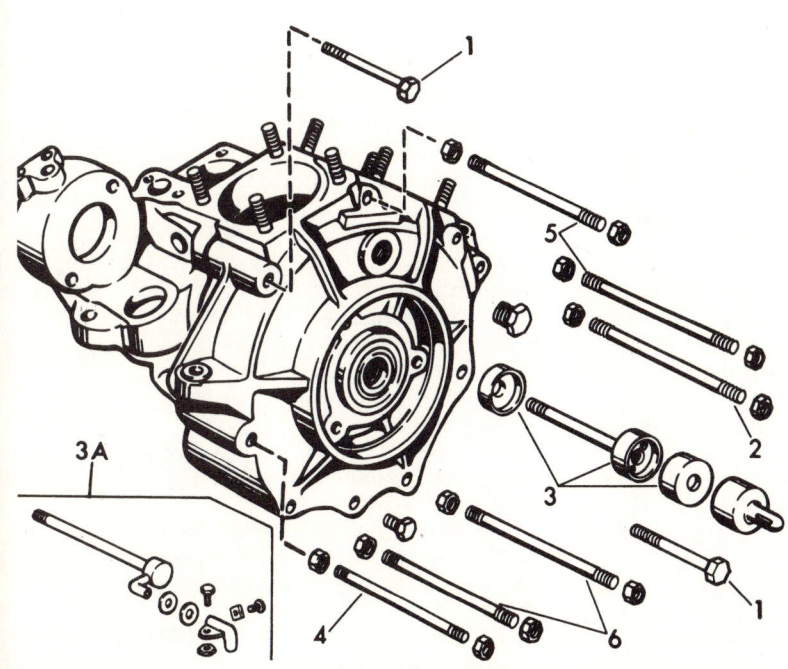

Crankcase studs, exploded view, Glide models.

The Bottom End

⑩ Put case on table and press outer races and bearing spacer from case, using sprocket shaft bearing outer race press plug, part No. 97194-57.

⑪ If flywheels are to be disassembled, install pinion shaft in vise and pull bearing from sprocket shaft, using the bearing puller, part No. 96015-56.

⑫ Place hooked end of the puller halves behind the bearing and hold the collar over puller halves.

⑬ Engage puller screw cross in puller slots and pull bearing off by tightening puller screw against sprocket shaft center.

⑭ Keep bearings in a set with proper bearing outer races.

Reassembly calls for full seating of the bearings in their recesses. The recommended order for assembly is as follows:

① Install flywheel side outer race snap ring in case.

② Use arbor press and outer race press plug, part No. 97194-57, to install outer races and bearing spacer in crankcase bushing one at a time with widest ends outward to match taper of bearings. Be sure that the first race bottoms on the snap ring and each successive part is snug against the one before.

③ To install bearing and spacer on sprocket shaft, use bearing tool, part No. 96015-56, as follows: (a) turn tool screw onto sprocket shaft thread and tighten securely; (b) remove tool handle and slip the bearing small end up over sprocket shaft, starting it squarely; (c) install the small bearing spacer and the sprocket shaft spacer; and (d) place tool sleeve on spacers and press bearing against flange on flywheel, using the tool driver and handle as shown in the illustration.

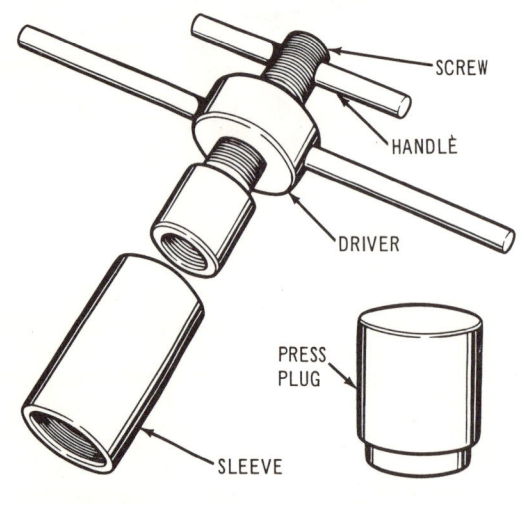

Sprocket shaft bearing installing tools.

Pressing bearing on sprocket shaft, Glide models.

④ Position flywheel assembly in vise with sprocket shaft up.

⑤ Put crankcase half, with outer race parts installed, over the shaft.

⑥ Slide bearing over tool screw, small end down.

⑦ Position tool sleeve screw and turn. Turn driver down against sleeve, pressing bearings tightly together.

Note: Bearings must be tight against the bearing spacer to provide correct bearing clearance.

⑧ Install left-hand thread bearing lock nut in crankcase, using sprocket shaft bearing nut wrench, part No. 97235-55A. Final tightening may be left until case is assembled.

⑨ Remove assembly from vise and install bearings and washers to shaft.

⑩ Fit a new spiral lock ring to groove in pinion shaft.

⑪ Apply a coat of non-hardening gasket sealer to mating surfaces and put case halves together.

⑫ Insert the studs and bolts, tapping the case as necessary to align. Tighten nuts evenly, working across the case in an "X" pattern.

CRANK AND RODS

To separate the flywheels for access to rod bearings and crank pin:

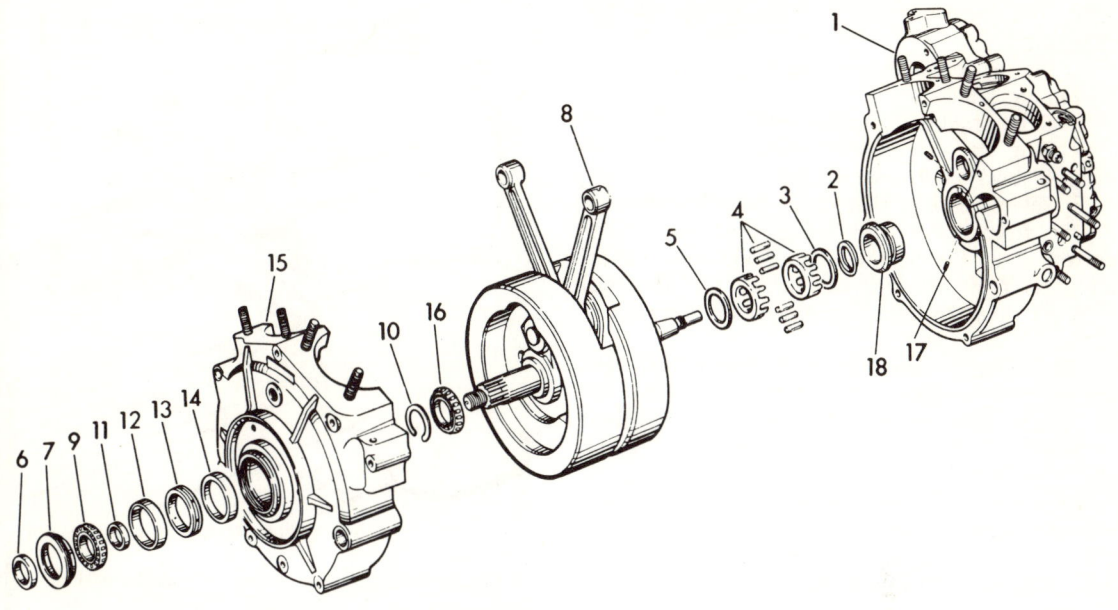

Crank and Rods

Crankcase, exploded view, Glide models.

1. Right crankcase half
2. Spiral lock ring
3. Bearing washer (2)
4. Bearings and retainer
5. Bearing washer (see item 3)
6. Sprocket shaft spacer
7. Sprocket shaft bearing nut
8. Flywheel and rod assembly
9. Sprocket bearing half
10. Flywheel side outer race snap ring
11. Bearing spacer
12. Bearing outer race
13. Bearing spacer
14. Bearing outer race
15. Left crankcase half
16. Sprocket bearing half
17. Pinion shaft bearing race lock screw (2)
18. Pinion shaft bearing race

Note: Keep parts 9, 11, 12, 13, 14 and 16 as a set. Do not transpose or interchange parts. Figure following name of part indicates quantity necessary for one complete assembly.

① Install pinion shaft vertically in soft vise jaws.

② Insert a rod through holes in flywheels to keep them from turning.

③ Remove lock plate screw, lock plate and crank pin nut.

④ Tap edge of left flywheel with soft mallet at about 90 degrees from crank pin hole to loosen.

⑤ Lift left flywheel off crank pin.

⑥ Hold down bearing assembly with a short length of pipe or tubing so connecting rods can be slipped off bearings.

⑦ Remove bearings and keep together.

⑧ Wash parts in solvent and blow dry with compressed air.

⑨ Examine crank pin for wear, grooving and pitting. If the surface is at all worn, replace with a new pin.

⑩ Examine flywheel washers. If either washer is worn and grooved, it should be renewed.

⑪ Check connecting rod races. If slightly grooved or shouldered where edge of bearing rollers ride, they may be lapped out and oversize bearing rollers installed. If badly worn, new rods should be installed as an assembly with new bearings and crank pin.

⑫ Inspect pinion shaft and right crankcase bushing for pitting, grooving and gouging at point where right main roller bearings ride.

⑬ Examine sprocket shaft outer races for wear, grooving and pitting and bearing rollers for wear, grooving, pitting and heat discoloration. The Timken tapered roller bearings are manufactured in sets. The same serial number appears on all parts. If any part is unusable, the complete set must be replaced.

If rods are worn, they may be enlarged and trued to take oversize roller bearings. This calls for a rod lapping arbor, part No. 96740-36, and a lathe. Lap the rods just enough to eliminate shiny spots, pits, grooves, etc., and to produce a velvety-metallic appearance.

The arbor is turned at about 150 rpm and adjusted to a drag fit in the rod. No. 220 grit compound mixed with oil is suggested, and the rod should be worked the full length of the tool to avoid tapering (see drawing).

After cleanup, the selection of proper oversize rollers is important. By finding a plug fit and

The Bottom End

subtracting one-half of the running clearance, the roller size necessary for a running fit can be determined.

① Put approximate-size bearings in rod and hold in one hand.

② Drop crank pin into bearings.

③ Plug fit is achieved when pin will slide through slowly of its own weight.

④ Select bearings that make plug fit, subtract .0005" from roller size being used to obtain correct size. Err on the side of looseness, if at all. Too tight bearings can seize. (If one rod is larger than the other, lap the smaller diameter out to the same size.)

This method seems to work better than attempting to measure I.D. of rod and O.D. of pin minus clearance to calculate roller diameter.

Note: All fitting should be done with parts *dry,* not oiled.

When rods are correctly fitted, extreme upper end of forked rod will have just barely noticeable side shake. The upper end of the male rod will have .025" to .031" side shake.

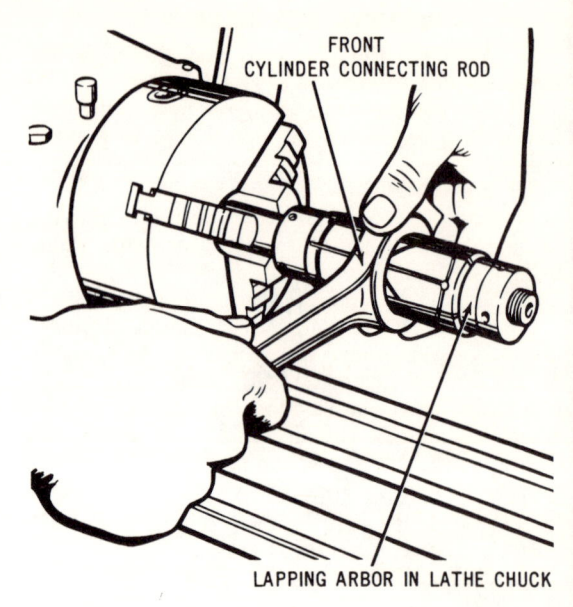

Lapping connecting rod bearing race, Glide models.

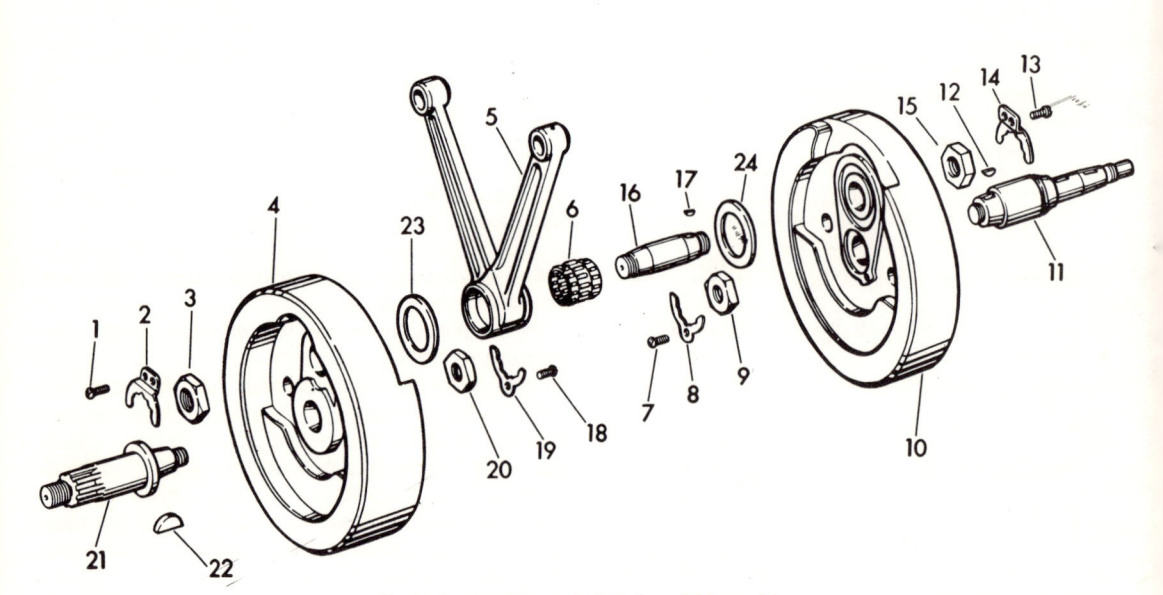

Flywheel assembly, exploded view, Glide models.

1. **Lock plate screw (4)**
2. **Lock plate (2)**
3. **Crank pin nut (2)**
4. **Left flywheel**
5. **Connecting rods (one forked, one single end)**
6. **Bearing rollers and retainers**
7. **Lock plate screw (see item 1)**
8. **Lock plate (2)**
9. **Gear shaft nut (2)**
10. **Right flywheel**
11. **Pinion shaft**
12. **Pinion shaft key**
13. **Lock plate screw (see item 1)**
14. **Lock plate (see item 2)**
15. **Crank pin lock out (see item 3)**
16. **Crank pin**
17. **Crank pin key**
18. **Lock plate screw (see item 1)**
19. **Lock plate (see item 8)**
20. **Sprocket shaft nut (see item 9)**
21. **Sprocket shaft**
22. **Sprocket shaft key**
23. **Flywheel washer (2)**
24. **Flywheel washer (see item 23)**

Figure following name of part indicates quantity necessary for one complete assembly.

TRUING FLYWHEELS

① Assemble the pin, rods and shafts to the flywheels with forked rod to rear cylinder.

② Put assembly in soft-jaw vise with left flywheel up and a rod through a hole to prevent turning.

③ Tighten left flywheel nut slightly.

④ Check edges of flywheels with straightedge and tap left wheel into alignment with right, using a soft hammer.

⑤ Tighten nut and recheck as you go.

⑥ When nut is fairly tight, install flywheel assembly in flywheel truing device, and adjust so centers are snug. Wheels must turn freely but shafts may not be loose in centers. If flywheel assembly is either loose or squeezed, indicators will not be accurate. Adjust indicators to take reading as near to flywheels as possible so pointers read at about the middle of the scales.

⑦ Turn flywheels slowly and observe the movement of indicator pointers. Movement toward flywheels indicates high points of shafts.

⑧ Find highest point of each shaft and chalk-mark flywheel rims at those points.

⑨ Loosen centers slightly, just enough so looseness may be detected, and make corrections as required.

Flywheels may be out of true three ways (see drawing) or a combination of two of the three ways:

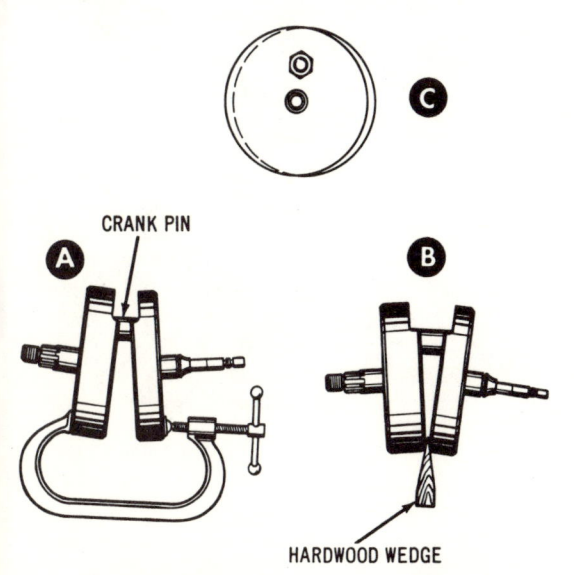

Correcting flywheel alignment, Glide models.

(A) When wheels are both out of true as indicated in "A," tighten a C-clamp on rims of wheels opposite crank pin and lightly tap the rim at the crank pin with soft mallet.

(B) When wheels are both out of true as indicated in "B," drive a hardwood wedge between the wheels opposite the crank pin and lightly tap the rims near the crank pins with a mallet.

(C) When wheels are out of true as indicated in "C," strike the rim of the wheel a firm blow at about 90° from crank pin on high side.

(D) When wheels are out of true in a combination of any of the conditions shown, correct "A" or "B" first, tapping rim of offending wheel only, and then correct condition "C."

⑩ Remember that centers must be loosened slightly before striking flywheels. Making them too loose may result in damaged centers. Never strike wheels a hard blow near crank pin. This could result in a broken crank pin.

⑪ Repeat truing operation until indicated run out does not exceed .001″ (each graduation on indicator is .002″). If it is impossible to true wheels, check for a cracked flywheel, damaged or enlarged tapered hole, or a sprocket or pinion shaft worn out of round at surface where indicator reading is being taken.

⑫ When wheels are true, position in vise and draw crank pin nuts very tight, using crank pin and flywheel nut wrench, part No. 94545-26.

⑬ Check connecting rod side play with thickness gauge. If it is greater than tolerance shown in SPECIFICATIONS, draw up crank pin nuts until within tolerance.

⑭ Insufficient play between rods and flywheel face is caused by one of the following conditions:

(A) Flywheels and crank pin assembled with oil on tapers and nuts over-tightened. Disassemble, clean, and reassemble.

(B) Taper holes enlarged as a result of having been taken apart several times. Replace wheel seating deepest.

(C) Cracked flywheel at tapered hole. Replace flywheel.

(D) New flywheel washers installed and not fully seated. Disassemble, inspect, replace deepest seating flywheel or exchange crank pin. As a last resort, grind down width of forked rod.

If sides of forked rod are ground to get desired clearance, backs of bearing retainers must be ground down to remain narrower than width of female rod.

After rod sideplay is checked and adjusted, crank pin nut pulled very tight and lock plate and screw installed, again recheck wheel trueness on truing device.

Installing flywheel washers

Proper installation of flywheel washers is highly important to the side clearance of connecting rods and flywheel alignment.

The washers are a close fit in the flywheel and are secured by punching flywheel metal against the washers at several points. It is usually necessary to drill a small hole at the outer edge of a washer to pry it out. Before installing a new washer, scrape the outer edge of the washer recess where metal was punched against it so new washer may seat fully against recess bottom.

Sprocket side bearing

If Timken tapered roller bearings and races pass visual check and have no apparent wear, the same set may be reinstalled. Make certain all parts of bearing are installed in exactly the same order they were removed. If any part of bearing assembly is worn, entire assembly should be replaced.

Pinion side bearing

If bearing clearance is too great, replacement with oversize rollers is called for. This is accomplished in much the same manner as installing oversize rod bearings. The race must be lapped to clean it up and to achieve a fit with the proper oversize. The tool is part No. 96718-58, main-bearing lap, and is operated by hand, rather than on a lathe.

Oversize rollers are available in .0002", .0004", .0006", .0008" and .001" sizes, and running fit is about .0008" to .001" over the plug fit.

Determine plug fit by using the mainshaft (without flywheel) as outlined in section on rod

Engine, right side view (1967 model XLH shown), Sportster series.

1. Gasoline line
2. Gasoline tank interconnecting line
2A. Vent line (1966 and later)
3. Cleaner assembly
4. Throttle cable connection
5. Engine support bolt location
6. Exhaust pipe port clamp (2)
9. Starter crank clamp bolt
10. Starter spring
11. Footrest
12. Foot shift lever
13. Cover bolt (2)
14. Rear chain
15. Oil return line
16. Oil vent line
17. Oil feed line
18. Breather pipe
19. Oil pressure switch wire
20. Clutch cable
21. Clip
22. Choke connection

Figure following name of part indicates quantity necessary for one complete assembly.

Tappets, Cams and Gear Train

Engine, left side view (1967 model XLH shown), Sportster series.

23. Top front end mounting bolt
24. Engine mounting bolts
25. Safety guard bolt hole
26. Battery (1967 XLH)
27. Battery carrier (1967 XLH)
28. Ground wire
29. Spark plugs
30. Horn cover
31. Wire
32. Support bracket and choke control (1966)
33. Support bracket bolt
35. Regulator ground strap
36. Engine mounting bolt
37. Oil tank
38. Foot lever and spring
39. Left footrest

bearings. Remember to check these fittings with all parts clean, dry and free from oil.

Sportster Models

TAPPETS, CAMS AND GEAR TRAIN

Sportster engine tappets are roller-mechanical and suffer from very few problems unless a seized valve has caused a broken roller. Ordinarily, the tappets are only removed for checking cam-gear end play. However, if there is excessive clearance between tappet and guide, a new tappet or guide can be installed. Individual parts of the tappet can be replaced if damaged or worn. (The adjusting screw is a good example.)

To pull guide-tappet assembly, proceed as follows:

① Remove tappet guide screw and tappet adjusting screw.

② Install tappet guide puller, part No. 95724-57, in mating grooves of tappet guide.

③ Before turning tappet guide from crankcase, be sure cam gear is installed in case for tappet to butt against when using puller.

④ Mark tappets in some manner to identify them as to location. It is good practice to reassemble valve tappets and valve tappet guides in the same place from which they were removed. This will ensure an even-wear pattern between tappet, guide and cam surface.

The gearcase cover and gears can be removed with the engine in the frame, as follows:

① Loosen exhaust pipe and muffler clamps

and pull exhaust pipe free of gearcase cover.

② Remove footrest, gear shift foot lever and breather pipe.

③ Remove distributor or magneto.

④ Remove pushrods.

⑤ Place a pan under gearcase to collect oil when cover is removed.

⑥ Remove gearcase cover screws evenly.

⑦ The cover must be worked off the pins carefully to avoid damage to joint faces. Do not pry off with a screwdriver inserted between joint faces. Use a hammer and a block of wood, and tap lightly at the end where the cover projects beyond the gearcase.

⑧ Remove valve tappets and valve tappet guides only to establish correct cam gear end play.

⑨ Pull clutch cable forward, and at the same time press cable inward and down to free from gearcase cover.

⑩ Refer to exploded drawing of gearcase and remove cam gears and cam gear plates. (Cam gears are numbered on cam lobe from one to four, from the rear exhaust valve cam forward.) When cam gears are removed, note whether or not cam gears one, three and four have thin steel spacing washers on either end of the cam gear shafts. If any of the cam gears mentioned have spacing washers, be sure the same number are used on each shaft when reassembling, if the same cam gears and case cover are used again.

⑪ Remove idler gear with fiber washer by lifting generator up and away from crankcase. Discard gasket.

⑫ Use pinion gear puller, part No. 96830-51, to remove pinion gear from pinion shaft splines.

⑬ Remove spiral oil pump gear, which is a slip fit on splined shaft.

Replacement should be carried out in reverse order of the above, after first checking end play of cam gears (.001″ to .006″), as follows:

① Temporarily install the two cam gear plates, less shims, against crankcase with beveled side of holes for cam shaft facing outward.

② Install cam gears one, three and four.

③ Assemble the case cover with a dry gasket and securely tighten in place (less generator bolts).

④ Turn the engine over until the number one gear lobe is facing up as indicated through the tappet guide hole in the crankcase.

⑤ Use a long-shank screwdriver to pry the cam gear toward the case cover.

⑥ Measure the clearance (end play) between the cam shaft shoulder and the gear plate.

⑦ If end play exceeds specifications, add steel shims to obtain recommended running clearance. After adding shims, turn engine over to be sure cam gears turn freely.

⑧ Repeat on other gears.

Then proceed with final installation:

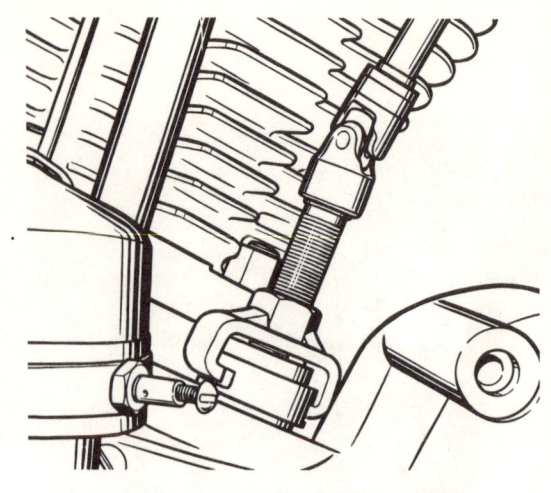

Removing tappet guide, Sportster models.

Removing gearcase cover, Sportster models.

1. Exhaust pipe port clamp (2)
2. Footrest
3. Gear shift foot lever
4. Breather pipe
5. Circuit breaker
6. Gearcase cover
7. Push rod (4)
8. Gearcase cover screw (11)
9. **Clutch cable**

Tappets, Cams and Gear Train

① Lubricate timing gear shafts and position in crankcase with marks on gears one, two, three, four and five in alignment.

② Install idler gear in crankcase with fiber washer toward the cover side.

③ Use sealer to hold gearcase cover gasket in place. (Be sure to install a new factory-made gasket. Never use a homemade gasket. The cover gasket has holes especially located for oil passages and if a hole is left out or put in the wrong place, the oiling system will not function normally.)

④ With a small paintbrush, put a liberal coating of oil on the gears.

⑤ Carefully align cover and tap into position. Cover should slip into place easily and should never be forced or driven into place.

⑥ Tighten all screws evenly, working opposite from one another.

⑦ Install generator and gasket in place.

⑧ Tilt generator back end down as it is inserted in gearcase opening to lift oil slinger over intermediate gear, and then up to mesh generator and intermediate gears.

⑨ Turn engine over to make sure gears turn freely.

Note: Do not overlook the important fact that the breather valve must be retimed (if it has been disengaged from the oil pump drive gear) before the gear train can be properly aligned.

Time it as follows:

① Flywheel timing mark should be exactly in center of timing inspection hole in left side of crankcase.

② Oil pump drive gear is located on splined shaft behind pinion gear. A mark is cut on one side of spiral gear, which should face outward against pinion gear when assembled to shaft.

③ Assemble spiral gear against shoulder on pinion shaft engaging breather sleeve gear tooth which will register timing hole in breather sleeve in center of slot in breather bushing as shown in the drawing.

④ Install pinion gear, using gear puller and installer tool. (This positions pinion gear outer face exactly 5/16" from gearcase joint face, the running position for the gear when the case cover is in place.)

⑤ Once the breather valve is correctly timed, the position of the flywheel timing mark and breather valve timing mark, registered in the slot of the breather sleeve gear, can be disregarded when installing timing gears.

Parts inspection

Follow general recommendations under this heading in GLIDE MODELS section.

Specified clearance for cam gear shafts in cover bushings and for pinion gear shaft in cover bushing is .0005" to .001". Specified clearance for cam gear shafts in **crankcase needle roller**

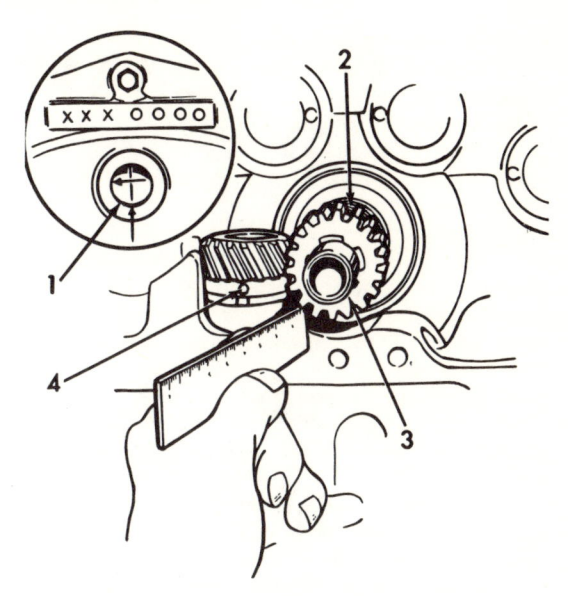

Timing crankcase breather, Sportster models.

1. Flywheel timing mark
2. Oil pump drive gear (spiral gear)
3. Pinion gear
4. Timing hole in breather sleeve gear

Installing pinion gear, Sportster models.

bearings is .0005" to .0025".

When bushings are worn to the extent of increasing clearance to .001" or more over specified limits, they should be replaced, for the cam gears are likely to become very noisy with excessive clearance in the bushings. Examine the face of each bronze bushing flange for wear. If bushing flanges are badly worn, **replace the bushings.**

The Bottom End

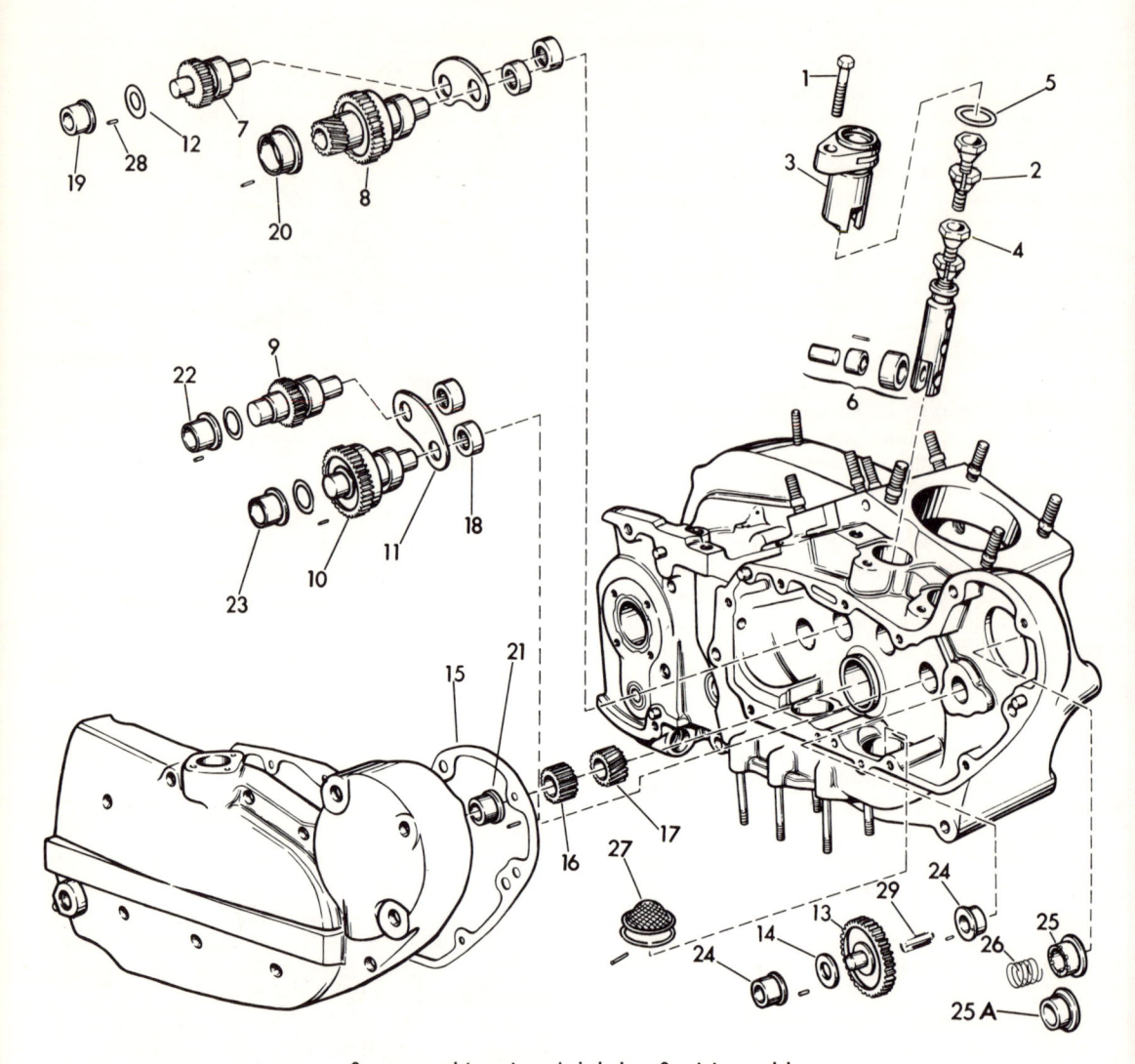

Gearcase and tappet, exploded view, Sportster models.

1. Tappet guide screw
2. Tappet screw with nut
3. Tappet guide
4. Tappet and roller
5. Tappet guide "O" ring
6. Tappet roller kit
7. Rear cylinder exhaust cam gear
8. Rear cylinder intake cam gear
9. Front cylinder intake cam gear
10. Front cylinder exhaust cam gear
11. Cam gear plate (2)
12. Cam shaft washer—.006 in.
13. Idler gear
14. Idler gear shaft fiber washer
15. Gearcase cover gasket
16. Flywheel shaft pinion gear
17. Oil pump drive gear
18. Cam gear needle roller bearing (4)
19. Rear exhaust cam gear shaft bushing
20. Cam gear and time shaft bushing
21. Pinion gear shaft bushing
22. Front intake cam gear shaft bushing
23. Front exhaust cam gear shaft bushing
24. Idler gear shaft bushing (2)
25. Oil separator bushing assembly (1962 and earlier)
25A. Oil separator bushing (1963 and later)
26. Breather oil separator seal ring spring (1962 and earlier)
27. Crankcase oil strainer, retaining pin and gasket
28. Gearcase cover bushing pin (7)
29. Idler gear shaft

Figure following name of part indicates quantity necessary for one complete assembly.

Oil Pump

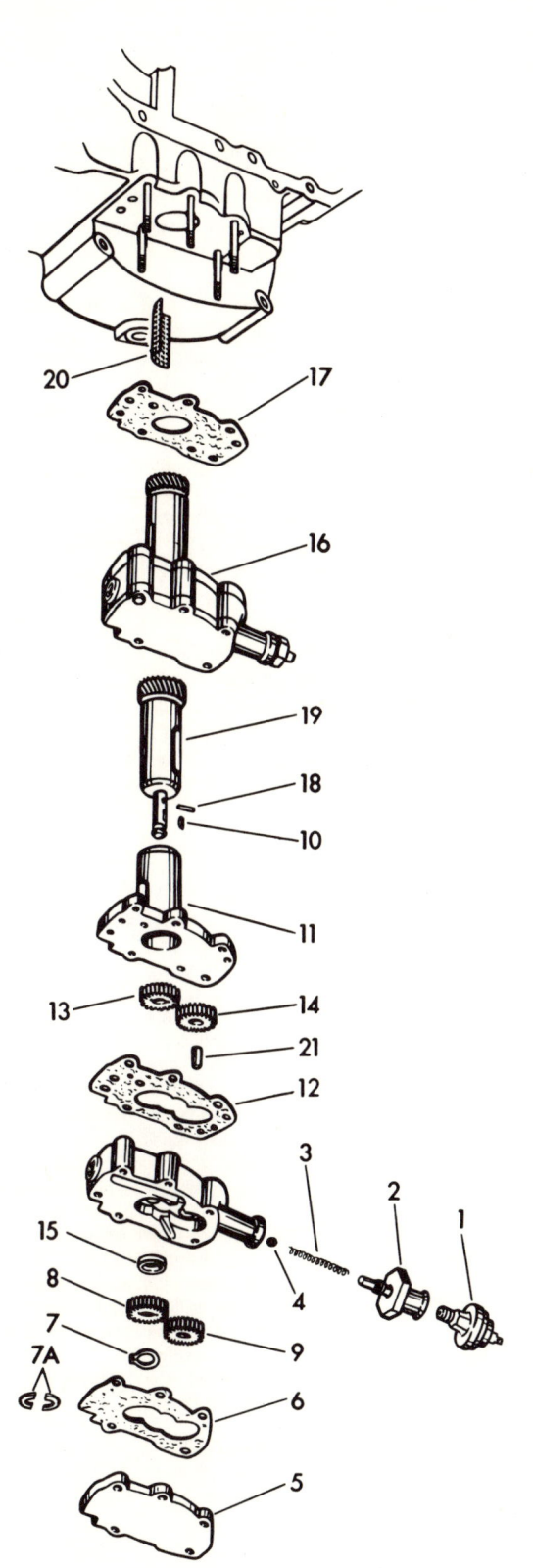

Examine the cam gear plate for excessive wear or damage. Replace if necessary. Check the operation of the oil separator bushing assembly used on 1962 and earlier models. The bushing is spring-loaded and should have free action and be fully extended in gearcase cover.

Fixed-type bushing should have $1/16''$ running clearance with the generator oil slinger washer.

Inspect the crankcase oil strainer to make sure it is not plugged with any foreign material.

OIL PUMP

See GLIDE MODELS heading for general instructions.

The check valve should be checked and cleaned if there is any doubt as to pump operation.

① Clean exterior of pump in solvent before disassembly.

② Disconnect oil pressure switch wire and disassemble switch from motorcycle.

③ Remove oil pump nipple.

④ Free check valve spring and valve from pump body.

⑤ Clean all parts in solvent.

⑥ Blow out pump nipple oil passage and the nipple valve spring guide.

⑦ Examine the nipple for any damage that would bind or hinder the free operation of the spring.

⑧ Examine the nipple threads for wear; if badly worn, replace nipple.

⑨ Replace spring if worn, rusted or damaged. Free length of new check valve spring is approximately $1\,15/64''$.

⑩ Check valve ball may have rings formed by action on valve seat. Valves not perfectly smooth and round should be replaced.

1. Oil pressure switch
2. Oil pump nipple
3. Check valve spring
4. Ball valve
5. Body plate
6. Body plate gasket
7. Retaining ring
7A. Retainer (2) (half ring)
8. Scavenger pump gear
9. Scavenger pump idler gear
10. Breather valve key
11. Oil pump cover
12. Body cover gasket
13. Pump gear
14. Pump idler gear
15. Oil pump seal
16. Oil pump body
17. Body gasket
18. Drive lock pin
19. Breather valve gear and shaft
20. Crankcase breather valve screen
21. Idler gear shaft

Oil pump, exploded view, Sportster models.

⑪ Use bright light to inspect valve seat in pump body for pits and dirty condition. A small particle of foreign matter lodged on valve seat will prevent check valve ball from seating. If seat is only slightly damaged, place check valve ball on seat and with a drift lightly tap it against its seat to remove slight striation marks or pits. Replace pump body if valve seat is badly damaged.

Assemble in the reverse order of disassembly. Apply a light coating of oil to all moving parts. Make sure that check valve ball is correctly seated and valve action is free. Be extremely careful to prevent dust, dirt or other foreign particles from getting on the parts when reassembling.

CRANKCASE ASSEMBLY

The crank assembly of the Sportster is like that of the larger models, but the case is different and several added steps in disassembly are required.

Preliminary steps

① Remove all components from engine as described in THE TOP END chapter.

② Disconnect spark control wire from distributor or magneto (1964 and earlier XLH and 1965 XLCH).

③ Remove starter crank clamp bolt and with a screwdriver pry crank from shaft. Press down on end of starter spring and at the same time pry spring off shaft.

④ Shift into high gear and remove footrest and foot shift lever.

⑤ Remove transmission sprocket cover.

⑥ Disengage clutch cable end from clutch release lever by moving lever forward (as positioned on motorcycle) and disengage cable from lever.

⑦ Disconnect rear chain.

⑧ Remove oil return line and vent line at oil tank and oil feed line at engine.

⑨ Remove breather pipe and disconnect oil pressure switch wire from switch.

⑩ Pull clutch cable forward until approximately 1" of cable remains in gearcase cover. At the same time press cable inward (toward oil pump) and down to free from cover.

⑪ Remove oil pressure switch.

⑫ Use vise grip pliers to disconnect the speedometer cable from speedometer drive unit (located under transmission sprocket cover) and free cable from clip.

⑬ Remove lower front safety guard bolt.

⑭ Loosen, but do not remove, the top front engine mounting bolt.

⑮ Remove three remaining engine mounting bolts and lower front safety guard bolt.

⑯ Remove tool box (1966 and earlier XLH

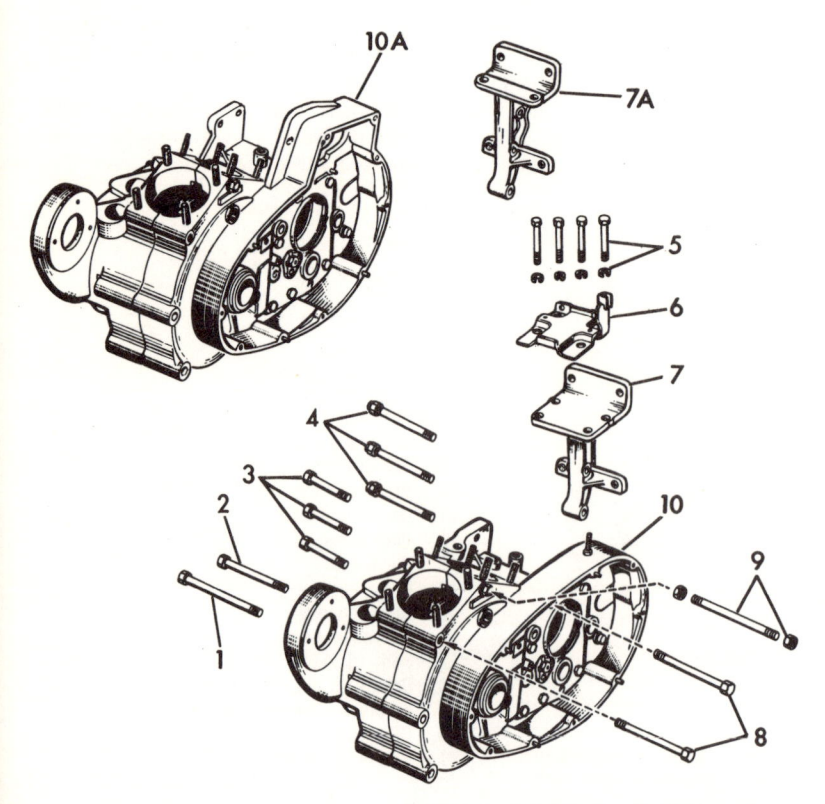

1. Crankcase mounting bolt 5/16 x 4 7/16"
2. Crankcase mounting bolt 5/16 x 4 1/16"
3. Crankcase mounting bolt 5/16 x 2 3/8" (3)
4. Crankcase rear mounting stud and lock nut (3)
5. Engine rear mounting bolt and lock washer (4) (1966 and earlier), (2) (1967)
6. Battery carrier (1966 and earlier)
7. Engine rear mount (1966 and earlier)
7A. Engine rear mount (1967)
8. Crankcase bolt (2)
9. Crankcase stud and lock nut (center)
10. Crankcase (1966 and earlier)
10A. Crankcase (1967)

Figure following name of part indicates quantity necessary for one complete assembly.

Crankcase, exploded view, Sportster engine.

Crankcase Assembly

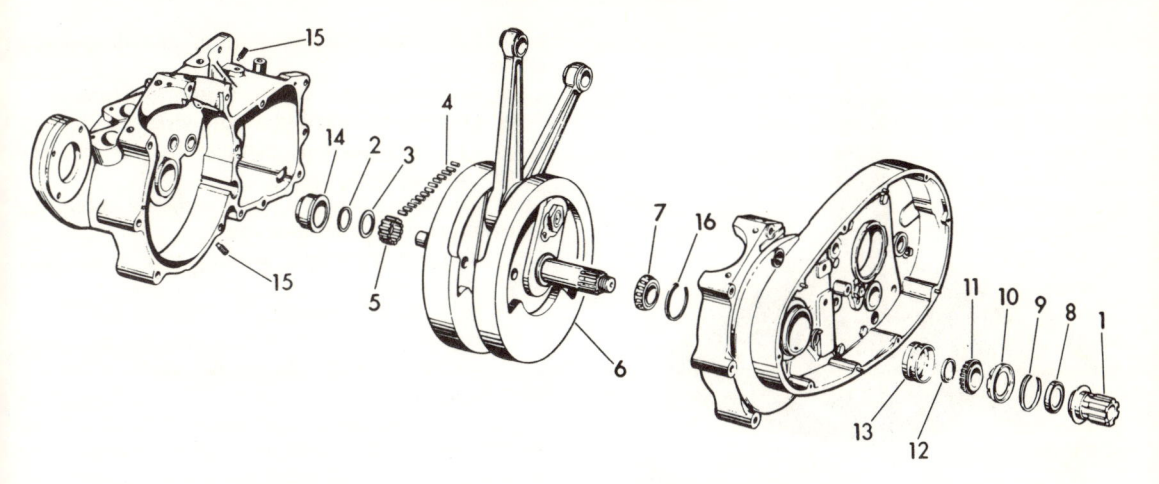

Sportster model crankcase and flywheel assembly, exploded view.

1. Sprocket shaft extension
2. Pinion shaft bearing snap ring
3. Pinion shaft bearing washer
4. Pinion shaft roller bearing (13)
5. Pinion shaft roller bearing retainer
6. Connecting rod and flywheel assembly
7. Sprocket shaft Timken bearing right half
8. Sprocket shaft oil seal
9. Sprocket shaft bearing spring ring (outer)
10. Sprocket shaft bearing spacer
11. Sprocket shaft Timken bearing left half
12. Sprocket shaft Timken bearing spacer
13. Sprocket shaft Timken bearing outer race
14. Pinion shaft bushing
15. Pinion shaft bearing bushing screw (2)
16. Sprocket shaft bearing spring ring (inner)

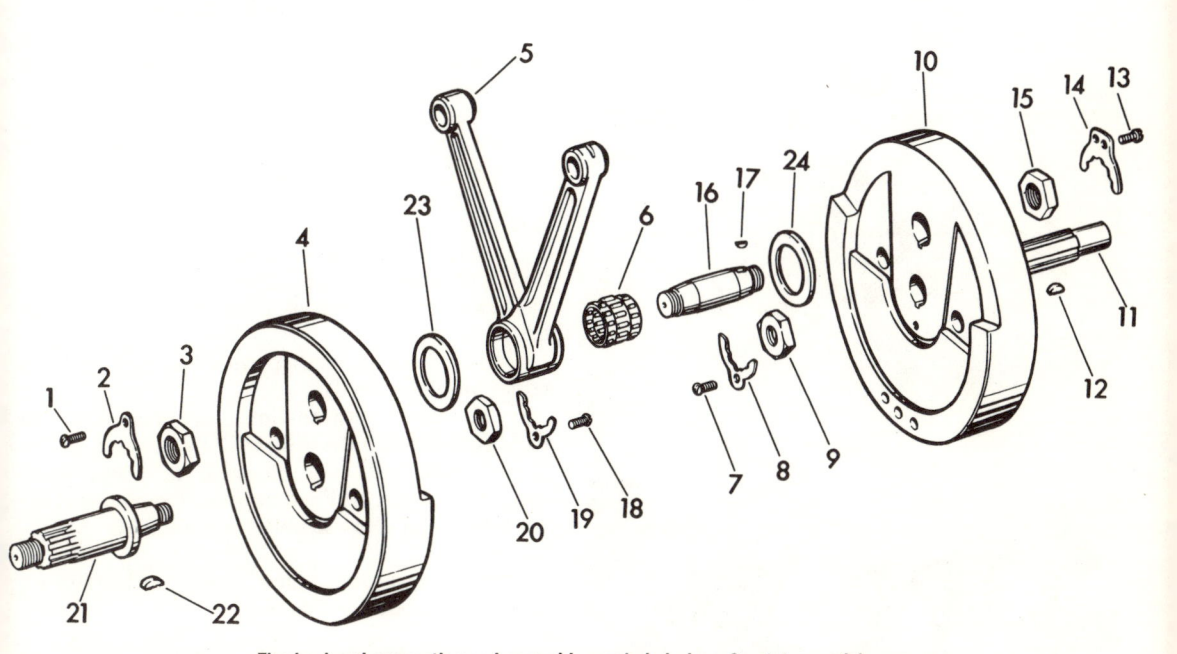

Figure following name of part indicates quantity necessary for one complete assembly.

Flywheel and connecting rod assembly, exploded view, Sportster models.

1. Crank pin lock plate screw
2. Crank pin nut lock plate
3. Crank pin nut
4. Flywheel (left)
5. Connecting rods
6. Crank pin roller and retainer set
7. Pinion shaft lock plate screw
8. Pinion shaft nut lock plate
9. Pinion shaft nut
10. Flywheel (right)
11. Pinion shaft
12. Pinion shaft key
13. Crank pin lock plate screw
14. Crank pin nut lock plate
15. Crank pin nut
16. Crank pin
17. Crank pin key
18. Sprocket shaft lock plate screw
19. Sprocket shaft nut lock plate
20. Sprocket shaft nut
21. Sprocket shaft
22. Sprocket shaft key
23. Crank pin boss washer (left)
24. Crank pin boss washer (right)

The Bottom End

Installing bearing (right half) and spacer, Sportster models.

Installing sprocket shaft extension, Sportster models.

model) by removing two Phillips screws and one nut at base.

⑰ Remove battery tie rod support, if fitted.

⑱ Disconnect distributor coil wire.

⑲ On 1967 models, remove battery, battery carrier and oil tank.

⑳ Remove two top rear engine mounting bolts and regulator ground strap.

㉑ Remove stop light switch, rear brake foot lever and spring.

㉒ Remove left footrest.

㉓ Remove two lower rear engine mounting bolts (located directly above rear brake crossover shaft.)

㉔ On 1964 and earlier XLH models remove battery wire (red wire with white tracer) and generator wires (red wire with black tracer and black wire with white tracer) from voltage regulator.

㉕ Free oil switch wire from behind generator (green wire with white tracer).

㉖ Remove front top engine mounting bolt.

㉗ With the help of an assistant, lift engine up off mounting pad. Then slip engine from left side of frame with top of engine tipped slightly toward right.

With heads, cylinders, clutch, gearcase assembly, generator, magneto or distributor and oil pump removed (as previously described):

① Take speedometer drive unit from the right case and remove right crankcase bolts and stud nuts.

② Remove bolts, battery carrier or oil tank bracket on magneto models, engine rear mount, studs, and top center crankcase stud.

③ Position crankcase on work bench, gearcase side up.

④ Tap crankcase with mallet to loosen top half, and separate cases.

⑤ Remove snap ring from pinion shaft with tip of screwdriver.

⑥ Lift bearing washer with bearings and retainer off pinion shaft.

⑦ Remove transmission as described in CLUTCH AND TRANSMISSION chapter.

⑧ Mount left case on table of arbor press and proceed as outlined under "Crankcase Disassembly and Reassembly" in GLIDE MODELS section.

Check specifications and actual measurements on all components as you work.

CRANK AND RODS

See this section under GLIDE MODELS.

CHAPTER 4

Clutch and Transmission

Most transmission problems can usually be traced to a lack of attention to the clutch or an effort to "get by" without gearbox maintenance or repair. Proper lubrication is very important, and keeping the clutch and shift mechanism adjusted so clean, crisp gear changes can be made is equally so. When any slight problem develops, take care of it immediately.

Although adjustments and many repairs can be made with only common hand tools, extensive gearbox work is best referred to the authorized Harley-Davidson shop. An outline of these repair procedures will be included, however, so that the rider will know what is involved and the skilled mechanic can perform certain services in an emergency.

CLUTCH

Any rider can recognize a dragging, chattering or slipping clutch. And any rider can adjust the clutch properly, but he may not know the cause behind the symptoms. Therefore, we will begin with a diagnosis.

Diagnosis
1. *Slipping*
    (a) Improper adjustment
    (b) Weakened springs
    (c) Worn discs
    (d) Oil on discs
2. *Dragging*
    (a) Improper advances
    (b) Excess spring tension
    (c) Warped discs
    (d) Dirty discs
3. *Chattering*
    (a) Loose rivets
    (b) Worn hub key
    (c) Spring disc flattened

Glide Models

ADJUSTMENT

Foot control

① With foot pedal in fully disengaged position (heel down), the clutch lever should strike the transmission case cover. Adjust length of the foot pedal rod to just clear the foot pedal bearing cover so the rod is not bent down by the bearing cover.

② On 1964 and earlier models, remove the chain guard clutch cover. On 1965 models, remove the chain housing cover.

③ Move the foot pedal to a toe down or fully engaged position.

④ Loosen the lock nut and readjust the pushrod adjusting screw with a screwdriver so that the end of the clutch lever rod has about ⅛" free movement before the clutch disengages. (Turn the screw right for less movement and left for more.)

⑤ On 1964 models, clutch lever should strike the transmission case cover.

⑥ On 1965 models, the clutch lever should be ¼" away from the starter drive housing.

Hand control

Normally, the only attention that the clutch hand control requires is occasional adjustment of control coil adjusting sleeve and the clutch lever rod to maintain the correct amount of free movement for the hand lever on the handlebar and the clutch actuating lever.

If major readjustment is indicated by the hand lever becoming hard to operate, the clutch con-

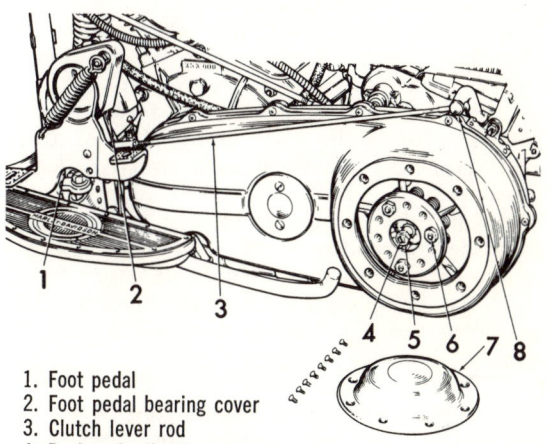

1. Foot pedal
2. Foot pedal bearing cover
3. Clutch lever rod
4. Push rod adjusting screw
5. Push rod adjusting screw lock nut
6. Spring tension adjusting nuts (3)
7. Clutch cover
8. Clutch actuating lever

Adjusting foot clutch control (1964 Glide model shown).

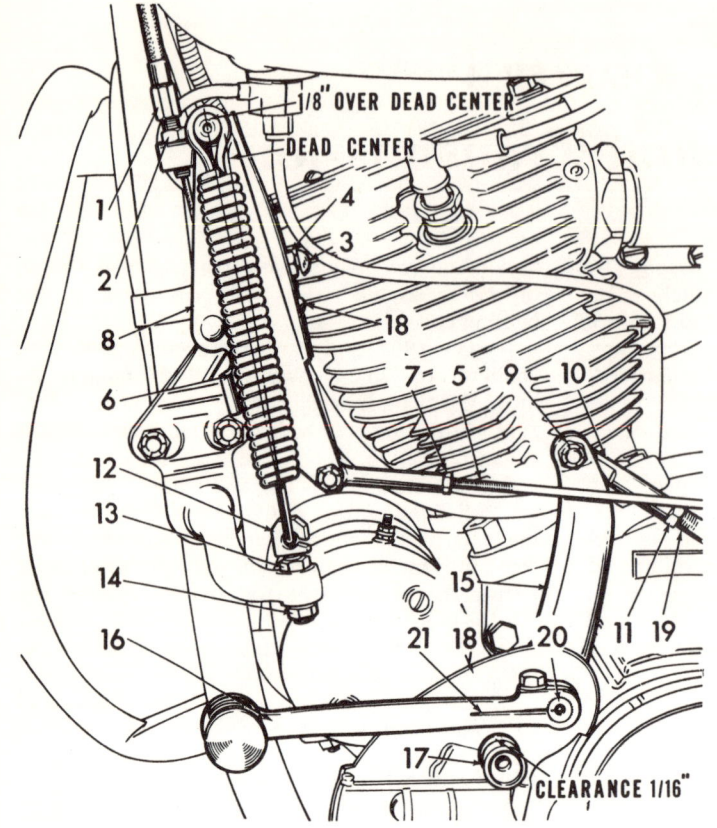

Clutch and Transmission

1. Control coil adjusting sleeve
2. Control coil adjusting sleeve lock nut
3. Bell crank adjusting screw
4. Bell crank adjusting screw lock nut
5. Clutch lever rod
6. Clutch control booster spring
7. Clutch lever rod lock nut
8. Clutch control booster bell crank
9. Shifter rod end bolt
10. Shifter rod end
11. Shifter rod end lock nut
12. Clutch booster spring tension adjuster
13. Clutch booster spring tension upper adjuster nut
14. Clutch booster spring tension lower adjuster nut
15. Gear shifter lever
16. Gear shifter foot lever and rubber pedal
17. Foot lever cover mounting stud (1964 and earlier models)
18. Grease gun fittings (2)
19. Shifter rod
20. Foot lever positioning mark
21. Foot lever clamping slot

Figure following name of part indicates quantity necessary for one complete assembly.

Adjusting hand clutch booster, Glide models.

trol booster bellcrank failing to return to the forward position when the hand lever is released, a slipping clutch, or dragging clutch manifested by gear clash when shifting, the following adjustments should be made:

① Loosen clutch lever rod lock nut and adjust clutch lever rod far enough so the clutch actuating lever has about ½″ free movement.

② Move end of actuating lever forward to a position where it becomes firm, indicating that all slack in the actuating mechanism has been taken up.

③ On 1964 and earlier models, the distance from the foot shifter housing on the transmission to the outer edge of chamfered slot in lever should be 4¼″. On 1965 and later models, the distance between the chain housing and clutch lever rod should be ¼″.

④ Remove clutch cover or chain housing cover, loosen pushrod adjusting screw lock nut and turn pushrod adjusting screw in (clockwise) to move lever to rear; out (counterclockwise) to move lever forward.

⑤ When correct position of lever has been attained, tighten lock nut.

⑥ Loosen control coil adjusting sleeve lock nut and turn in adjusting sleeve until clutch hand grip has an inch or more free play.

⑦ Loosen bell crank adjusting screw lock nut and tighten bell crank adjusting screw until bell crank fails to go across top dead center when moved back and forth by hand.

⑧ Loosen clutch booster spring tension upper adjusting nut as far as it will go.

⑨ Turn out bell crank adjusting screw a little at a time until bell crank moves over top dead center and remains in that position when released. (Move bell crank by hand, not with control hand lever. Bell crank should find locked position at about ⅛″ over dead center.)

⑩ Tighten adjusting screw lock nut.

⑪ Adjust clutch lever rod so clutch actuating lever has 1/16″ free movement.

⑫ Tighten clutch lever rod lock nut.

⑬ Turn adjusting sleeve upward until end of clutch hand lever has ½″ free movement before releasing pressure is applied to clutch.

⑭ Tighten lock nut.

⑮ Depress clutch hand lever fully.

⑯ Tighten clutch booster spring tension lower adjusting nut until hand lever remains depressed.

⑰ Slowly loosen lower adjusting nut enough to allow hand lever to return to fully extended position.

Disassembly and Reassembly

⑱ Tighten upper adjusting nut.

Spring tension

If the clutch still skips with controls properly adjusted, increase the spring tension. If it drags, spring tension may be too high.

A new clutch is assembled so the distance from the inner edge of spring collar to the surface of the outer disc is exactly $31/32''$. If this distance is $7/8''$ or less, the clutch probably cannot be fully disengaged.

To increase or decrease tension, turn the three slotted clutch spring nuts ½ turn at a time until the desired effect is attained. You can test for slip by cranking the engine. Generally a slipping clutch will hold in use if it will hold for cranking.

DISASSEMBLY AND REASSEMBLY

It is not necessary to remove transmission from chassis to disassemble clutch, starter, main drive gear oil seal or clutch release mechanism.

① Remove outer chain guard or chain housing cover.

② Remove pushrod adjusting screw lock nut.

③ Place a flat washer about ⅛" thick with 1¾" outside diameter and ⅜" hole over the adjusting screw.

④ Replace lock nut and turn down until three spring tension adjusting nuts are free.

⑤ Remove nuts and the spring collar-springs-outer disc assembly. (Do not disassemble these parts unless necessary to replace spring, spring collar or outer disc.)

⑥ Remove spring disc, three steel discs and three friction discs.

⑦ If motorcycle is equipped with compensating sprocket, use compensating sprocket shaft nut wrench, part No. 94557-55, to remove com-

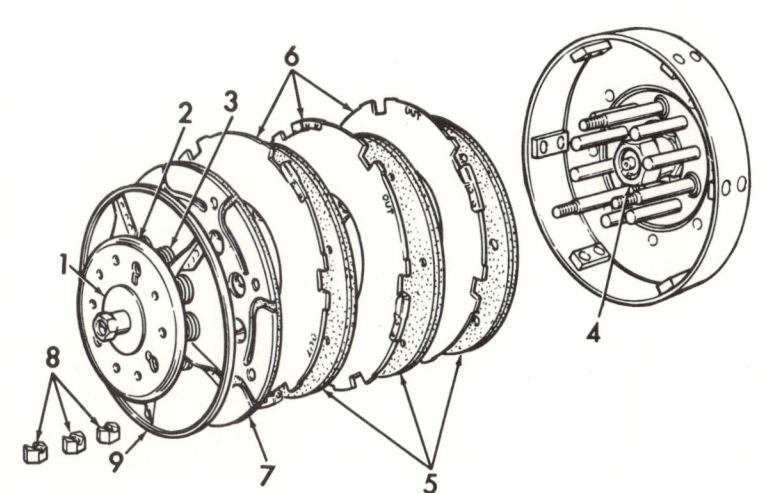

Positioning clutch actuating lever (1964 Glide model).

1. Clutch actuating lever
2. Clutch cover
3. Push rod adjusting screw
4. Push rod adjusting screw lock nut
5. Clutch lever rod

1. Flat washer
2. Spring collar
3. Springs
4. Clutch hub nut
5. Lined friction discs (3)
6. Steel discs (3)
7. Spring disc
8. Spring tension adjusting nuts (3)
9. Outer disc

Figure following name of part indicates quantity necessary for one complete assembly.

Clutch, exploded view, Glide models.

pensating sprocket shaft nut. If not, use 1⅜" socket or box wrench to remove nut. Loosen nut by striking wrench handle several sharp blows with hammer.

⑧ Remove clutch shell and primary chain from clutch hub.

⑨ Pry back ear on clutch hub nut lock washers.

⑩ Remove clutch hub nut, using clutch hub nut wrench, part No. 94645-41 (left-hand thread). Loosen nut by striking wrench handle several sharp blows with a mallet.

⑪ Remove clutch hub nut lock washer and on 1964 and earlier models, strip pushrod cork oil seal off pushrod.

⑫ Remove clutch hub, using clutch hub puller, part No. 95960-41A, to pull hub off tapered shaft.

⑬ Remove hub key.

When reassembling clutch

① Install a new cork oil seal on clutch pushrod.

② Make sure steel discs are installed with side stamped "OUT" facing outward.

③ Draw down stud nuts evenly until distance from back of pressure plate to front of clutch releasing disc is ³¹⁄₃₂".

④ Make final adjustments to clutch as described above.

Parts inspection

① Friction discs should be replaced if they appear:
  (a) Glazed or burned (smooth, shiny, dark)
  (b) Grooved
  (c) Worn down to near rivets
  (d) Oil soaked
  (e) Chipped around the edges or cracked.

In an emergency, oil soaked discs can be re-used if soaked overnight in solvent or white gasoline, dried thoroughly and roughened with sand paper. This won't be very satisfactory, but it might get you home from some far-off place.

② Check bearing race inside clutch shell. If it appears grooved or pitted, the shell should be replaced.

③ Revolve clutch hub roller bearing. If it sticks or feels rough, inner bearing race is probably pitted and should be replaced. Disassemble clutch hub as follows:
  (A) Remove three bearing plate springs.
  (B) Slip bearing plate off hub pins and remove bearing retainer. If inner race proves to be worn, replace hub.

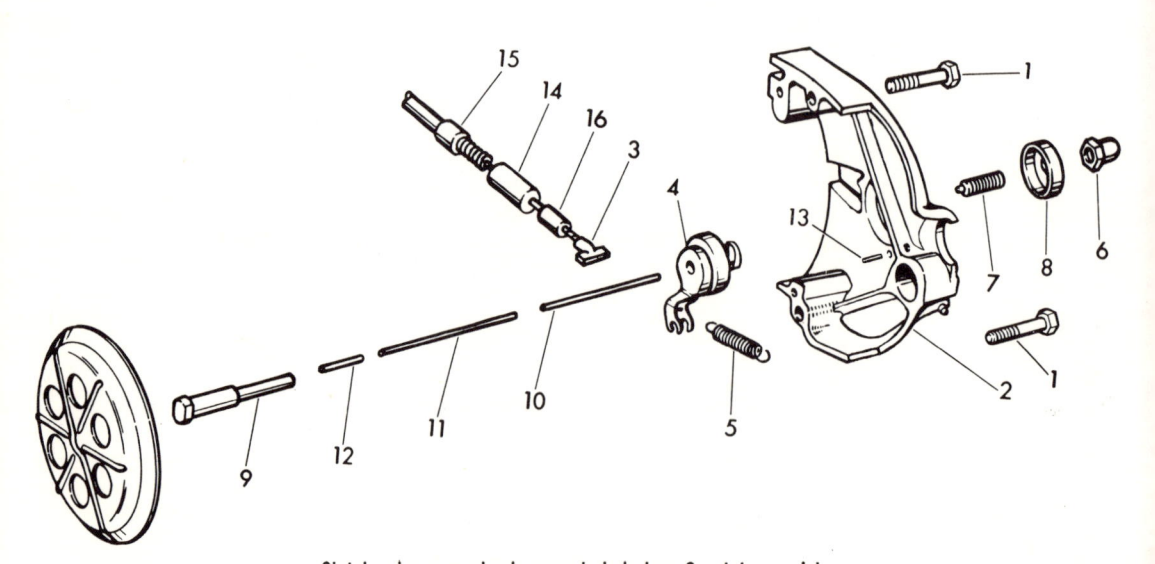

Clutch release mechanism, exploded view, Sportster models.

1. Sprocket cover bolt (2)
2. Sprocket cover
3. Control cable end
4. Clutch release worm and lever
5. Clutch release worm and lever spring
6. Clutch adjusting screw lock nut
7. Clutch adjusting screw
8. Clutch release worm cover
9. Clutch release rod—left
10. Clutch release rod—right
11. Clutch release rod—right center
12. Clutch release rod—left center
13. Sprocket cover roll pin
14. Clutch cable felt seal retainer
15. Clutch cable ferrule (2)
16. Clutch cable felt seal

Figure following name of part indicates quantity necessary for one **complete** assembly.

Disassembly and Reassembly

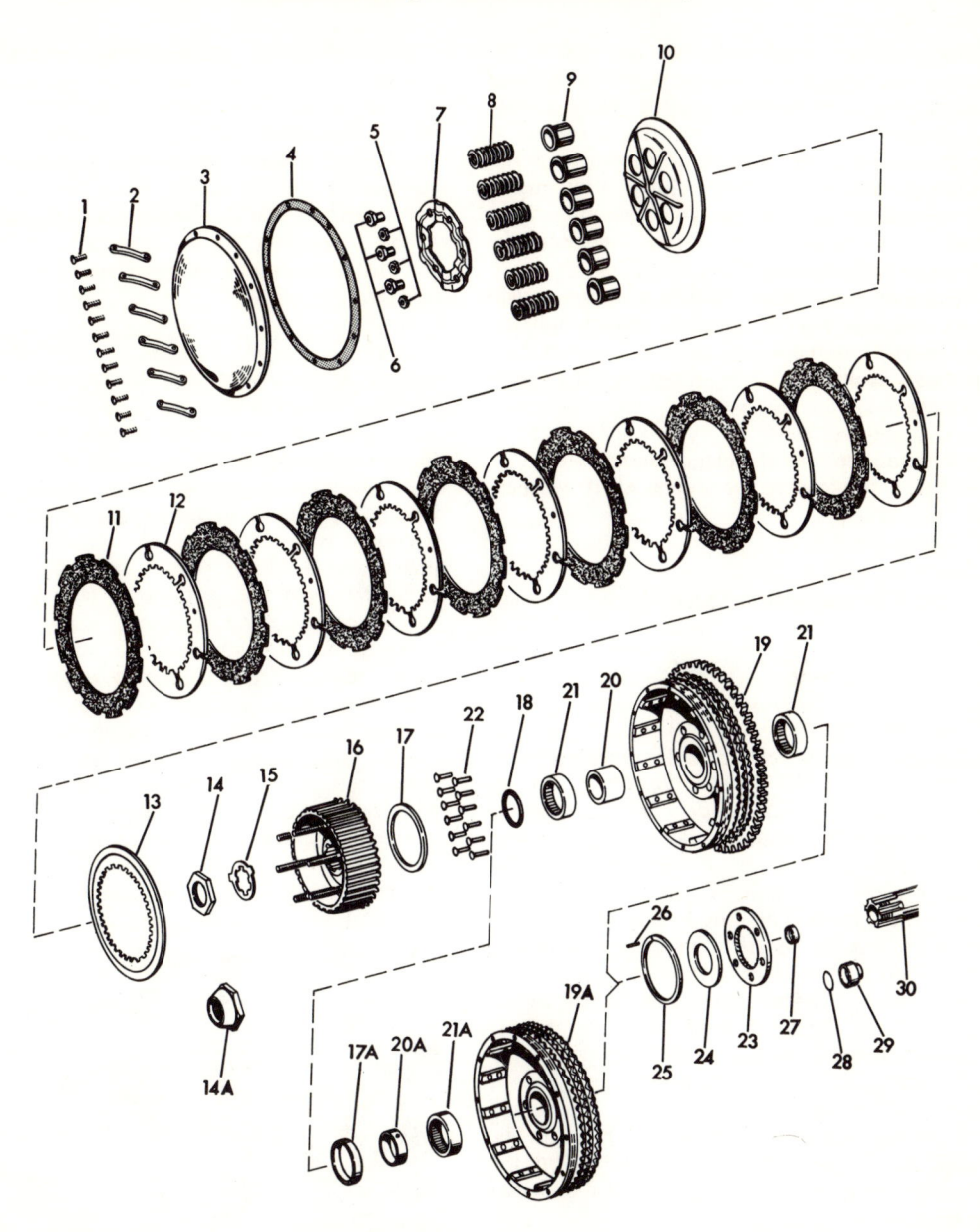

Clutch, exploded view, Sportster models.

1. Clutch cover screw (12)
2. Clutch cover screw retainer (6)
3. Clutch cover
4. Clutch cover gasket
5. Hub stud nut (3)
6. Hub stud nut—long (3)
7. Pressure plate
8. Clutch spring (6)
9. Backing plate cup (6)
10. Releasing disc
11. Friction drive plate (7)
12. Driven plate (7)
13. Backing plate
14. Hub nut (1967 XLH)
14A. Hub nut (1966 and earlier)
15. Hub nut lock washer
16. Clutch hub assembly
17. Clutch hub oil seal (1967 XLH)
17A. Clutch hub oil seal (1966 and earlier)
18. Clutch hub O-ring (1967 XLH)
19. Clutch shell (1967 XLH)
19A. Clutch shell (1966 and earlier)
20. Clutch hub spacer (1967 XLH)
20A. Clutch hub spacer (1966 and earlier)
21. Needle bearing (2) (1967 XLH)
21A. Needle bearing (1) (1966 and earlier)
22. Sprocket rivet (12)
23. Starter clutch
24. Sprocket bearing washer (variable-size)
25. Sprocket hub washer
26. Sprocket hub washer pin
27. Clutch gear (push rod) oil seal
28. Clutch gear extension O-ring (1966 and earlier)
29. Clutch gear extension (1966 and earlier)
30. Clutch gear

Note: 1966 and earlier parts also used for 1967 XLCH.
Figure following name of part indicates quantity necessary for one complete assembly.

Clutch springs occasionally set or become fatigued, especially when excessive heat has been produced by operating motorcycle with a slipping clutch. If this has been the case, or if clutch discs are in good condition but it was not possible to obtain a suitable clutch adjustment:

④ Check clutch spring free length. They should be $1\tfrac{31}{64}''$, and compression test should be from 43 to 52 pounds at $1\tfrac{1}{8}''$.

⑤ On 1964 and earlier models, compress pushrod oil seal spring locating inside clutch hub nut with fingertip. If the spring returns both washers to position against shoulder or spring ring, parts are serviceable.

⑥ On 1965 models, lip type seal should be inspected and replaced if worn or damaged.

Driven plates should be replaced if warped, scored or burned.

Sportster Models

ADJUSTMENT

Release mechanism

① Loosen clutch release rod adjusting screw lock nut and back off (counterclockwise) adjusting screw. Clutch release worm inside transmission sprocket cover should seat against its stop when clutch hand lever is in its fully extended position. If lever does not fully seat, check to see if cable is binding in housing.

② Adjust cable length by turning adjusting sleeve (hand lever end of cable housing) so that clutch releasing worm does not quite return against its stop. This will hold clutch hand lever in its fully extended position at all times.

③ Turn release rod adjusting screw inward until hand lever has $\tfrac{1}{8}$ of its full movement free before clutch starts to release. (This can be checked by a slight increase in tension on the hand lever as it is being moved to the released position.)

④ Tighten release rod lock nut without disturbing the setting of the adjusting screw.

Spring tension

See this heading under GLIDE MODELS for general hints.

① Remove left footrest, stoplight switch and rear brake foot lever.

② Place an oil drain pan under clutch and remove front chain cover and gasket.

Note: Three of the spring-tension adjusting nuts have $\tfrac{7}{16}''$ hex-heads, and three nuts have $\tfrac{1}{2}''$ hex-heads. All are recessed to conform to the raised portion of the spring-tension adjusting plate which provides a lock for the nuts.

③ Turn each of the six nuts one-half turn at a time.

Tightening the spring-tension adjusting nuts moves the spring-tension adjusting plate closer to the outside surface of the clutch releasing plate. The inner surface of the spring-tension adjusting plate should measure $\tfrac{3}{16}''$ from the outer surface of the flange on the clutch spring cups for normal clutch spring-tension adjustment. When increasing spring tension, do not reduce this distance to less than $\tfrac{7}{64}''$ or clutch will not release.

DISASSEMBLY AND REASSEMBLY

With chain cover and clutch cover removed as described above:

① Remove the three $\tfrac{7}{16}''$ hex-head nuts and three $\tfrac{1}{2}''$ hex-head nuts.

② Remove spring-tension adjusting plate, springs, spring cups, releasing disc, seven clutch friction-drive plates, seven clutch steel-driven plates and backing plate. (All plates may be easily removed with a piece of wire with a hook formed on one end.)

③ Remove front chain adjuster brace and three front chain adjuster cap screws. This will leave the chain adjuster loose behind the front chain. Install sprocket locking link tool, part No. 97200-55, between engine sprocket teeth and clutch sprocket teeth or put transmission in gear with rear wheel on floor to prevent clutch and compensating sprocket from turning.

④ Use tool No. 97175-55 or a pair of old drive and driven plates welded together to lock the clutch hub to outer shell.

Removing and installing clutch hub nut, Sportster models.

1. Front chain adjuster brace and cap screws
2. Front chain adjuster
3. Sprocket locking link tool
4. Clutch lock plate
5. Clutch hub
6. Clutch shell
7. Clutch hub nut wrench
8. Front chain
9. Compensating sprocket

Replacing Clutch Cable 45

Removing clutch hub; removing and installing compensating sprocket, Sportster series.

1. Clutch hub puller
2. Compensating sprocket shaft wrench

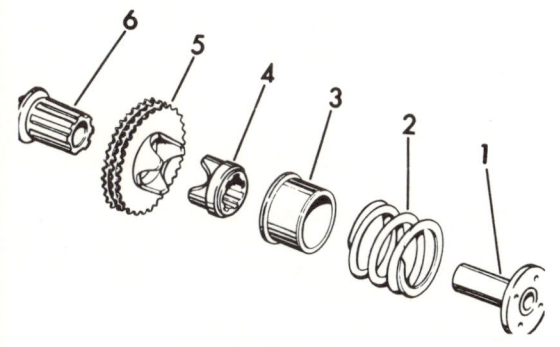

Compensating sprocket, exploded view, Sportster models.

1. Sprocket shaft nut
2. Sprocket spring
3. Sprocket sliding cam sleeve
4. Sprocket sliding cam
5. Engine sprocket
6. Sprocket shaft extension

⑤ Remove release rod.
⑥ Remove hub nut.
⑦ Use hub puller No. 95960-52 to pull clutch hub off splines.
⑧ Remove "O" ring if fitted to clutch gear.
⑨ Use tool No. 94557-55 to remove compensating sprocket.
⑩ Lift clutch shell, chain and sprocket off together.

During reassembly, note the following points:
1. Do not forget to insert clutch release rod.
2. Be sure chain adjuster is positioned loose behind chain.
3. Torque clutch hub nut to at least 150 lb./ft. Use a soft hammer to strike wrench handle if necessary.
4. Be sure clutch runs free on shaft after tightening nut.

5. If starter clutch, clutch shell or clutch gear has been replaced, it is necessary to check the clearance between teeth on the starter clutch gear and starter clutch as described in STARTER section, this chapter.
6. Draw the six spring-tension adjusting nuts down evenly until the inside of the spring-tension adjusting plate measures $3/16''$ out from the outside surface of flange of the clutch spring cups at the six stud locations. This is proper clutch spring-tension adjustment when new clutch plates are used.

Parts inspection

See under GLIDE MODELS for general hints.
Free length of Sportster clutch springs is $1 5/8''$. Any springs not meeting this specification should be replaced. Be sure clutch gear oil seal is not cracked. This seal prevents leakage between the end of the gear and the release rod.

Inspect the tips of clutch release rods for scoring or excessive wear. Damage to release rods is usually caused by excessive clutch spring tension.

When you assemble clutch release lever and worm, spring, cover, adjusting screw and lock nut, check the lever and worm action by moving lever back and forth. Engage cable end with fingers of lever and install sprocket cover with bolts. Then inject "Grease-All" grease through fitting to lubricate worm.

Check the operation of the release lever to be sure lever returns to stop pin, when clutch hand lever is released. A sticking worm or clutch control cable causes lever to stop short of pin, thus reducing effective clutch release rod travel, causing clutch to slip.

REPLACING CLUTCH CABLE

The clutch hand lever, control coil and cable are available from the factory completely assembled for speedster and buckhorn handlebars.

If cable only is to be installed, it should be approximately $47 3/4''$ long for speedster bars and $51 1/16''$ long for buckhorn bars.

To remove cable only, first remove sprocket cover from motorcycle and cut off cable end. Disengage cable from hand lever and pull out from upper end of coil.

To remove cable and coil:
① Remove starter crank, exhaust pipe and muffler.
② Remove right front footrest and two transmission sprocket cover bolts.
③ With a mallet, lightly tap cover, at the same time working cover off starter shaft.
④ Loosen adjusting screw lock nut and adjusting screw.
⑤ Disengage clutch cable end from clutch release worm and lever by moving lever forward until approximately $1''$ of cable remains in gear-

case cover. Press coil in (toward oil pump) and down to free from cover.

⑥ Loosen clip securing coil to left front frame member and disengage cable from hand lever.

⑦ Remove assembly from motorcycle.

To install, strip approximately $5/8''$ insulated covering from upper coil end and approximately $1\frac{1}{4}''$ from lower end before installing upper and lower ferrules. To attach rubber control housing oiler, simply strip off approximately $\frac{1}{4}''$ insulated covering, $7''$ from hand lever, and slip oiler in place.

① Lubricate cable with grease as it is being inserted in coil (hand lever end).

② Position upper cable end in hand lever bushing.

③ Insert felt seal retainer and felt seal on lower cable end.

④ Insert cable end on cable, $7\frac{11}{16}''$ from lower ferrule.

⑤ Cut cable off at end.

⑥ Spread cable strands in cable end countersunk hole and flow a hard solder in hole to securely join together.

⑦ Engage cable end with fingers of lever.

⑧ Install sprocket cover with bolts.

⑨ Install footrest, exhaust pipe and muffler and starter crank.

⑩ Adjust clutch release mechanism as described previously.

TRANSMISSION

Nearly all gearbox problems can be solved by attending to proper maintenance, lubrication and linkage adjustment. However, wear is inevitable and abuse takes its toll, so worn or bent forks or beat-up dogs are possibilities. Attending to the latter is a major job and requires putting the box on the bench. Several special Harley-Davidson tools are necessary for stipping and adjustment. However, adjusting the shift mechanism above the box is carried out with engine, etc., in the frame and without special tools.

Note: A main drive gear oil seal tool, part No. 95660-42, enables you to replace the seal without removing the gearbox from frame. Without it, the job is much harder, so it is usually wise to refer this operation (if it alone is required) to the Harley-Davidson dealer.

TROUBLE DIAGNOSIS

1. Difficult shifting
   (a) Dragging clutch
   (b) Oil too heavy
   (c) Improper adjustment of linkage
   (d) Bent shift rod
   (e) Bent shift forks
   (f) Worn dogs

2. Jumping out of gear
   (a) Improper adjustment of linkage
   (b) Bent shift forks
   (c) Improperly adjusted forks

Glide Models

LINKAGE ADJUSTMENT

Hand shift

① Move the shift lever to third position on four-speed transmissions and to second position on three-speed transmissions.

② Disconnect shift rod from lever.

③ With slight backward and forward movement, carefully "feel" the transmission lever into exact position where the shift spring plunger (inside transmission) seats fully in its retaining notch.

④ Carefully refit the rod to the lever, without disturbing the shift lever's exact positioning, by turning the clevis in or out.

Foot shift

Check to make sure that the clamping slot in shift lever is in alignment with notch or mark in end of shaft.

On 1964 and earlier models only, adjust length of shift rod so that the foot lever has about $\frac{1}{16}''$ clearance from the foot lever cover mounting stud when depressed.

① Remove shift rod end bolt.

② Loosen shift rod end lock nut.

③ Turn rod end farther on or off rod.

Note: Rod adjustment is important because interference between foot lever and cover mounting stud will prevent full engagement of shifting parts inside transmission.

When it is impossible to shift foot shifting mechanism into all gears, refer to SHIFTER COVER (FOOTSHIFT) below.

SHIFT MECHANISM AND GEARBOX

The gearbox can be removed from the frame separately or in unit with the clutch. The factory recommends the following steps to put the transmission on the bench:

Preliminary steps

① Remove chain cover and clutch assembly (with chain and drive sprocket) as outlined in CLUTCH and THE BOTTOM END sections.

② On 1964 and earlier models, remove cotter pin, nut, flat washer and spring from each of the two inner chain guard rear mounting bolts. Bend back the ears of the screw lock away from the three cap screws around the engine sprocket shaft that secure the front end of the inner chain guard to the engine crankcase, and remove cap

Shifter Cover (Handshift)

screws and lock. Remove oil drain pipe from inner chain guard.

③ Remove mainshaft key.

④ Loosen the five transmission base mounting bolts.

⑤ Remove the three bolts attaching the chain housing to the engine crankcase and four bolts attaching the housing to the transmission.

⑥ Remove the two chain housing stud nuts attaching the starter housing to the chain guard.

⑦ Remove wires connected to the starter solenoid terminals.

⑧ Pull the inner chain housing loose from mainshaft, using puller No. 95960-41A which has four screws to fit tapped holes in chain housing. (Care must be taken to be sure housing moves out squarely, for the front end is a snug fit on the shoulder of the crankcase.)

⑨ As the housing is pulled out, shake starter assembly shaft to free it from gear in the starter motor housing.

⑩ Remove the chain oiler hose at oil pump.

⑪ Remove chain housing oil return hose at rear of chain guard and vent hose at the T-connection and move housing away.

⑫ Remove battery carrier bracket and regulator ground strap from right side of transmission.

⑬ Remove right Buddy Seat footrest bracket.

⑭ Remove starter motor bracket and pull starter motor out left side.

⑮ Remove kickstarter crank.

⑯ Remove clutch control rod from clutch release lever at pedal (foot control clutch) or at booster connection (hand control clutch) and turn rod out until length has been increased enough to slide flat portion out of slot in clutch release lever.

⑰ Disconnect shift rod from transmission cover by removing nut and bolt or cotter pin and clevis pin.

⑱ Disconnect speedometer drive cable and housing from transmission.

⑲ Disconnect neutral indicator switch wire clip.

⑳ Remove rear chain connecting link and chain. Remove bolt that secures transmission to support bracket on right side of frame.

㉑ Remove bolts and cap screws that secure transmission mounting plate to chassis.

㉒ Remove complete transmission with mounting plate.

SHIFTER COVER (HANDSHIFT)

Disassembly and reassembly

① Remove cover screws, noting location of vented screw (adjacent to right side dowel pin).

② Remove cover.

③ Remove shaft lock screw.

④ Drift shaft out of cam. (An engine valve may be used for this: place edge of valve head

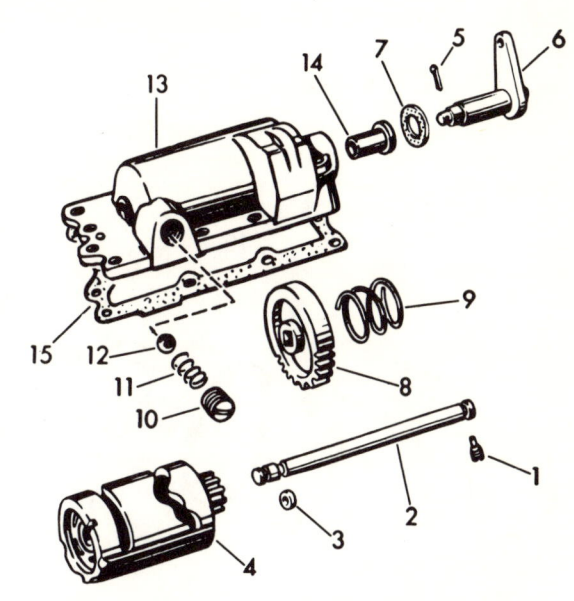

Hand shifter cover, exploded view, Glide models cover.

1. Shaft lock screw
2. Shaft
3. Oil seal
4. Shifter cam
5. Cotter pin
6. Shifter lever
7. Leather washer
8. Shifter gear
9. Shifter gear spring
10. Cam plunger cap screw
11. Ball spring
12. Plunger ball
13. Cover
14. Shifter lever bushing
15. Cover gasket

in groove and tap on stem end.)

⑤ Remove cam from cover.

⑥ Pull cotter key from shifter lever.

⑦ Pry shifter gear off shaft to free lever.

⑧ Unscrew cam plunger screw to remove spring and ball.

When reassembling cover, it is necessary to time the shifter gear to the cam gear. Proceed as follows:

① Install spring and shifter gear in cover with spring located over gear hub and with timing mark between gear teeth to the outside (facing cover bushing).

② Install cam so notch in gear tooth is aligned with timing mark on shifter gear.

③ Install shifter lever and shaft assembly with square end of shaft in hole in gear with shifting lever pointed toward left, front screw hole in cover, and leather washer between lever and cover bushing.

Install shifter camshaft and secure with lock screw. Be sure oil seal is in place in widest groove in right end of shaft. Shifter cam end play should be .0005" to .0065". If greater, install shim washer of desired thickness. If less than desired amount, file boss in case until recommended play has been achieved.

Be sure that vented screw is in proper hole when fitting cover to case.

Clutch and Transmission

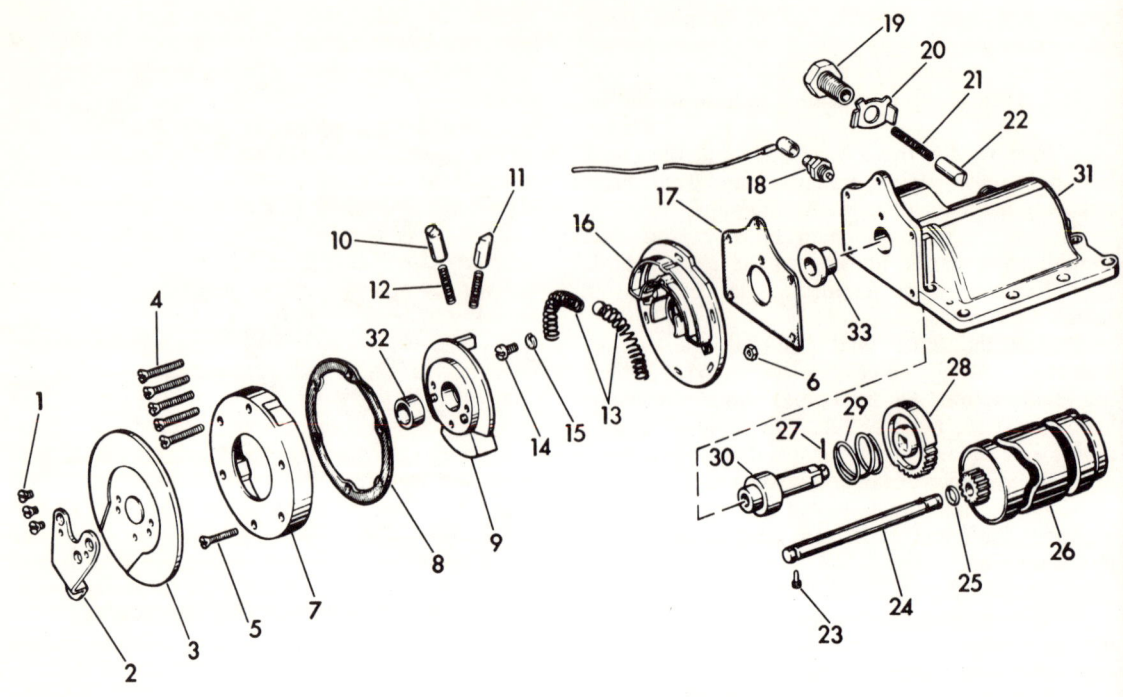

Foot shifter/cover, exploded view, Glide models.

1. Shifter lever screw (3)
2. Shifter lever
3. Dust shield
4. Shifter cover screw (5)
5. Shifter cover screw (short)
6. Cover screw nut
7. Pawl carrier cover
8. Cover gasket
9. Pawl carrier
10. Pawl (right)
11. Pawl (left)
12. Pawl spring (2)
13. Pawl carrier spring (2)
14. Adapter plate bracket screw
15. Adapter plate bracket screw washer
16. Adapter plate
17. Adapter plate gasket
18. Neutral indicator switch
19. Cam follower retainer
20. Cam follower retainer washer
21. Spring
22. Cam follower
23. Cam shaft lock screw
24. Cam shaft
25. Oil seal
26. Shifter cam
27. Cotter pin
28. Shifter gear
29. Shifter gear spring
30. Shifter shaft
31. Shifter cover
32. Pawl carrier bushing
33. Shifter shaft bushing

Figure following name of part indicates quantity necessary for one complete assembly.

Parts inspection

① Inspect shifter cam slots and plunger ball seats for excessive wear. Cam track and ball seats must be sharp-edged. Compare with new part if possible. Replace cam if slots are worn.

② Inspect oil seal and cover gasket and replace if broken or in questionable condition.

③ Inspect gear teeth on shifter cam and shifter gear. If wear is deep, replace parts. Slightly worn parts may be used safely with no impairment of proper function.

SHIFTER COVER (FOOTSHIFT)

Disassembly and reassembly

① Remove twelve screws that secure cover to case, noting position of long vented screw (adjacent to right side dowel).

② Remove three shifter lever screws, lever and dust shield.

③ Remove five long shifter cover screws and one short screw by removing nut located on rear of adapter plate.

④ Remove the pawl carrier cover, gasket and pawl carrier.

Note: Pawls and springs are under compression and will pop out when pawl carrier is removed.

⑤ Remove adapter plate bracket screw and washer, adapter plate and gasket.

⑥ Remove neutral indicator switch.

⑦ Remove retainer, washer, spring and cam follower.

⑧ Drift camshaft out of cam, using an engine valve as described in step ④ of HANDSHIFT above.

⑨ Remove cam from cover.

⑩ Remove cotter key from shifter.

⑪ Pry shifter gear off shaft and remove spring and shaft.

Shift Forks
49

washer in hole directly above end of shifter gear, but do not tighten.

⑤ Shift gear shift cam to any position but neutral.

⑥ Rock cam back and forth to make sure spring-loaded cam follower is seating exactly in one of the indexing notches, or "Vs", that determine cam position for one of the four gears.

⑦ Rotate adapter plate until timing notch in adapter plate, located at bottom of shifter gear hole, lines up with notch between two bottom shifter gear teeth.

⑧ Make alignment exact, then tighten adapter plate bracket screw to lock in position.

⑨ Install pawls in carrier so the notches in pawls face toward each other.

⑩ Lubricate pawl assembly and curved springs with "Grease-All".

⑪ Use Loctite sealant (part No. 99619-60) on the six end-cover screws, shift lever screw and the cover assembly screws *except* the long vented screw. Be sure vented screw is in correct hole.

⑫ Use Perfect Seal No. 4 on cover gasket.

Note: The neutral indicator switch cannot be repaired if faulty. It must be replaced.

SHIFT FORKS

The shift fork shaft is held in position by a lock screw which may be found in the gearbox cover joint surface in line with the right end of the shaft. With the lock screw removed, the shaft may be driven out by means of a drift inserted in the hole in the starter cover joint face of gearbox. Note that a rubber oil seal is assembled in the groove on the left end of the shifter fork shaft.

The two fork assemblies are not interchangeable. Note exactly the arrangement of parts and components in each. Keep parts separate to avoid needless adjusting when reassembling. If inspection shows fork assemblies are not dam-

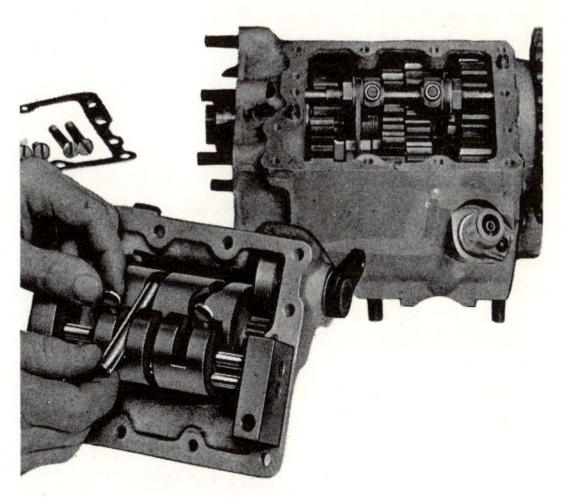

Timing shifter gear, Glide models.

Timing shifter notches, Glide models.

Reassemble in reverse order, paying special attention to the following procedures.

① Align the timing marks on shifter shaft, shifter gear and cam gear. The timing mark cut between the center teeth on one side of the **shifter gear is in line with the corner of the squared shaft end and just a little to the left of the last ratchet tooth on the shifter shaft.**

② After installing cam and indicator switch, **position** cover in vise with shifter mechanism **end** upward.

③ Place gasket and adapter plate over cover.

④ Insert adapter plate bracket **screw and**

Adjusting shifter gauge, Glide models.

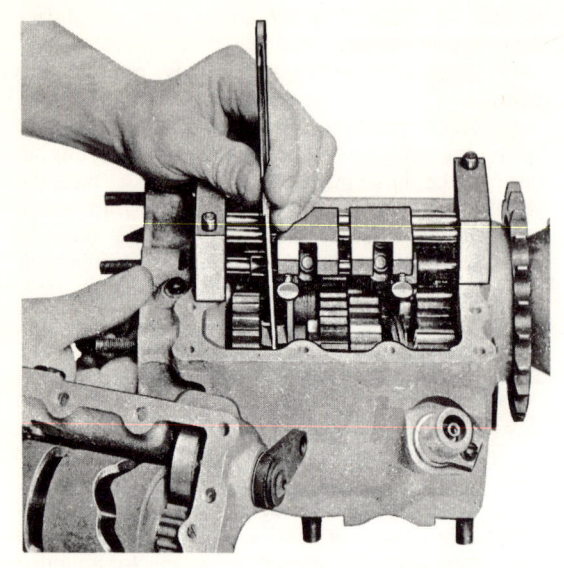

Clutch and Transmission

Checking shifter clutch clearance, Glide models.

aged, worn or bent, it may not be necessary to disassemble them unless shifter clutches are replaced.

Parts inspection

The factory advises that if shifter forks are bent or worn, replace them. Straightened forks are weak. They may break and cause extensive damage to gearbox parts.

Check fit of shifter fork bushings on shaft. If bushings are loose enough to give fork action lash, replace them. Check replacement part fit on shaft.

Lap out bushings if they bind. Shifting will be difficult unless bushings work freely on shaft.

Check adjustment of shifter forks with fork shifter gauge, part No. 96384-39 (see photo). With the ⅜" gauge rod furnished, set tool gauge blocks in exact alignment with straight sections of cam slots in shifter cam. Lock gauge blocks in place with thumb screws.

Remove tool from cover, turn it over, and place it on transmission case with shifter fingers engaged in slots on gauge blocks. Be sure shifter finger rollers are in place on shifter fingers.

With thickness gauges, check clearance on both sides of shifting clutches. All shifting clutches must be centered. Clearances between shifter clutch and gear are as follows:

Low and second gear: .075" clearance on both sides.

Third and high gear: .100" clearance on both sides.

Sliding reverse gear: .055" clearance between gear teeth.

Where shifter clutch engagement is with dogs protruding from face of gear, turn gear so dogs on shifter clutch and dogs on gear are over-lapping each other about ⅛" before checking clearance.

When clearances are not equal and correct, shifting fork assemblies must be corrected by increasing or decreasing the number of shims between shifter fork and shifter finger. To make this adjustment, remove shifter fork assemblies from transmission. Shims are available .007" and .014" thick.

After taking out or adding shims, be sure fork assembly lock nut is tight. However, excessive tightness may close up the hole in the bushing so it is no longer a free, sliding fit on the shaft.

GEARBOX

Disassembly and reassembly

① Remove cover and forks as noted above.

② Remove countershaft end cap (1964 and earlier) on left side of case.

③ Remove countershaft nut lock and plate on right side.

④ Drift countershaft out left (clutch) side. Note end play of adjusting washer (# 9 in exploded view). It does not stay with shaft and drops in case.

⑤ Remove speedometer drive housing screw and washer and lift out speedometer drive unit and gasket from gearcase.

⑥ If yours is a three-speed and reverse transmission, remove idler gear shaft, spacer washer, and idler gear. Thread a ¼-20 tap screw into end of shaft, grasp screw head in pliers and pull shaft out of case. (It may be necessary to heat the case.)

⑦ Remove the four bearing retaining plate screws, oil deflector and retaining plate.

⑧ Drive mainshaft assembly toward right side of case with plastic mallet or block of wood and hammer until mainshaft bearing or bearing housing with bearing are just free of opening in case.

⑨ With screwdriver or other suitable tool, pry lock ring out of groove in mainshaft and slide it onto mainshaft splines.

⑩ Pull ball bearing nut, washer, bearing, housing, low and second gear assembly and mainshaft out right side of case, slipping third gear, retaining washer, spring lock ring and shifter clutch off left end of mainshaft and out through shifter cover opening in case.

(If bearing housing does not come out with bearing when mainshaft assembly is being removed, slide low and second gear along mainshaft until edge of large gear is against bearing housing and drive out housing together with mainshaft. To avoid damage to the case, make sure gear is positioned so it does not overlap housing.)

Do not disassemble either shaft unless neces-

Gearbox

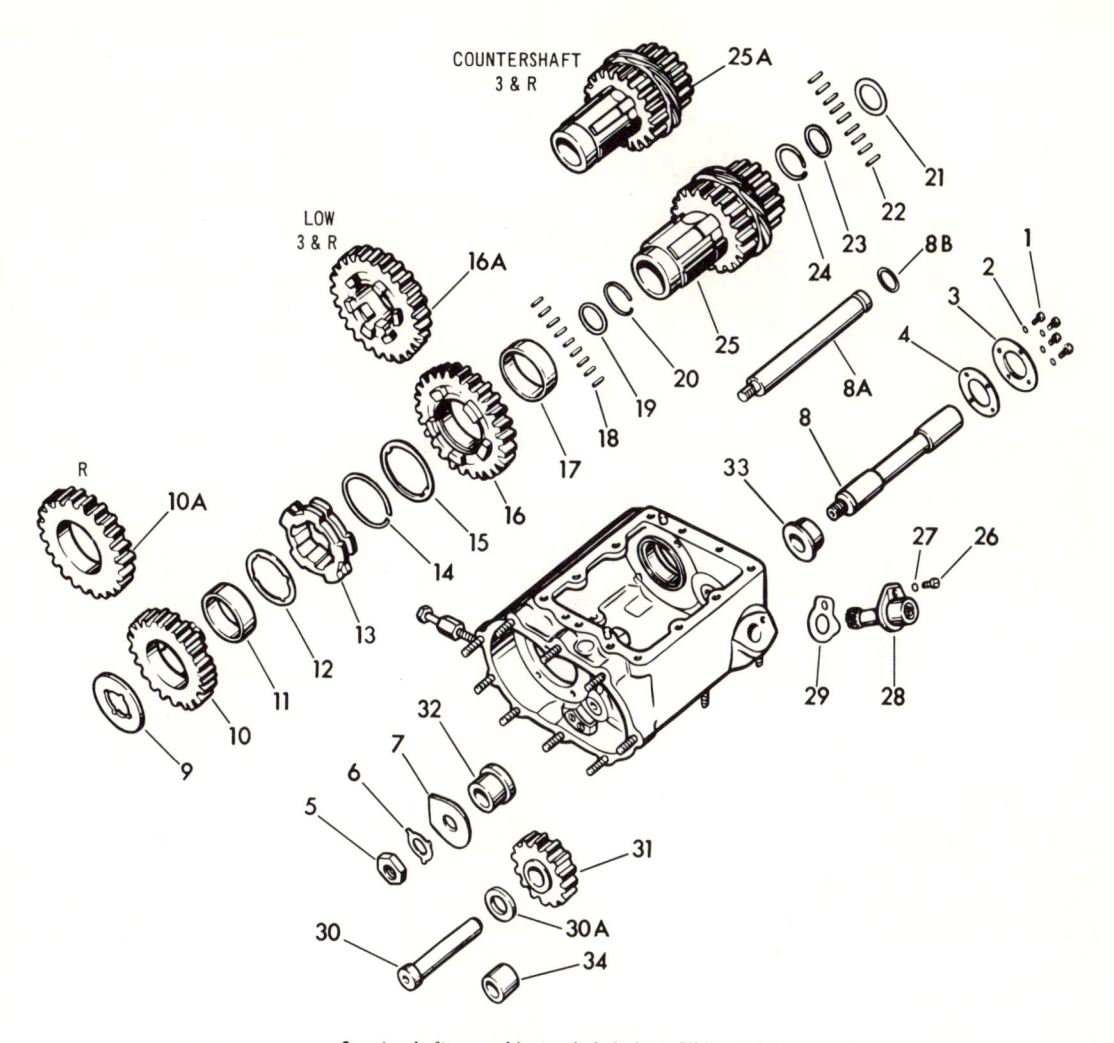

Countershaft assembly, exploded view, Glide models.

1. End cap screw (4) (1964 and earlier)
2. End cap screw washer (4) (1964 and earlier)
3. End cap (1964 and earlier)
4. End cap gasket (1964 and earlier)
5. Countershaft nut
6. Lock washer
7. Lock plate
8. Countershaft (1964 and earlier)
8A. Countershaft (1965)
8B. O-ring (1965)
9. Countershaft gear end washer
10. Low gear
10A. Countershaft reverse gear
11. Low gear bushing
12. Low gear bearing washer
13. Shifter clutch
14. Spring lock ring
15. Gear retaining washer
16. Countershaft second gear
16A. Countershaft low gear (3-speed and reverse)
17. Second gear bushing
18. Bearing rollers (22)
19. Roller retainer washer
20. Lock ring
21. Roller thrust washer
22. Roller bearing (22)
23. Retaining washer
24. Lock ring
25. Countershaft gear
25A. Countershaft gear (19-tooth for 3-speed and reverse)
26. Speedometer drive housing screw
27. Washer
28. Speedometer drive unit
29. Drive unit gasket
30. Idler gear shaft
30A. Spacer washer (1964)
31. Idler gear
32. Countershaft mounting collar (starter side)
33. Countershaft mounting collar (clutch side)
34. Idler gear bushing

Figure following name of part indicates quantity necessary for one complete assembly.

Clutch and Transmission

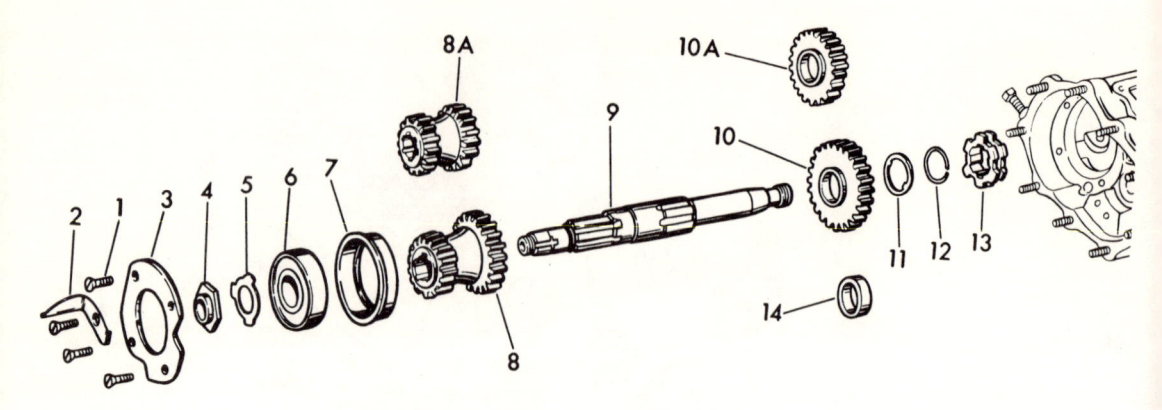

Mainshaft assembly, exploded view, Glide models.

1. Bearing housing retaining plate screw (4)
2. Oil deflector
3. Retaining plate
4. Ball bearing nut
5. Ball bearing washer
6. Mainshaft bearing
7. Mainshaft bearing housing
8. Low and second gear
8A. Low and reverse gear (handshift)
9. Mainshaft
10. Third gear
10A. Mainshaft second gear (handshift)
11. Retaining washer
12. Lock ring
13. Shifter clutch
14. Third gear bushing

Figure following name of part indicates quantity necessary for one complete assembly.

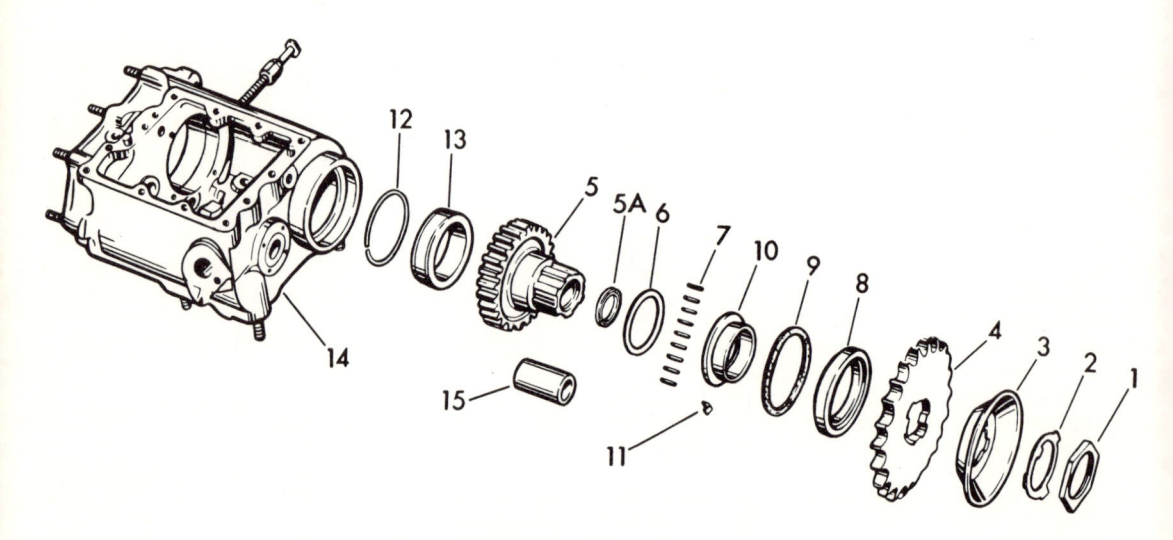

Main drive gear, exploded view, Glide models.

1. Sprocket lock nut
2. Sprocket lock washer
3. Oil deflector
4. Chain sprocket
5. Main drive gear
5A. Main drive gear shaft seal (1965)
6. Thrust washer
7. Roller bearings (4)
8. Main drive gear oil seal
9. Oil seal cork washer
10. Main drive gear spacer
11. Main drive gear spacer key
12. Bearing race retaining ring
13. Bearing race
14. Gear box
15. Main drive gear bushing

Figure following name of part indicates **quantity necessary** for one complete assembly.

Gearbox Disassembly and Reassembly

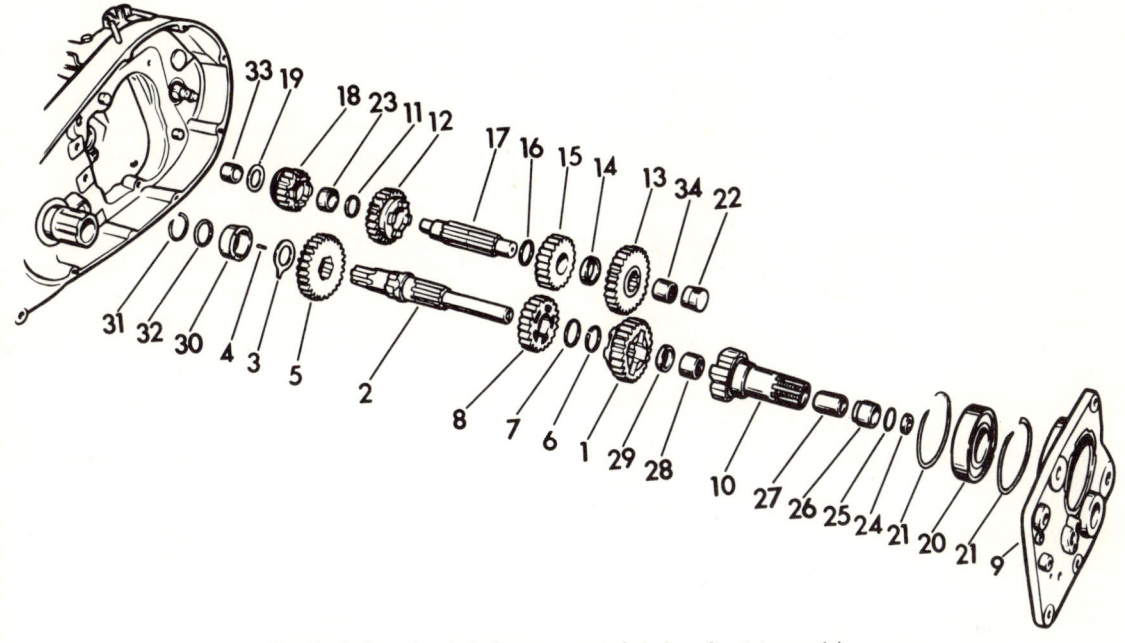

Countershaft and mainshaft group, exploded view, Sportster models.

1. Mainshaft second gear
2. Transmission mainshaft
3. Mainshaft thrust washer
4. Transmission mainshaft roller (23)
5. Mainshaft low gear
6. Mainshaft third gear retainer ring
7. Mainshaft third gear washer
8. Mainshaft third gear
9. Access cover
10. Clutch gear
11. Countershaft low gear washer
12. Countershaft third gear
13. Countershaft drive gear
14. Countershaft gear spacer
15. Countershaft second gear
16. Countershaft second gear thrust washer
17. Transmission countershaft
18. Countershaft low gear
19. Countershaft low gear washer
20. Mainshaft ball bearing
21. Mainshaft ball bearing snap ring (2)
22. Countershaft oiler plug
23. Countershaft low gear bushing
24. Clutch gear oil seal
25. Clutch hub nut "O"-ring
26. Clutch gear oil seal extension
27. Clutch gear bushing
28. Clutch gear needle roller bearing
29. Mainshaft thrust washer
30. Mainshaft roller bearing race
31. Mainshaft roller bearing retainer ring
32. Mainshaft roller bearing washer
33. Countershaft bearing—closed end
34. Countershaft bearing—open end

Figure following name of part indicates quantity necessary for one complete assembly.

sary. However, if necessary, study the exploded view drawings for proper order before attempting disassembly.

Note: 1. Roller bearings on the shafts are matched sets and not interchangeable. If rollers are mixed, two new sets must be installed.

2. Do not remove the main drive gear oil seal unless it is bad.

3. Countershaft end play must be adjusted to specifications by using washer of appropriate thickness. Hold the washer to the shaft with heavy grease while installing. Check clearance between washer and countershaft low gear.

Sportster Models

The gearbox can be serviced via the transmission cover or when the cases are split as described in THE BOTTOM END. If the problem is solely in the transmission, go through the cover.

If a general engine overhaul is also required, do not remove cover but refer to Chapter 3 for gaining access to the gearbox. Then proceed as follows:

① Remove spacer and low gear from countershaft.
② Remove mainshaft and gears.
③ Separate mainshaft second gear from fork.
④ Remove shift cam cap screw and retainer.
⑤ Remove countershaft spacer, third gear and shift fork.
⑥ Withdraw countershaft and gears.

GEARBOX DISASSEMBLY AND REASSEMBLY

Preliminary steps

① Select high gear.

② Put a pan under clutch cover to catch oil.
③ Remove the following: footrest, stop light switch, rear brake foot pedal, chain case cover, clutch, front chain compensating sprocket, starter crank assembly, right footrest and foot shift lever, exhaust pipe, transmission sprocket cover, starter crank gear, starter clutch gear and starter crankshaft. See CLUTCH and STARTER ASSEMBLY headings for details on these components.
④ Loosen mainshaft nut.
⑤ Disconnect master link and rear chain.
⑥ Remove transmission mainshaft nut and lock washer.
⑦ Use all purpose claw puller to remove sprocket.
⑧ Remove retainer screws, oil seal and gasket.
⑨ Remove four access cover cap screws.
⑩ Pry clutch gear oil seal from clutch gear with screwdriver.
⑪ Remove "O" ring (if fitted) from clutch gear extension.
⑫ Use transmission access cover puller, part No. 95560-57 or similar tool to remove access cover from crankcase.

Note: Shift mechanism and countershaft assembly stay with cover.

Transmission access cover, Sportster models.

1. Access cover
2. Access cover cap screws (4)
3. Clutch gear oil seal
4. Hub nut rubber "O"-ring (XLCH, 1966 and earlier XLH)

Shift mechanism and cover assembly

① Remove mainshaft second gear.
② Remove cam cap screw and retainer.
③ Remove cam retainer ring (with Tru-Arc pliers).
④ Separate cam, pawl carrier and support from cover (note number of shims used, if any).
⑤ Remove pawl carrier springs, shifter pawls and springs.
⑥ Remove countershaft, forks and rollers.

Do not disassemble the units farther than necessary to make repairs. The mainshaft third gear is retained by a ring—discard it and use a new one if removed. The clutch gear is pressed into the ball bearing and the main drive gear is pressed onto the shaft. A suitable press must be employed for removal and replacement. Similarly, the shift fork shaft is factory-aligned and should not be tampered with. If bent or worn, replace cover.

Note: Be sure to specify model and year when ordering a replacement cover. The 1957 and later covers (part No. 34844-57) are not interchangeable with older ones.

In reassembling the gearbox, pay particular attention to the following procedures:
① Check the height of the shifter assembly (see drawing) to assure correct operation of forks. Rotate cam to third gear position and shim as required to make the 3½" dimension shown. Shims are .010" thick.
② If gears have been replaced, select the thinnest countershaft low gear spacer washer (.065", .075", .085" and .100" are available) and check clearance between low and third. Add washers or substitute to bring clearance up to .038" to .058".
③ With all parts assembled except mainshaft thrust washer and countershaft low spacer washer, rollers, washer and retainer ring, check operation of the transmission by shifting through range of gears several times. Then shift into neutral and check clearance between clutch faces of countershaft third and second gears. If correct clearance of .038" to .058" is not obtained, it is possible that shifter forks are bent and should be replaced.
④ Check end play of countershaft and mainshaft.
⑤ Select the thinnest countershaft low gear washer and mainshaft thrust washer and install in their respective positions. Install thrust washer ear down as positioned in transmission compartment, using grease to hold in place.
⑥ Temporarily install cover to crankcase with all transmission parts.
⑦ Align cover on dowel pins and gently tap cover into position.
⑧ Secure cover with four cap screws.
⑨ Use a dial indicator to check end play of mainshaft, gauging from sprocket side of shaft. Move shaft back and forth and measure end play. With access cover still in place, measure end play of countershaft from access cover side using a dial indicator.
⑩ Bend a discarded spoke and wedge in coun-

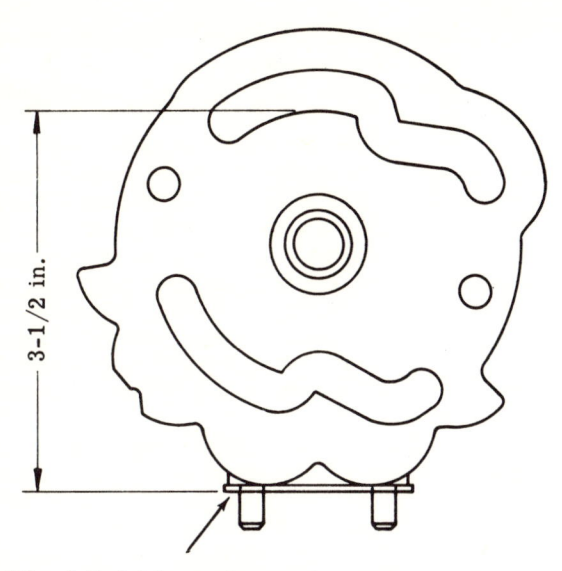

Shims (indicated by arrow) are used to correct dimension on shifter assembly, Sportster models.

tershaft end hole. Pull and push countershaft and at the same time measure amount of end play. If end play of either transmission mainshaft or countershaft is not within .004" to .009" limits, it is necessary to remove access cover and install correct fit. (Spacer washers are available in .050", .055", .060", .065", .070" and .075".)

Parts inspection

Refer to GLIDE MODELS heading for general hints. Note the following procedures particularly in the SPORTSTER box.

① Inspect gear shifter pawl carrier for depressions or grooves worn in fingers that engage shifter lever arm shaft. A badly worn yoke is caused by rubbing action of lever arm shaft ball, and will result in transmission jumping out of gear.

② Examine pawl carrier springs for breakage or damage caused by acids in oil. If possible, compare old springs with new springs. New spring free length is approximately $2\tfrac{25}{32}$".

③ Do not use cadmium plated, 14-coil pawl carrier springs. Use only cadmium plated, 16-coil springs or black phosphatized springs, 14 or 16-coil, when reassembling pawl carrier support.

④ Examine shifter pawls and springs for wear, grooves, cracks or breakage. Insert right and left pawl springs in their respective carrier holes and check operation. Pawl must be free in carrier. Free length of new springs is approximately $1\tfrac{7}{32}$".

⑤ Inspect shifter cam follower and spring for wear and damage, especially on thrust face of follower. Check movement of follower and spring in retainer. Free length of new spring is approximately $1\tfrac{19}{32}$".

STARTER ASSEMBLY

GLIDE MODELS

Kick-starter disassembly and assembly

① Place a pan under transmission to catch oil.

② Remove starter cover nuts and plain washers.

③ Remove clutch lever rod from left end of clutch release lever.

④ Remove cover with clutch release lever assembly. (Clutch release bearing will come off with cover.) If starter cover binds, the release bearing is binding on the starter clutch. Pry bearing off starter clutch. *Do not* pry cover.

⑤ Put crank in a vise, remove nut and lock washer, crank nut.

⑥ Pull starter gear, using the all purpose claw puller, part No. 95635-46, or if puller is not available, drive crank out of gear with plastic mallet. (Be sure to hold starter crank and cover from swinging when shaft is free from gear.)

⑦ Pull crank out of cover. *Note:* Thrust washer is installed between starter crank spring and cover with chamfered side of washer facing spring.

⑧ Remove nut and lock washer and pull release lever from end of clutch release lever shaft, using claw puller.

⑨ Remove cotter key and plain washer from lower end of release lever shaft, which can then be pulled out of cover, freeing release finger and thrust washer.

Do not disassemble unit any farther than required to effect repairs. If it is necessary to disassemble the starter clutch, it must be pulled from the tapered mainshaft with puller No. 95650-42 or similar tool.

Reassemble starter unit in reverse order, with attention to the following procedures.

① Install starter crank spring and thrust washer on starter crank with chamfer side facing spring. Apply a film of light grease on oil seal and on end of starter crank shaft before installing crank.

② Hold crank in vise and wind spring by turning cover clockwise. Install starter crank gear so dowel pin holds crank in normal, upward position.

③ Before starter cover is installed, clutch release bearing is inserted into cover with slot in outer bearing race engaging clutch release finger.

④ Groove in clutch release bearing inner race and ball plunger in starter clutch must align so they will be engaged when assembly is completed.

⑤ Refill unit with 1½ pints of same grade oil used in engine.

Electric starter

If starter problem is not in solenoid, starter or switch and drive unit must be removed. Proceed as follows:

Clutch and Transmission

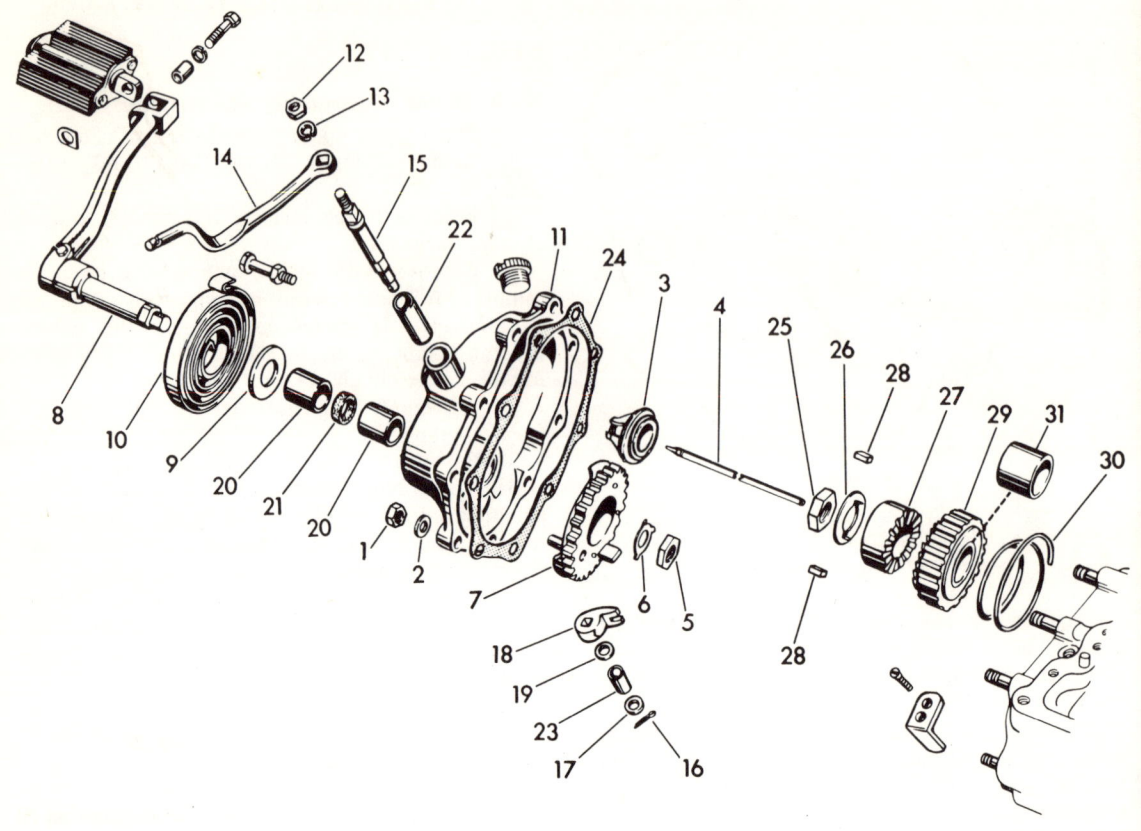

Kickstarter assembly, exploded view, Sportster models.

1. Starter cover nut (9)
2. Plain washer (9)
3. Clutch release bearing
4. Push rod
5. Starter crank nut
6. Eared lock washer
7. Starter gear
8. Crank
9. Thrust washer
10. Starter crank spring
11. Starter cover
12. Release lever nut
13. Lock washer
14. Release lever
15. Release lever shaft
16. Cotter pin
17. Plain washer
18. Release finger
19. Thrust washer
20. Starter crank bushing (2)
21. Oil seal
22. Release lever bushing
23. Release lever bushing
24. Starter cover gasket
25. Starter clutch nut
26. Starter clutch washer
27. Starter clutch
28. Starter clutch key (2)
29. Starter mainshaft gear
30. Starter clutch spring
31. Mainshaft gear bushing

Figure following name of part indicates quantity necessary for one complete assembly.

① Disconnect battery ground wire from battery terminal post.

② Remove cover and disconnect wires from starter solenoid terminals held by nuts and lock washers.

③ Remove chain housing cover.

④ Depress retainer cup, remove pin from hole in plunger shaft and remove spring.

⑤ Remove solenoid attaching bolts and lock washers, spacer bar, solenoid complete with boot, gasket, plunger and plunger spring.

⑥ Turn starter pinion lever end forward and disengage lever fingers from pinion gear shifting collar.

⑦ Pull pinion gear and shaft assembly from housing. (Drive gear will remain in drive shaft housing.)

If you disassemble the pinion gear/shaft, remember that the nut has a left-hand thread.

To remove starter shift lever, it is necessary to remove oil tank.

Reassemble in reverse order.

SPORTSTER MODELS

Kick-starter

Complaints generally center around slippage, caused by worn starter clutch teeth, binding

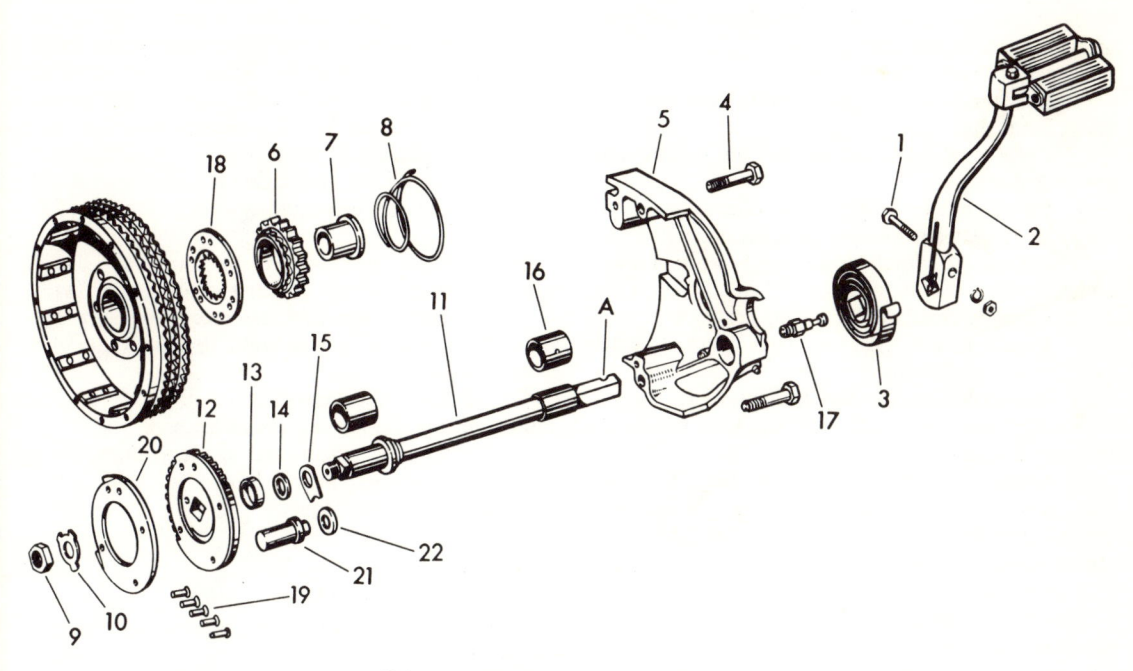

Starter Assembly

Kickstarter, exploded view, Sportster models.

1. Crank clamp bolt, lock washer and nut
2. Crank and pedal assembly
3. Crank spring
4. Sprocket cover bolt (2)
5. Sprocket cover
6. Starter clutch gear
7. Clutch sprocket spacer available (long or short)
8. Clutch spring
9. Shaft nut
10. Crank gear lock washer
11. Crankshaft
12. Crank gear
13. Crank oil seal
14. Crankshaft shim—.007"
15. Shaft thrust plate
16. Shaft bushing (2)
17. Spring stud
18. Starter clutch
19. Crank gear cam plate rivet (5)
20. Crank gear cam plate
21. Crank gear stop pin
22. Crank gear stop pin washer

Figure following name of part indicates quantity necessary for one complete assembly.

Positioning starter crank gear on starter shaft, Sportster models.

Starter drive, Sportster models.

1. Armature shaft
2. Shifter lever
3. Shifter collar
4. Pinion gear
5. Clutch ring gear
6. Starter shaft
7. Overrunning clutch

clutch gear, or clicking while the engine is running, caused by too much crankshaft end play or a loose crank gear cam plate.

To get at these components:

① Remove starter crank clamp bolt and pry crank from shaft.

② Press down on end of starter spring and pry it off shaft.

③ Loosen exhaust pipe and muffler.

④ Remove transmission sprocket cover.

⑤ Disengage clutch cable end from release lever.

⑥ Remove clutch as described previously.

⑦ Rotate crank gear to free starter clutch gear, spacer and spring.

⑧ Remove crank nut and lock washer.

⑨ Tap end of shaft with a soft mallet to loosen from gear.

⑩ Remove shaft, oil seal, shims (if fitted) and thrust plate. (Shims are used to establish correct crankshaft end play when crankshaft and thrust washer are worn.)

Replacement is the reverse of above steps.

However, before installing the assembly permanently, check crankshaft end play. Temporarily install starter shaft, seal and washer, gear, washer and nut in left case and check crankshaft end play with dial indicator. If end play is not within specified limits of .001" to .007", it is absolutely necessary to shim the crankshaft. Use .007" thickness shim, part No. 6802, between crankshaft and thrust washer to obtain correct fit (see illustration).

Also if a clutch sprocket spacer only is replaced, the new spacer must be exactly the same length as the old spacer. Spacers are available in two lengths, 1.025" and 1.047". If starter clutch gear, starter clutch, clutch sprocket hub or clutch gear are replaced, it is absolutely necessary to check the clearance between teeth on starter clutch gear and starter clutch as follows:

① Measure distance from end of clutch sprocket spacer to top of starter clutch gear teeth.

② On clutch sprocket assembly, measure distance from top of starter teeth to clutch sprocket thrust washer.

③ Subtract the sprocket reading from the clutch gear reading to obtain clearance.

④ If resulting clearance is less than .040" using short spacer, install long spacer to obtain .040" minimum clearance.

Parts inspection

① Compare clutch spring with new one if possible to ascertain condition. Spring is approximately 1" long.

② Check camplate ears for wear and note if rivets are loose. If re-riveting is required, insert rivets from gear side.

Electric starter

See this heading under GLIDE MODELS.

CHAPTER 5

Electrical Systems

Electrical systems in the Harley-Davidson line include DC generator/coil ignition; DC generator/magneto ignition; and alternator.

The most-used is the conventional DC generator (or alternator)-regulator-battery-coil-distributor setup analogous to that of the automobile. Some Sportsters have generators for lighting and magneto ignition.

Glide and Sportster Models

GENERATOR

The standard generator is a direct current two-pole, two-brush unit with charging rate governed entirely by a voltage regulator. The regulator functions to increase charging rate when the battery charge is low or current is used, and to decrease charging rate when no current is being used and the battery is nearing full charge.

If battery is low or dead, or if generator warning light is on, first check the warning light to see if it is grounded.

① Remove the wire or wires from the generator "A" terminal.

② Turn ignition on.

③ If generator light on instrument panel goes on, light circuit is grounded and may be the reason for the generator not charging.

If the generator signal light circuit tested OK, or if a grounded condition has been corrected, test generator, as follows:

① Remove wire from "F" terminal of generator.

② Connect a jumper wire from generator "F" terminal to ground on cycle.

③ Remove wire or wires from generator "A" terminal and connect the positive lead of a 0-30 ammeter.

④ Start engine and run at a speed of 2000 rpm (approximately 40 mph).

⑤ Momentarily connect negative lead of ammeter to motorcycle battery positive terminal. If the ammeter reads 15 amperes or more for a 6-volt generator or 10 amperes or more for a 12-volt generator, the generator is not at fault. If generator shows no charge or charge below minimum rate, it must be removed for further checking.

Note: Avoid running with this hook-up for extended periods. Also, the factory says it is advisable to flash the field coils whenever wires have been removed from the generator or regulator, or after generator or battery has been removed and is reinstalled. This is done to make sure generator has correct polarity. If polarity of generator is reversed, relay points will vibrate and burn. Flash the field coils by momentarily touching a jumper wire between "BAT" terminal and "GEN" terminal on regulator after all wires have been properly connected and before starting engine. The momentary surge of current from battery to generator will correctly polarize generator.

Removal and replacement

On the Duo-Glide:

① Disconnect wires from generator "F" and "A" terminals.

② Remove two long screws through timing gearcase cover that secure generator to gearcase.

③ Move generator to left side of motorcycle and remove, gear end first, between frame members.

On the Sportster:

① Disconnect red wire from "BAT" terminal on voltage regulator. On standard Sportster, disconnect black wire from "GEN" terminal.

② Remove two long screws through timing gearcase cover that secure generator to gearcase.

③ Remove regulator from generator.

④ Remove black or green wire from "F" terminal and red wire from "A" terminal on generator.

⑤ Remove generator from chassis from left side of motorcycle.

When replacing, make sure connections are correct, clean and tight.

Inspection

① Remove commutator end cover nuts, washers and frame screws.

② Pry or gently tap commutator end cover off frame and armature shaft.

③ Remove brush holder mounting plate from frame.

④ Disconnect both black brush wires and generator positive brush cable from brush holder terminals.

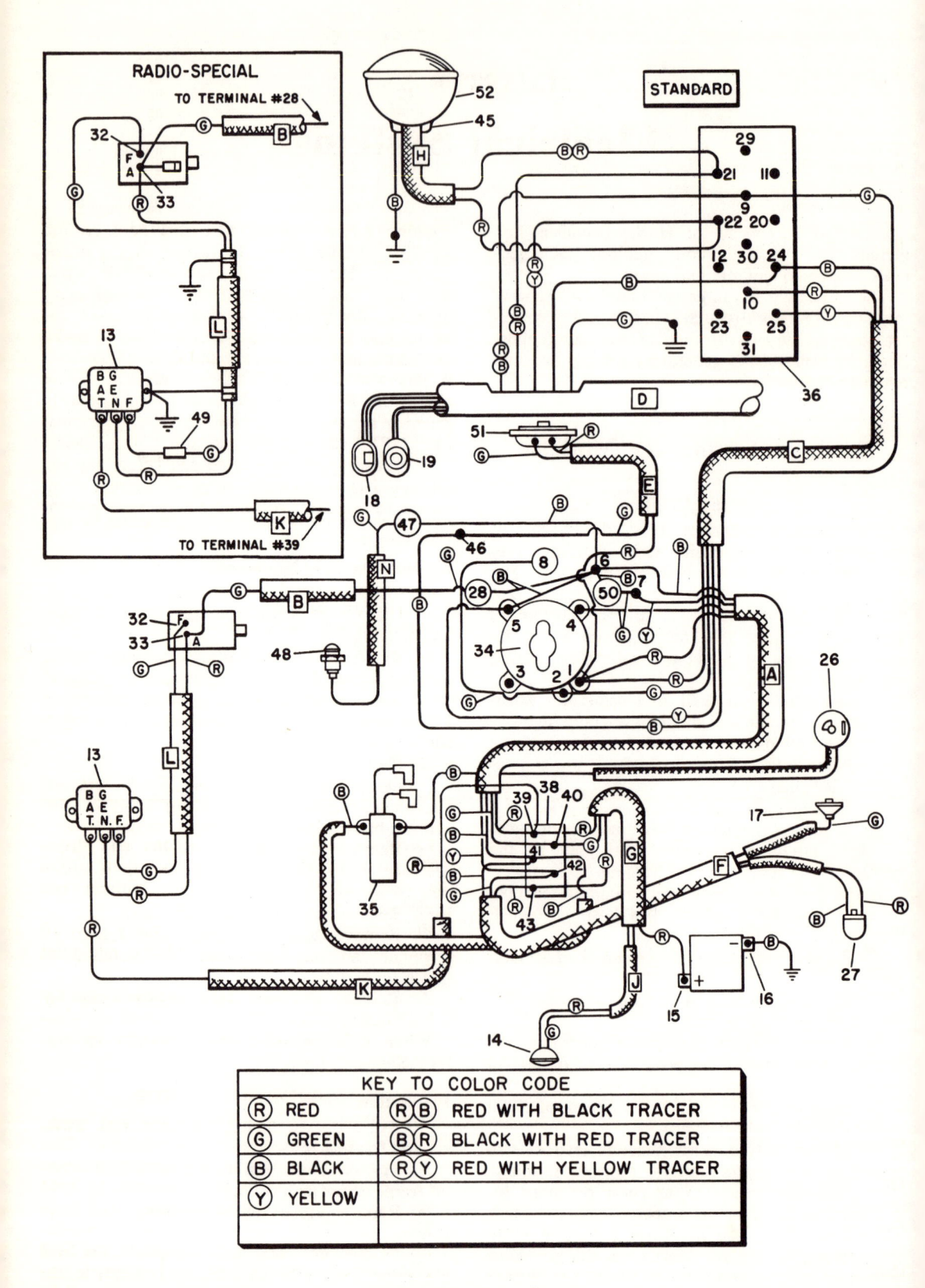

1959 Duo-Glide wiring diagram.

Voltage Regulator

A. Conduit (four wire)—Red, green, black and yellow
B. Conduit (one wire)—Green
C. Conduit (four wire)—Red, green, yellow and black
D. Handlebar (loose wires)—Red with black tracer, black with red tracer, red with yellow tracer, black and green
E. Conduit (two wire)—Red and green
F. Conduit (three wire)—Black, green and red
G. Conduit (three wire)—Red, green and red
H. Conduit (two wire)—Black with red tracer and red
J. Conduit (two wire)—Red and green
K. Conduit (one wire)—Red
L. Conduit (two wire)—Green and red
N. Conduit (one wire)—Green

1. Switch terminal—3 red wires
2. Switch terminal—2 green wires
3. Switch terminal—Not used with standard wiring
4. Switch terminal—Green wire
5. Switch terminal—Black and yellow wires
6. Junction terminal—5 black wires
7. Junction terminal—Green, yellow wires
8. Speedometer light—Green wire
9. Terminal—Red with black tracer, green wire
10. Terminal—Red wire
11. Terminal—Not used with standard wiring
12. Terminal—Not used with standard wiring
13. Regulator—2 red, green wires
14. Tail and stop lamp—Green, red wires
15. Battery positive terminal—Red wire
16. Battery negative terminal—Black wire
17. Oil pressure signal switch—Green wire
18. Handlebar headlamp switch—Red with black tracer, black with red tracer, red with yellow tracer
19. Horn switch—Black, green wires
20. Terminal—Not used with standard wiring
21. Terminal—2 black wires with red tracer
22. Terminal—Red wire, red with yellow tracer
23. Terminal—Not used with standard wiring
24. Terminal—2 black wires
25. Terminal—Yellow wire
26. Ignition circuit breaker—Black wire
27. Stop lamp switch—Black, red wires
28. Generator signal light—Green, black wires
29. Terminal—Not used with standard wiring
30. Terminal—Not used with standard wiring
31. Terminal—Not used with standard wiring
32. Generator "F" terminal—Green wire
33. Generator "A" terminal—Red and green wires
34. Ignition—Light switch—See terminals 1 through 5
35. Ignition coil—2 black wires
36. Terminal place—See 10 and terminals 20 through 24
38. Terminal box—See terminals 39 through 43
39. Terminal—3 red wires
40. Terminal—2 green wires
41. Terminal—3 black wires
42. Terminal—Yellow, green wires
43. Terminal—2 red wires
45. Headlamp bracket—Black wire
46. Junction terminal—Black, green wires
47. Neutral indicator light—Black, green wires
48. Neutral indicator switch—Green wire
50. Oil signal light—Black and green wires
51. Horn—Red and green wires
52. Headlamp—Red wire, black with red tracer

KEY TO WIRING DIAGRAM (RADIO-SPECIAL)

Wiring with radio equipment is unchanged except for regulator, generator and battery connections.

B. Conduit (one wire)—Green
G. Conduit (two wire)—Red and green
K. Conduit (one wire)—Red
L. Cable (two wire)—Red and green
M. Conduit (one wire)—Red (not shown)

13. Regulator—Green and red wires
32. Generator "F" terminal—Green wire
33. Generator "A" terminal—Red wire
39. Terminal—Red wire
49. Fuse

---

⑤ Remove brushes from brush holders and clean brush holders with cleaning solvent.
⑥ Blow dry with compressed air.
⑦ Replace brushes when longest side of brush measures ½" or less.

To check generator condition, hook jumper wires from battery "F" terminals and case (ground) of generator to "motor" it. If armature revolves, the generator is good.

If it does not motor, field or armature is faulty and should be checked by a specialist.

ALTERNATOR

The GM Delcotron alternator is used on late models and is similar to the generator except that alternating current (AC) is produced rather than DC. This current is rectified (changed to DC) immediately by means of diodes—electro-sensitive crystals which permit the flow of electricity only one way. Advantage of the alternator is that it produces high voltage at low rpm and does not require as much power to turn it.

Checking the wiring connections and drive-belt tension are about the only operations within the range of the average rider, without test equipment.

Belt tension is correct when it takes 8 to 10 pounds to deflect the belt ¼" at the mid-point between the pulleys.

Note: The alternator can be ruined quickly if wiring connections are reversed, such as when charging a battery or using a booster battery. Be extremely careful.

VOLTAGE REGULATOR

If the battery is consistently low and weak, the trouble may be in the voltage regulator. This is a simple electro-mechanical device between the generator and the battery designed to hold generator output to a specified voltage.

The regulator is set to maintain a pre-determined generator voltage at all speeds, the field strength being controlled by the automatic insertion of a resistance in the generator field

62 *Electrical Systems*

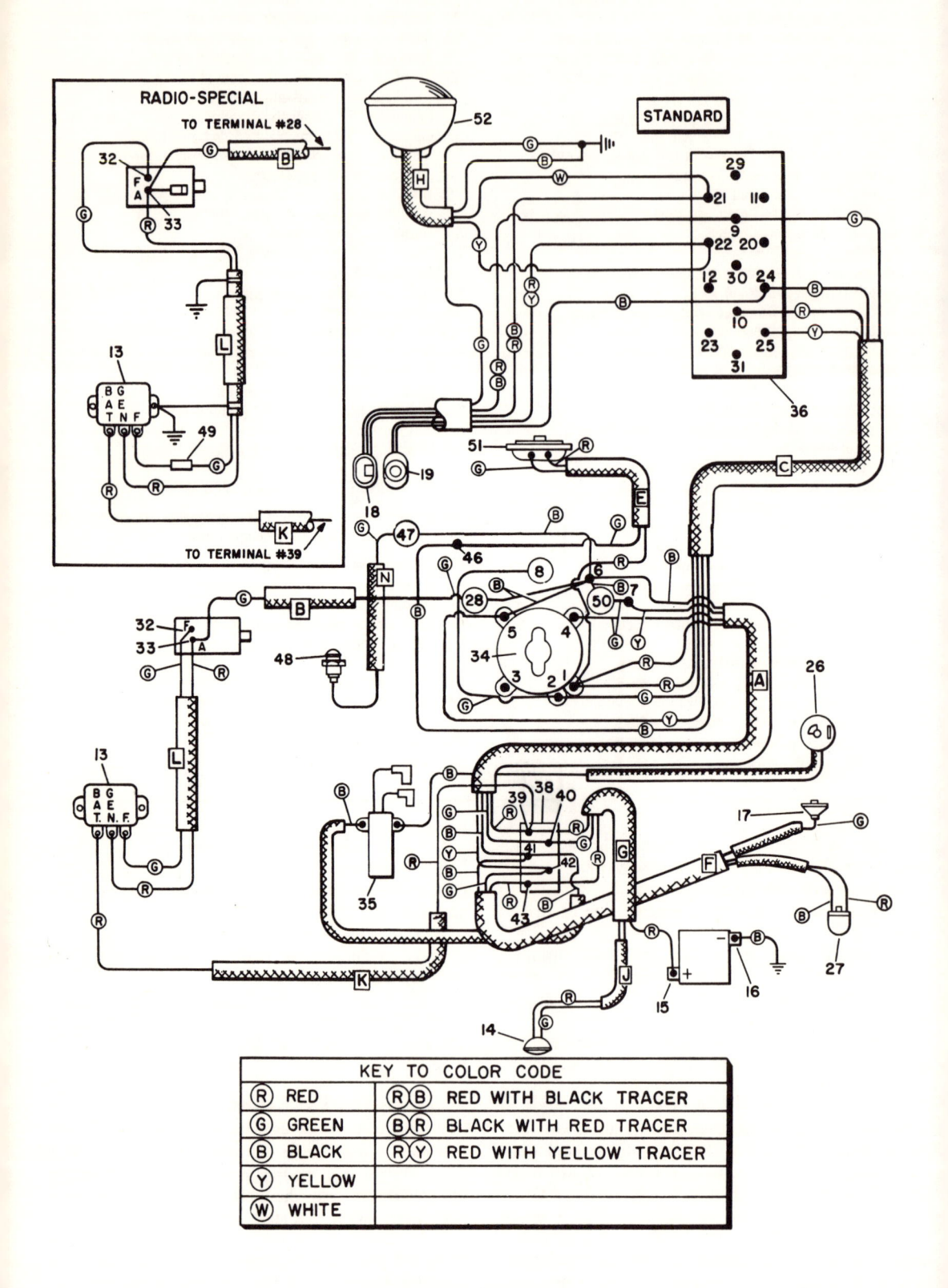

1960 Duo-Glide wiring diagram.

Voltage Regulator

A. Conduit (four wire)—Red, green, black and yellow
B. Conduit (one wire)—Green
C. Conduit (four wire)—Red, green, yellow and black
D. Handlebar (loose wires)—Red with black tracer, black with red tracer, red with yellow tracer, black and green
E. Conduit (two wire)—Red and green
F. Conduit (three wire)—Black, green and red
G. Conduit (three wire)—Red, green and red
H. Conduit (three wire)—Black, white and yellow
J. Conduit (two wire)—Red and green
K. Conduit (one wire)—Red
L. Conduit (two wire)—Green and red
N. Conduit (one wire)—Green

1. Switch terminal—3 red wires
2. Switch terminal—2 green wires
3. Switch terminal—Not used with standard wiring
4. Switch terminal—Green wire
5. Switch terminal—Black and yellow wires
6. Junction terminal—5 black wires
7. Junction terminal—Green, yellow wires
8. Speedometer light—Green wire
9. Terminal—Red with black tracer, green wire
10. Terminal—Red wire
11. Terminal—Not used with standard wiring
12. Terminal—Not used with standard wiring
13. Regulator—2 red, green wires
14. Tail and stop lamp—Green, red wires
15. Battery positive terminal—Red wire
16. Battery negative terminal—Black wire
17. Oil pressure signal switch—Green wire
18. Handlebar headlamp switch—Red with black tracer, black with red tracer, red with yellow tracer
19. Horn switch—Black, green wires
20. Terminal—Not used with standard wiring
21. Terminal—2 black wires with red tracer
22. Terminal—Red wire, red with yellow tracer
23. Terminal—Not used with standard wiring
24. Terminal—2 black wires
25. Terminal—Yellow wire
26. Ignition circuit breaker—Black wire
27. Stop lamp switch—Black, red wires
28. Generator signal light—Green, black wires
29. Terminal—Not used with standard wiring
30. Terminal—Not used with standard wiring
31. Terminal—Not used with standard wiring
32. Generator "F" terminal—Green wire
33. Generator "A" terminal—Red and green wires
34. Ignition—Light switch—See terminals 1 through 5
35. Ignition coil—2 black wires
36. Terminal place—See 10 and terminals 20 through 24
38. Terminal box—See terminals 39 through 43
39. Terminal—3 red wires
40. Terminal—2 green wires
41. Terminal—3 black wires
42. Terminal—Yellow, green wires
43. Terminal—2 red wires
45. Terminal plate top mounting screw (ground)
46. Junction terminal—Black, green wires
47. Neutral indicator light—Black, green wires
48. Neutral indicator switch—Green wire
50. Oil signal light—Black and green wires
51. Horn—Red and green wires
52. Headlamp—Black, white and yellow wires

KEY TO WIRING DIAGRAM (RADIO-SPECIAL)

Wiring with radio equipment is unchanged except for regulator, generator and battery connections.

B. Conduit (one wire)—Green
G. Conduit (two wire)—Red and green
K. Conduit (one wire)—Red
L. Cable (two wire)—Red and green
M. Conduit (one wire)—Red (not shown)

13. Regulator—Green and red wires
32. Generator "F" terminal—Green wire
33. Generator "A" terminal—Red wire
39. Terminal—Red wire
49. Fuse

---

circuit. A current in a series winding on the regulator compensates this voltage figure in accordance with the output current to make sure that the battery does not receive an excessive charging current when in a discharged condition.

Normally, during daytime running, when the battery is in good condition, the generator gives only a trickle charge.

The cut-out is an automatic switch which is connected between the generator and battery. It consists of a pair of contacts held open by a spring and closed magnetically. When the engine is running fast enough to cause the voltage of the generator to exceed that of the battery, the contacts close and the battery is charged by the generator. On the other hand, when the speed is low or the engine is stationary, the contacts open, thus disconnecting the generator from the battery and preventing current flowing from the battery through the windings.

Here are some regulator troubles that can cause it to work improperly or not at all.

1. Dirty contact points
2. Burned contact points
3. Broken or shorted wiring in coil
4. Loose or bad connections
5. Poor ground

Vibration of the cycle causes most problems, and if the regulator is not operating at all, search for bad connections first.

Dirty points can best be shined up by inserting a piece of paper or a business card between them and burnishing by rotating the paper or card. Burned points can be dressed with very fine emery cloth used in the same way.

A check can be made for a bad coil by running the engine and holding the armature down so that points open. If they won't stay open, the series winding is bad. If the coil pulls the contacts apart but voltage doesn't drop (as indicated by a voltmeter), the shunt windings are broken.

With a voltmeter and an ammeter, the regulator settings can be checked against specifications

64   *Electrical Systems*

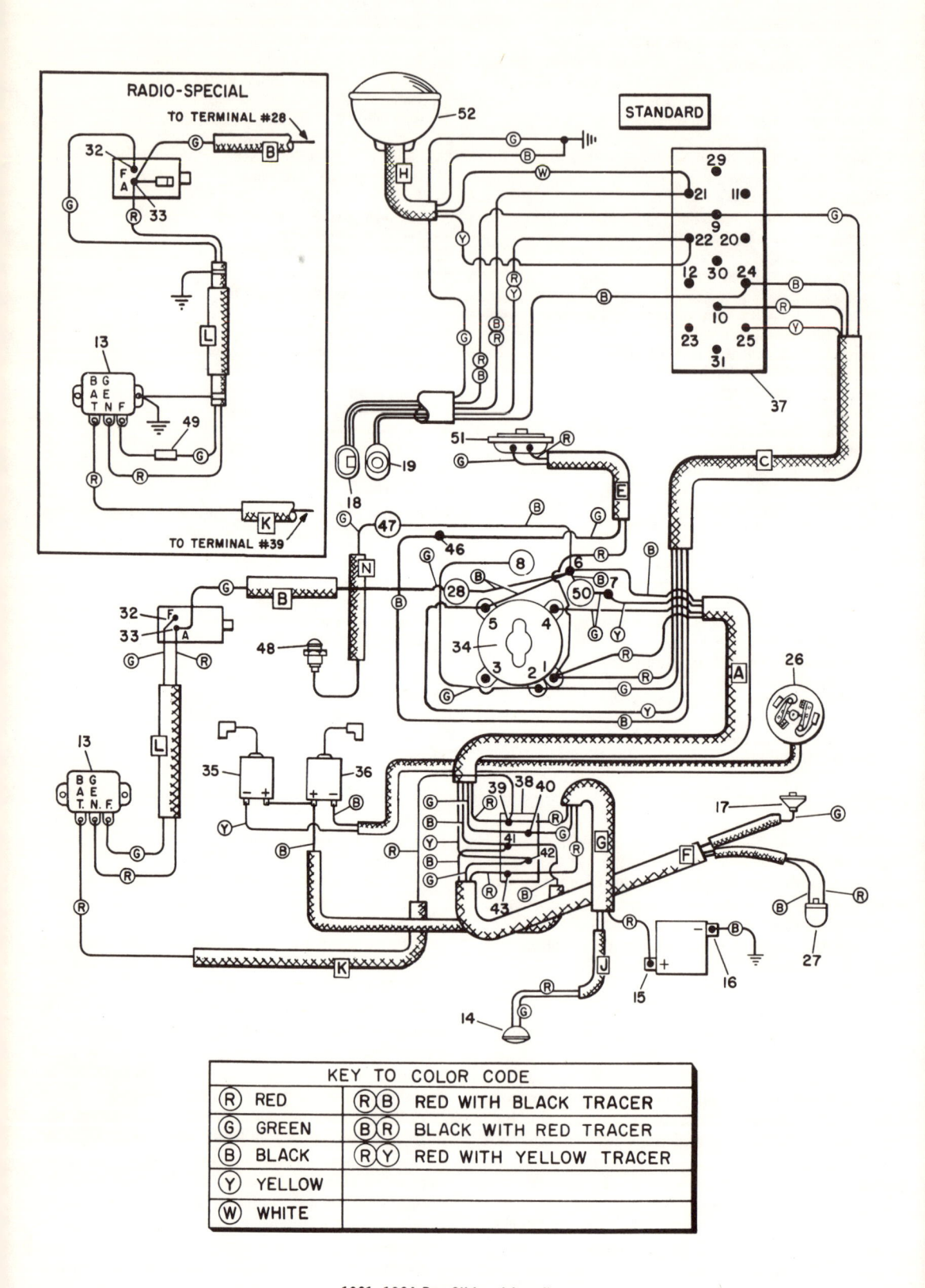

1961–1964 Duo-Glide wiring diagram.

Starter

A. Conduit (four wire)—Red, green, black and yellow
B. Conduit (one wire)—Green
C. Conduit (four wire)—Red, green, yellow and black
D. Handlebar (loose wires)—Red with black tracer, black with red tracer, red with yellow tracer, black and green
E. Conduit (two wire)—Red and green
F. Conduit (three wire)—Black, green and red
G. Conduit (three wire)—Red, green and red
H. Conduit (three wire)—Black, white and yellow
J. Conduit (two wire)—Red and green
K. Conduit (one wire)—Red
L. Conduit (two wire)—Green and red
N. Conduit (one wire)—Green

1. Switch terminal—3 red wires
2. Switch terminal—2 green wires
3. Switch terminal—Not used with standard wiring
4. Switch terminal—Green wire
5. Switch terminal—Black and yellow wires
6. Junction terminal—5 black wires
7. Junction terminal—Green, yellow wires
8. Speedometer light—Green wire
9. Terminal—Red with black tracer, green wire
10. Terminal—Red wire
11. Terminal—Not used with standard wiring
12. Terminal—Not used with standard wiring
13. Regulator—2 red, green wires
14. Tail and stop lamp—Green, red wires
15. Battery positive terminal—Red wire
16. Battery negative terminal—Black wire
17. Oil pressure signal switch—Green wire
18. Handlebar headlamp switch—Red with black tracer, black with red tracer, red with yellow tracer
19. Horn switch—Black, green wires
20. Terminal—Not used with standard wiring
21. Terminal—2 black wires with red tracer
22. Terminal—Red wire, red with yellow tracer
23. Terminal—Not used with standard wiring
24. Terminal—2 black wires
25. Terminal—Yellow wire
26. Ignition circuit breaker—Black, yellow wires
27. Stop lamp switch—Black, red wires
28. Generator signal light—Green, black wires
29. Terminal—Not used with standard wiring
30. Terminal—Not used with standard wiring
31. Terminal—Not used with standard wiring
32. Generator "F" terminal—Green wire
33. Generator "A" terminal—Red and green wires
34. Ignition light switch—See terminals 1 through 5
35. Ignition coil front cylinder—Yellow wire
36. Ignition coil rear cylinder—2 black wires
37. Terminal plate—See 10 and 20 through 24
38. Terminal box—See terminals 39 through 43
39. Terminal—3 red wires
40. Terminal—2 green wires
41. Terminal—3 black wires
42. Terminal—Yellow, green wires
43. Terminal—2 red wires
45. Terminal plate top mounting screw (ground)
46. Junction terminal—Black, green wires
47. Neutral indicator light—Black, green wires
48. Neutral indicator switch—Green wire
50. Oil signal light—Black and green wires
51. Horn—Red and green wires
52. Headlamp—Black, white and yellow wires

KEY TO WIRING DIAGRAM (RADIO-SPECIAL)

Wiring with radio equipment is unchanged except for regulator, generator and battery connections.

B. Conduit (one wire)—Green
G. Conduit (two wire)—Red and green
K. Conduit (one wire)—Red
L. Cable (two wire)—Red and green
M. Conduit (one wire)—Red (not shown)

13. Regulator—Green and red wires
32. Generator "F" terminal—Green wire
33. Generator "A" terminal—Red wire
39. Terminal—Red wire
49. Fuse

---

in the accompanying table. The identification number is stamped on the base of the regulator or the bracket.

Accompanying wiring diagrams show hookups for various tests of regulator and generator output or condition:

(A) To test generator system and cutout shut-off voltage

(B) To test generator system 1964 and earlier XLCH (no battery)

(C) To test voltage regulator setting

(D) To test current control on three-unit regulator

(E) To test Bosch regulator

(*Note:* This unit is not adjustable and must be replaced if faulty.)

BATTERY

See MAINTENANCE AND TUNING chapter.

STARTER

Two types of starters are fitted, Prestolite and Delco. Both are 12-volt, series field or 4-pole. The motor engages the clutch ring gear through a Bendix-type drive and a reduction gear unit. A solenoid relay is controlled by a button switch on the handlebar. On some models the control circuit has a cutout switch in the transmission cover to prevent starter operation when transmission is in gear.

The starter requires very little maintenance. Periodic inspection of brushes and commutator should be made. If the starter fails to operate, the following checks should be made:

① Make sure the mounting and wiring connections are tight and in good condition. The solenoid switch should be firmly mounted and all wiring connections should be clean and tight.

② Inspect the connections to the battery and return circuit.

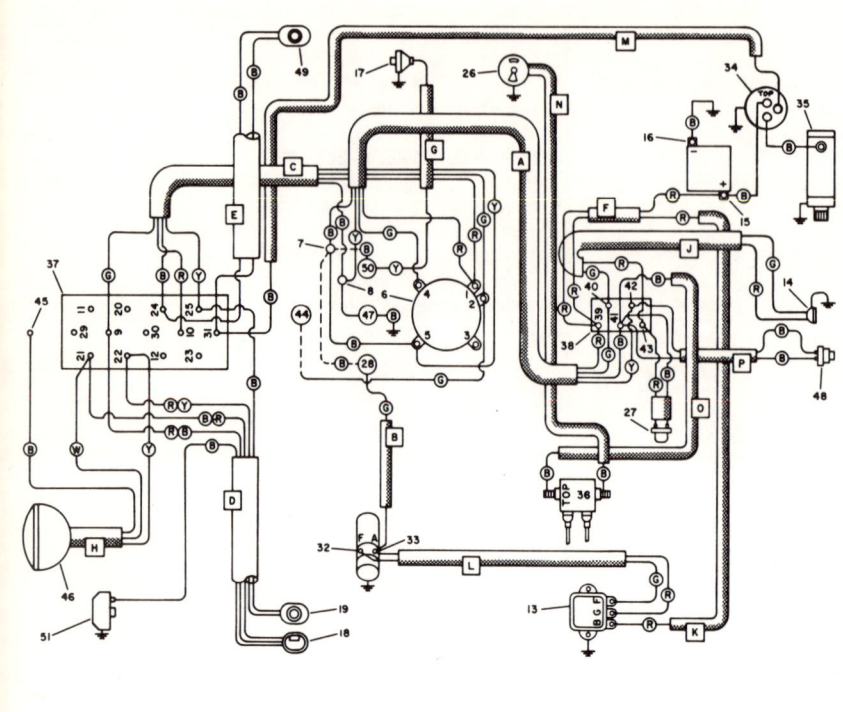

66 Electrical Systems

KEY TO COLOR CODE
- R RED
- G GREEN
- B BLACK
- Y YELLOW
- W WHITE
- RB RED WITH BLACK TRACER
- BR BLACK WITH RED TRACER
- RY RED WITH YELLOW TRACER

LATE 1966 CIRCUIT BREAKER

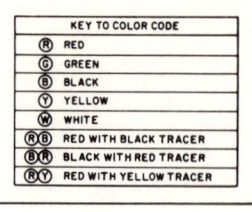

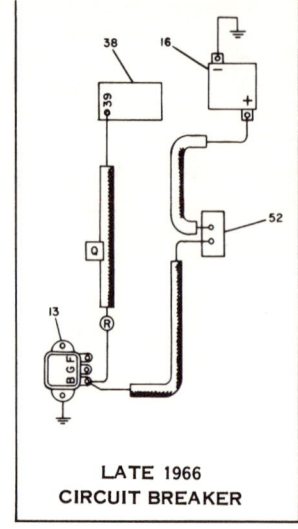

1965–1967 Electra-Glide wiring diagram.

A. Conduit (four wire)—Red, green, black and yellow
B. Conduit (one wire)—Green
C. Conduit (four wire)—Red, green, yellow and black
D. Left handlebar (loose wires)—Red with black tracer, black with red tracer, red with yellow tracer, 2 black wires
E. Right handlebar (loose wires)—2 black wires
F. Conduit (two wire)—2 red wires
G. Conduit (one wire)—Yellow
H. Conduit (three wire)—Black, white and yellow
J. Conduit (two wire)—Red and green
K. Conduit (one wire)—Red
L. Conduit (two wire)—Green and red
M. Conduit (one wire)—Black
N. Conduit (one wire)—Black
O. Conduit (one wire)—Black
P. Conduit (two wires)—2 black wires
Q. Conduit (one wire)—Red

1. Switch terminal—Switch supply
2. Switch terminal—Headlamp
3. Switch terminal—Not used with standard wiring
4. Switch terminal—Tail lamp
5. Switch terminal—Ignition coil
6. Ignition—Light switch—See terminals 1 through 5
7. Junction terminal
8. Junction terminal
9. Terminal
10. Terminal
11. Terminal—Not used with standard wiring
12. Terminal—Not used with standard wiring
13. Regulator
14. Tail and stop lamp
15. Battery positive terminal
16. Battery negative terminal
17. Oil pressure signal switch
18. Handlebar headlamp switch
19. Horn switch
20. Terminal—Not used with standard wiring
21. Terminal
22. Terminal
23. Terminal—Not used with standard wiring
24. Terminal
25. Terminal
26. Ignition circuit breaker
27. Stop lamp switch
28. Generator signal light
29. Terminal—Not used with standard wiring
30. Terminal—Not used with standard wiring
31. Terminal
32. Generator "F" terminal
33. Generator "A" terminal
34. Starter solenoid
35. Starter motor
36. Ignition coil
37. Terminal plate
38. Terminal box—See terminals 39 through 43
39. Terminal
40. Terminal
41. Terminal
42. Terminal
43. Terminal
44. Speedometer light
45. Terminal plate top mounting screw (ground)
46. Headlamp
47. Neutral indicator light
48. Neutral switch
49. Starter button
50. Oil signal light
51. Horn
52. Circuit breaker

Starter   67

Generator output wiring diagram.

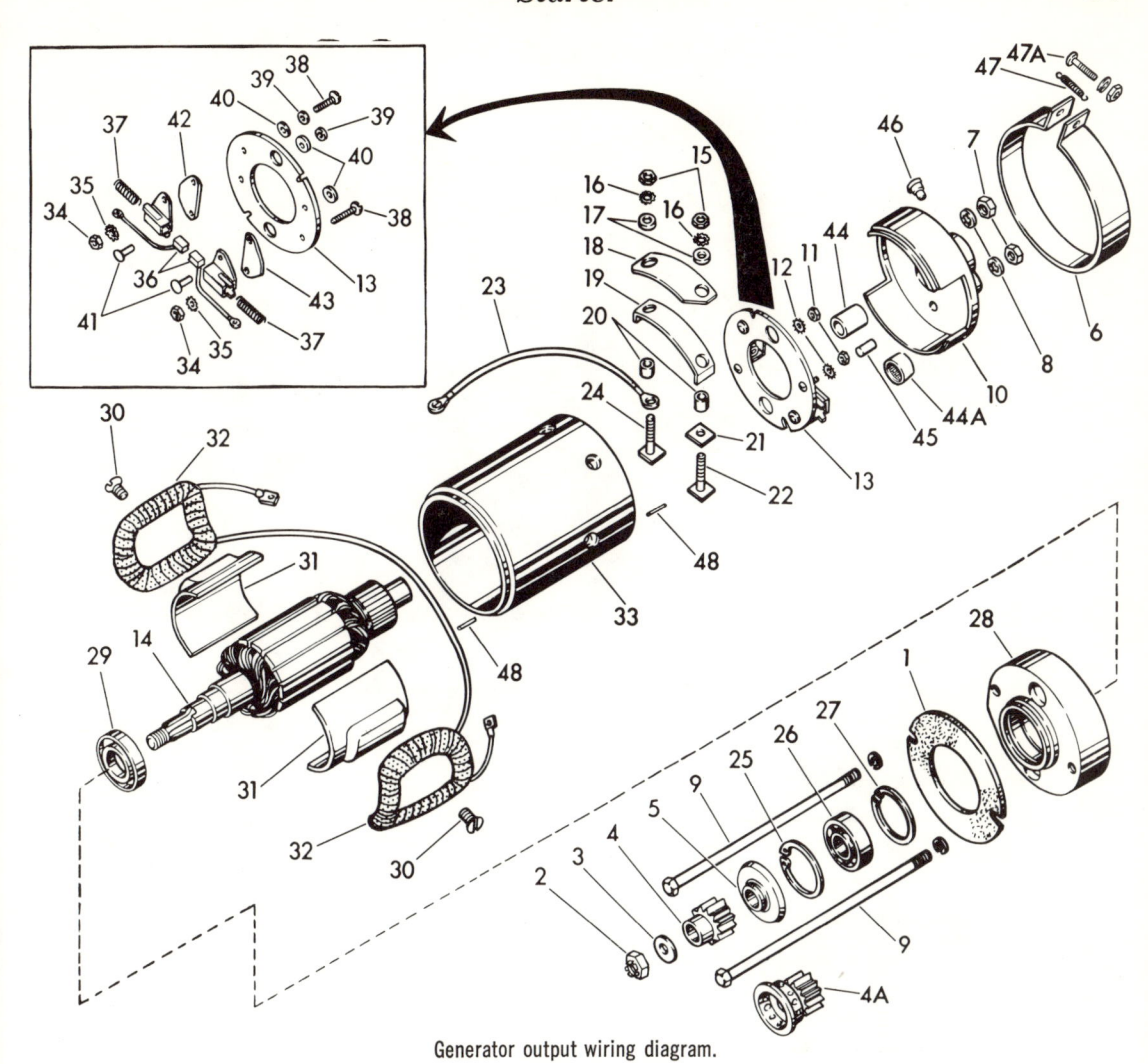

1. Mounting gasket
2. Gear shaft nut
3. Gear shaft washer
4. Drive gear
4A. Drive gear with oil slinger
5. Drive end oil deflector
6. Brush cover strap
7. Commutator end cover nut (2)
8. Commutator end cover washer (2)
9. Frame screw (2)
10. Commutator end cover
11. Brush cable nut (2)
12. Brush cable washer (2)
13. Brush holder mounting plate
14. Armature
15. Terminal screw nut (2)
16. Terminal screw lock washer (2)
17. Insulating washer (2)
18. Terminal insulator
19. Terminal bolt clip
20. Terminal screw bushing (2)
21. Bracket insulator
22. Terminal screw (2)
23. Positive brush cable
24. Terminal screw (see item 22)
25. Bearing retainer
26. Armature bearing
27. Bearing retainer
28. Drive end plate
29. Armature oil seal
30. Pole shoe screw (2)
31. Pole shoe (2)
32. Field coil (2)
33. Frame
34. Terminal screw nut (2)
35. Terminal screw lock washer (2)
36. Brush (2)
37. Brush spring (2)
38. Brush holder plate screw (2)
39. Brush holder plate screw washer (2)
40. Brush holder plate screw washer (3)
41. Brush holder plate rivet (2)
42. Brush holder insulation
43. Brush holder spacer
44. End cover bushing
44A. End cover bearing
45. Generator oil wick
46. Commutator end cover oil cup
47. Brush cover strap spring
47A. Brush cover screw, lock washer and nut (1966 model)
48. End locating pin (2)

Figure following name of part indicates quantity necessary for one complete assembly.

68 *Electrical Systems*

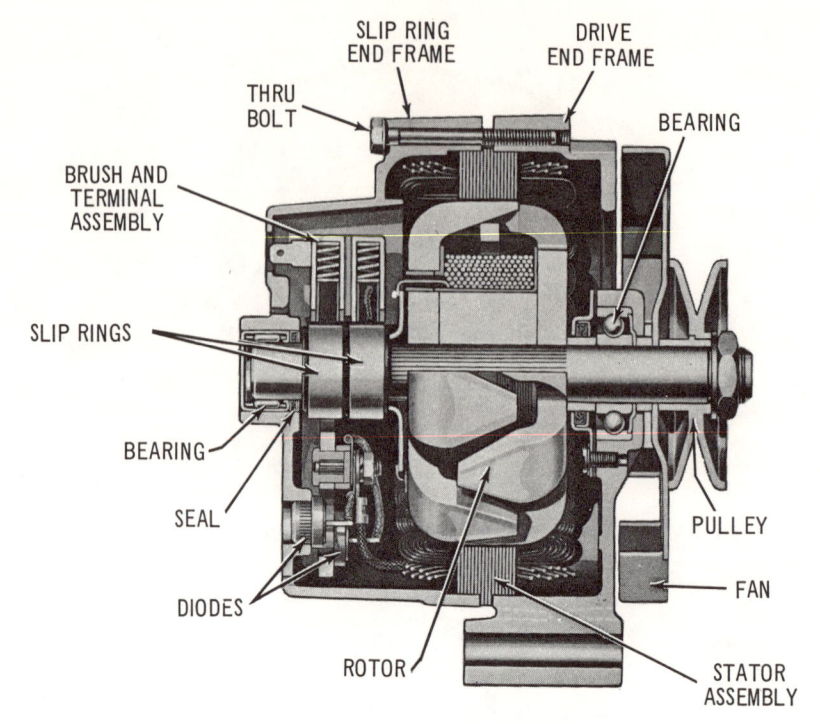

Delcotron alternator cross-section view.

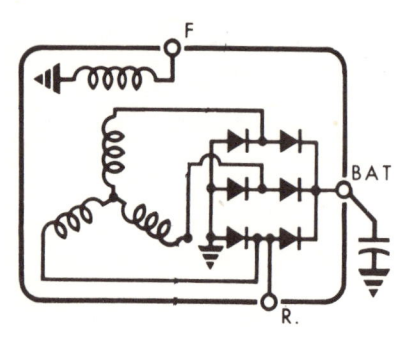

Delcotron wiring diagram.

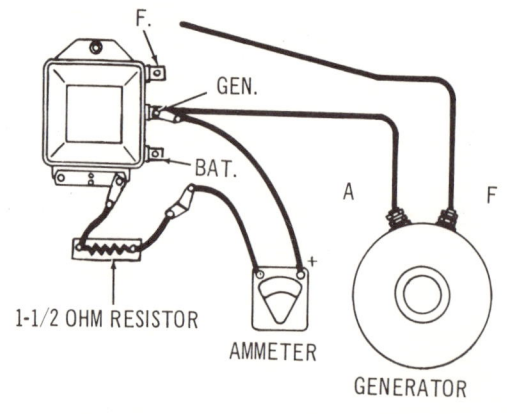

To test generator system 1964 and earlier XLCH (no battery).

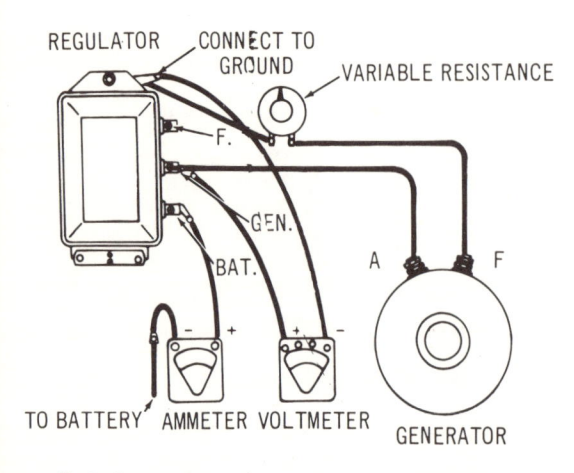

To test generator system and cutout shutoff voltage.

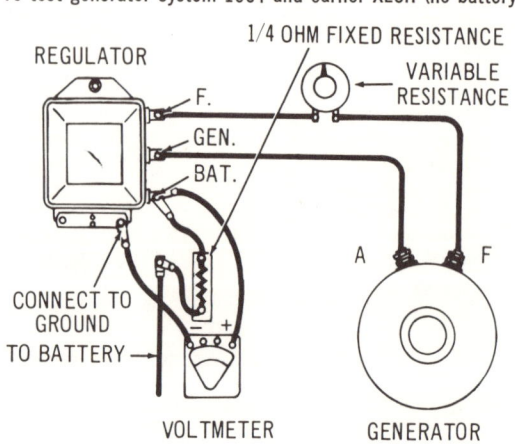

To test voltage regulator setting.

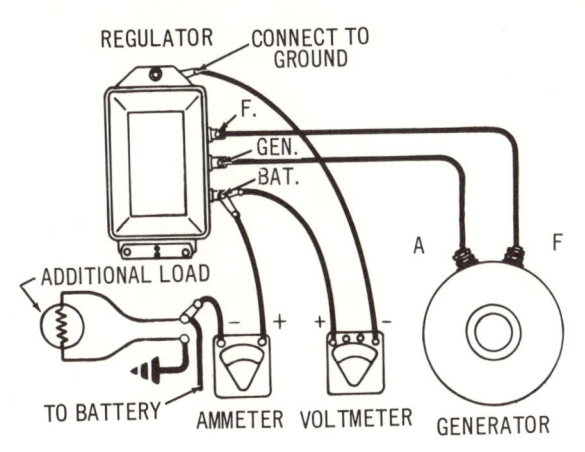

Starter

To test current control on three-unit regulator.

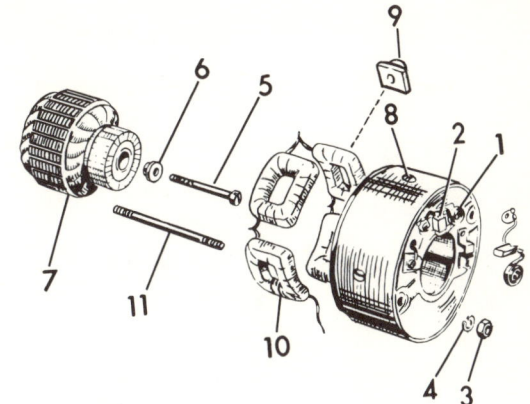

Generator, exploded view, Sprint models.

1. Brush spring (2)
2. Generator brush (2)
3. Mounting nut (2)
4. Mounting nut lockwasher (2)
5. Armature mounting screw
6. Armature mounting screw spacer
7. Armature
8. Pole shoe screw (4)
9. Pole shoe (4)
10. Field coil (set of four)
11. Generator frame stud (2)

Figure following name of part indicates quantity necessary for one complete assembly.

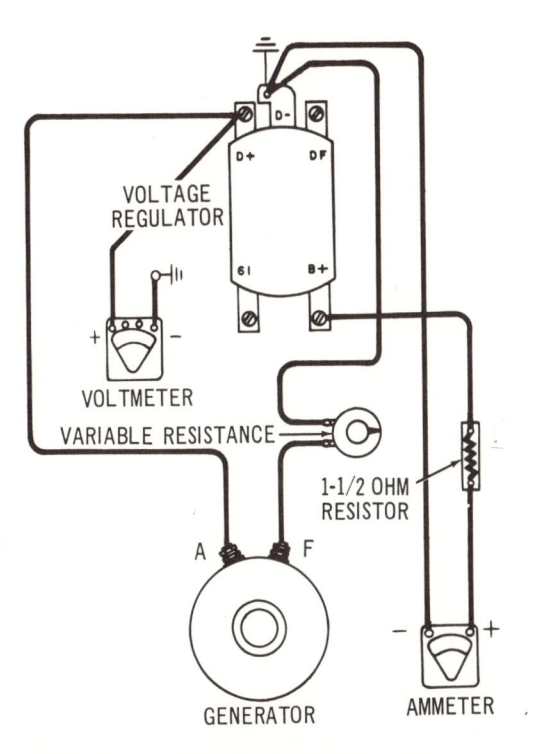

③ If the connections and wiring are found to be satisfactory, the battery should be checked to determine its state of charge.

If the battery is charged but there is no current flow to starter, bypass the switch with a jumper wire from battery to starter (see wiring diagram).

Removal and replacement

ELECTRA-GLIDE MODELS

① Disconnect solenoid cable from starter motor terminal.

② Remove attaching nuts and lock washers that fasten starter housing to studs on chain housing.

③ Remove end support plate from transmission. (It may be necessary to loosen and raise battery carrier to provide clearance.)

④ Remove starter and shaft housing from motorcycle as an assembly.

SPORTSTER MODELS

① Disconnect solenoid cable from starter terminal.

② Remove starter clamp bolt and lock washer from crankcase.

③ Unscrew motor through-bolts from shaft housing.

④ Remove starter and clamp as an assembly.

To test Bosch regulator.

Releasing brush springs, Sprint models.

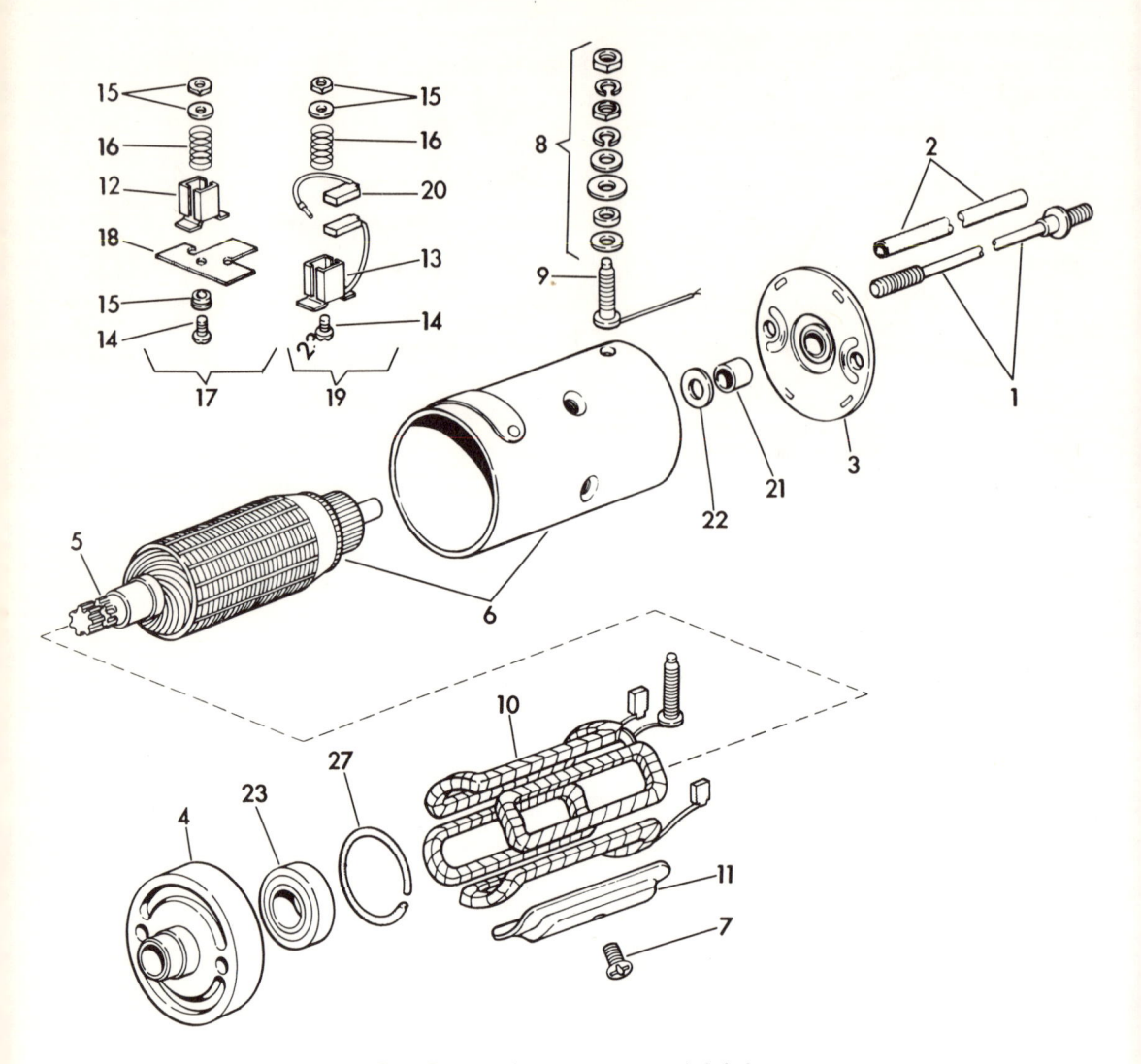

Delco-Remy 4-pole starter motor, exploded view.

1. Through bolt (2)
2. Insulating sleeve
3. Commutator end frame
4. Drive end frame
5. Armature
6. Frame and field assembly
7. Pole shoe screw (2 or 4)
8. Terminal nuts, lockwashers and insulating washers
9. Terminal screw
10. Set of field coils
11. Pole shoe (2 or 4)
12. Brush holder (2 or 4)
13. Grounded brush and holder (1 or 2)
14. Brush holder mounting screw (2 or 4)
15. Brush holder mounting nut and lockwasher (2 or 4)
16. Brush spring (2 or 4)
17. Insulated brush holder set
18. Insulator
19. Grounded brush holder set
20. Insulated brush (1 or 2)
21. Bushing
22. Thrust washer
23. Ball bearing
24. Bearing retainer

Figure following name of part indicates quantity necessary for one complete assembly.

Disassembly and Reassembly

DISASSEMBLY AND REASSEMBLY

PRESTOLITE

① Remove through-bolts with washers and lock washers.

② Remove commutator end cover, holding brush plate in place if necessary.

③ Remove armature and drive end cover with bearing as an assembly. (Bearing is a light press fit on armature shaft and is staked in end cover.)

Note: To prevent brushes escaping from holders, insert a spool of slightly larger diameter than the commutator underneath brushes when brushes are half-exposed as armature is withdrawn from frame. In this way armature can be reinstalled without removing brushes from holders.

Reassemble in reverse order, paying attention to the following:

End cover is marked with a double line next to the motor terminal. Also, brush holder has a positioning notch which registers on the motor terminal insulator. Parts must be located correctly when reassembled.

Replacing brushes

① Remove the terminal and insulated brush assembly from slot in frame and install new terminal and brush assembly.

② To replace ground brushes, attached to the field coils, cut off old brush lead wire where it is attached to the field coil lead.

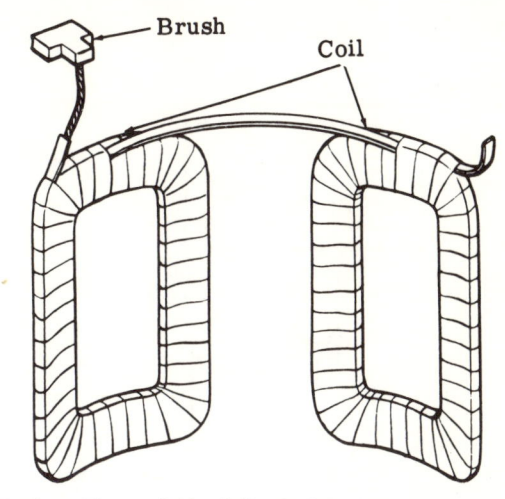

Brush position on field coil (2-pole Delco-Remy starter motor shown).

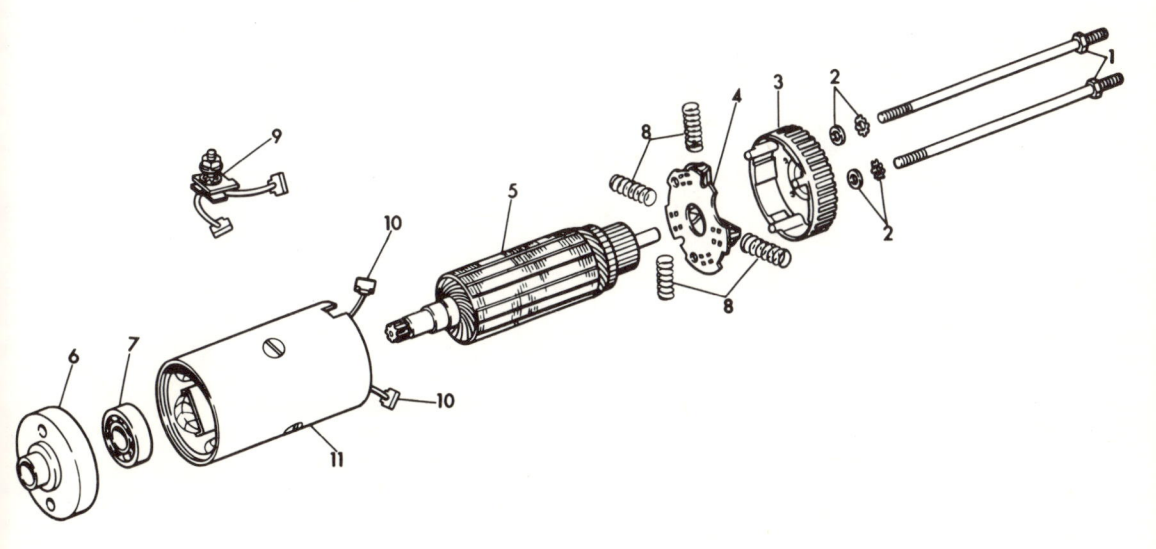

Prestolite 4-pole starter motor, exploded view.

1. Through bolt
2. Washer and lockwasher (2)
3. Commutator end cover
4. Brush plate and holder assembly
5. Armature
6. Drive end cover
7. Drive end ball bearing
8. Brush spring (4)
9. Terminal and brush assembly
10. Ground brush (2)
11. Frame and field coil assembly

Figure following name of part indicates quantity necessary for one complete assembly.

72　　　　　　　　*Electrical Systems*

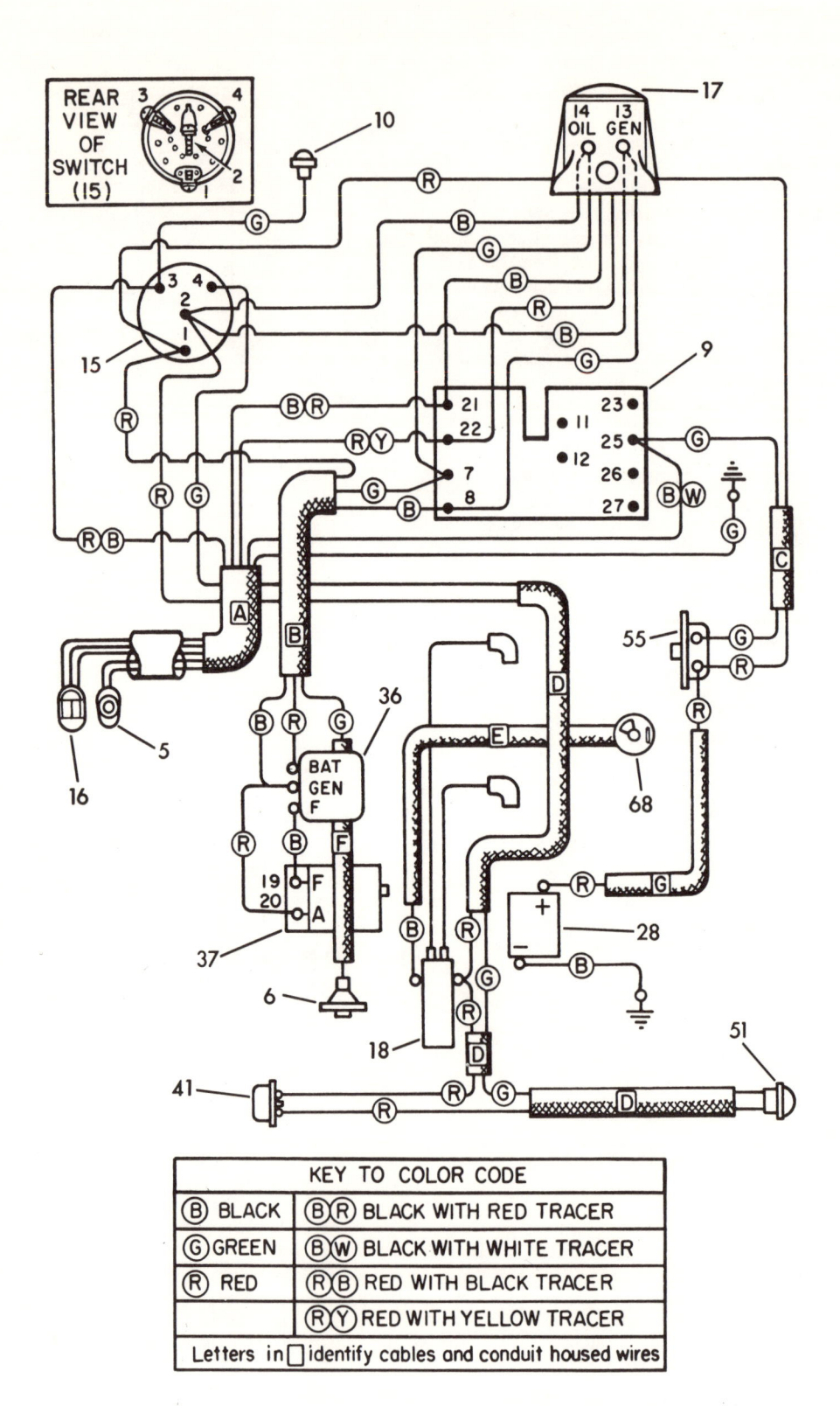

1959–1964 Sportster H wiring diagram.

Disassembly and Reassembly

A. Handlebar—Red wire with black tracer, black wire with red tracer, red wire with yellow tracer, green wire and black wire with white tracer
B. Conduit (three wires)—Green, red and black
C. Conduit (two wires)—Red and green
D. Conduit (two wires)—Red and green
E. Conduit (one wire)—Black
F. Conduit (one wire)—Green
G. Conduit (one wire)—Red
H. Conduit (two wires)—Black and red

5. Horn switch—Green wire and black wire with white tracer
6. Oil signal light switch—Green wire
7. Terminal—2 green wires
8. Terminal—Black and green wires
9. Terminal plate
10. Speedometer light—Green wire
11. Terminal—Not used with standard wiring
12. Terminal—Not used with standard wiring
13. Generator signal light—Green and black wires
14. Oil signal light—Green and black wires
15. Ignition—Light switch—Terminal No. 1 2 red wires; terminal No. 2 red wire and 2 black wires; terminal No. 3 green wire, and red wire with black tracer; and terminal No. 4 green wire
16. Headlamp switch—Red wire with black tracer, black wire with red tracer, and red wire with yellow tracer
17. Headlamp—Black and red wires
18. Ignition coil—2 red wires and black wire
19. Generator "F" terminal—Black wire
20. Generator "A" terminal—Red wire
21. Terminal—Black wire with red tracer and black wire
22. Terminal—Red wire with yellow tracer and red wire
23. Terminal—Not used with standard wiring
25. Terminal—Black wire with white tracer and green wire
26. Terminal—Not used with standard wiring
27. Terminal—Not used with standard wiring
28. Battery—Red and black wires
36. Regulator—"B" terminal, red wire; "G" terminal, black and red wires; "F" terminal, black wire
37. Generator
41. Stop light switch—2 red wires
51. Tail lamp—Green and red wires
55. Horn—Green wire and 2 red wires
68. Ignition circuit breaker—Black wire

---

③ Thoroughly clean coil lead by filing off old connection. Insulation on field coil lead should be removed only as far back as necessary to make new solder connection.

④ Using rosin flux, solder the brush lead to field coil lead, making certain that the brush lead is in the same position as the original.

⑤ Do not overheat brush lead or solder will run on wire strands and brush lead will no longer be flexible.

⑥ Before reassembling motor, check brush connections for sufficient clearance from frame and from armature.

DELCO-REMY

① Remove through-bolts. (Note that the bolt which passes near field coil connection has insulating sleeve.)

② Remove commutator end frame and drive end frame.

③ Remove armature from drive end of frame and field assembly.

Reassembly is essentially the reverse of the disassembly procedure. Note that pole shoes are notched on one end to accommodate connections at field coils.

Replacing brushes

① Remove pole shoe screws, terminal nuts, lockwashers and insulating washers and terminal screw.

② Remove set of field coils with brush and pole shoes. (It is unnecessary to remove brush holders except when defective or when replacing grounded brushes.)

③ Remove by cutting off or drilling out rivets. Replacement brushes are complete with screws, washers, and nuts for attaching to frame.

④ To remove brush springs, compress one side of spring with a small screwdriver until it flips out of its seat. Then turn spring clockwise until it comes out of holder.

⑤ Cut off old insulated brush lead where it is attached to field coil wire. Coil wire must then be prepared for soldering on new lead. Lead should be soldered to back side of coils so that excessive solder will not rub on armature.

⑥ Thoroughly clean coil lead end by filing or grinding off old connection. Varnish should be removed only as far back as necessary to make new solder connection.

⑦ Using rosin flux, solder the brush lead to field coil lead, making certain brush is in the right position to reach brush holders.

Note: Do not overheat brush lead or solder will run on wire strands and lead will no longer be flexible.

⑧ Attach new grounded brush holder and brush assembly with hardware included in package.

⑨ After tightening nuts on both brush holders, peen the screws with a hammer so nuts cannot vibrate loose.

74 Electrical Systems

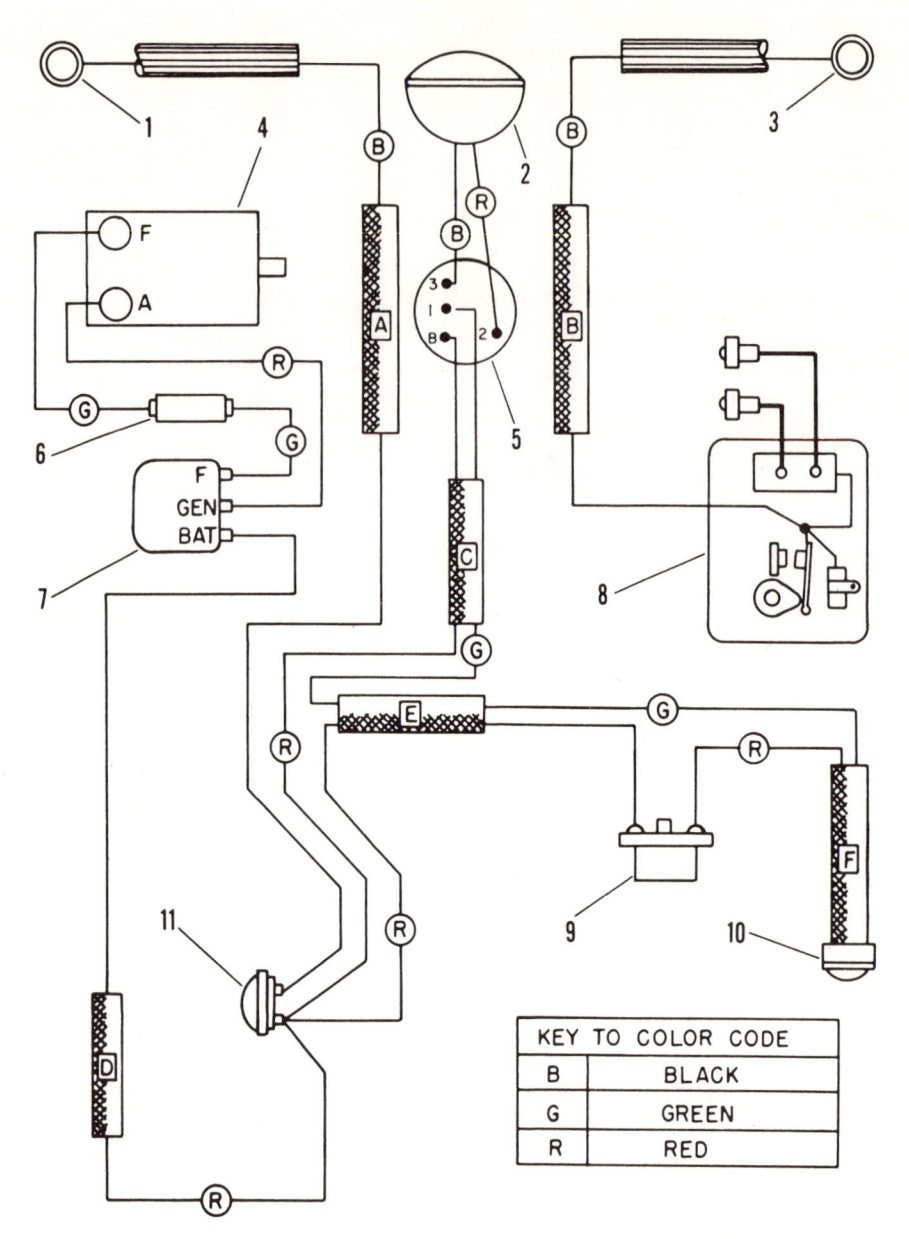

1959–1962 Sportster CH wiring diagram.

A. Conduit (one wire)—Black
B. Conduit (one wire)—Black
C. Conduit (two wires)—Red and green wires
D. Conduit (one wire)—Red
E. Conduit (two wires)—Red and green wires
F. Conduit (two wires)—Red and green wires

1. Horn switch—Black wire
2. Headlamp—Black and red wires
3. Ignition cutout switch—Black wire
4. Generator—
    "F" terminal—Green wire
    "A" terminal—Red wire
5. Headlamp switch—
    Terminal "B"—Red wire
    Terminal 1—Green wire
    Terminal 2—Red wire
    Terminal 3—Black wire
6. Fuse—2 green wires
7. Voltage regulator—
    "F" terminal—Green wire
    "GEN" terminal—Red wire
    "BAT" terminal—Red wire
8. Magneto—Black wire
9. Stoplight switch—2 red wires
10. Tail and stop lamp—Red and green wires
11. Horn—
    Upper terminal—Black wire
    Lower terminal—3 red wires

KEY TO COLOR CODE	
B	BLACK
G	GREEN
R	RED

Disassembly and Reassembly

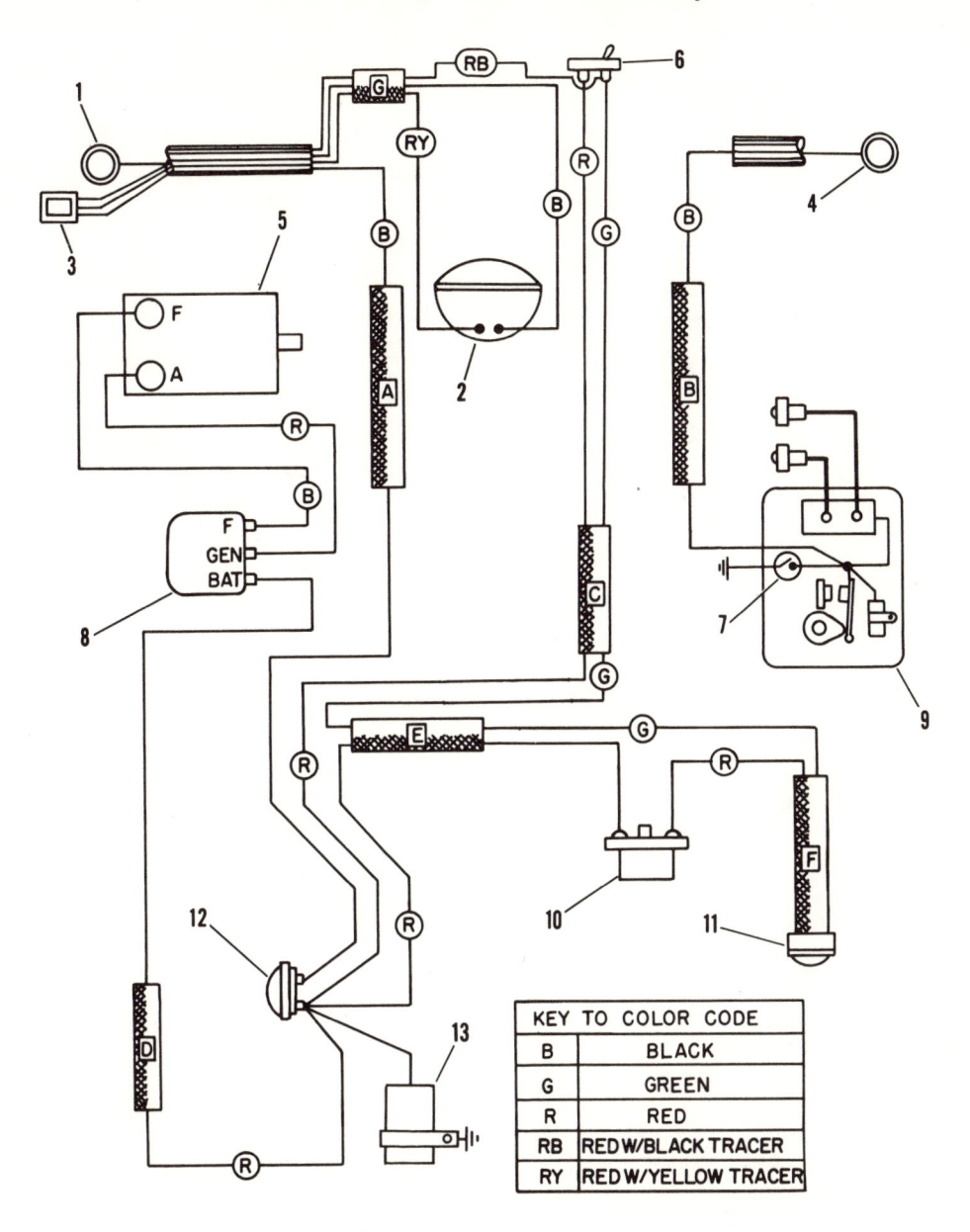

KEY TO COLOR CODE	
B	BLACK
G	GREEN
R	RED
RB	RED W/BLACK TRACER
RY	RED W/YELLOW TRACER

1963–1964 Sportster CH wiring diagram.

A. Conduit (one wire)—Black
B. Conduit (one wire)—Black
C. Conduit (two wires)—Red and green wires
D. Conduit (one wire)—Red
E. Conduit (two wires)—Red and green wires
F. Conduit (two wires)—Red and green wires
G. Conduit (three wires)—2 red and 1 black wire

1. Horn switch—Black wire
2. Headlamp—Black and red wires
3. Dimmer switch—2 red and 1 black wire
4. Ignition cutout switch—Black wire
5. Generator—
   "F" terminal—Black wire
   "A" terminal—Red wire
6. Light switch—2 red and 1 green wire
7. Ignition ground switch lock
8. Voltage regulator—
   "F" terminal—Black wire
   "GEN" terminal—Red wire
   "BAT" terminal—Red wire
9. Magneto—Black wire
10. Stop light switch—2 red wires
11. Tail and stop lamp—Red and green wires
12. Horn—
    Upper terminal—Black wire
    Lower terminal—3 red wires and capacitor wire
13. Capacitor

Electrical Systems

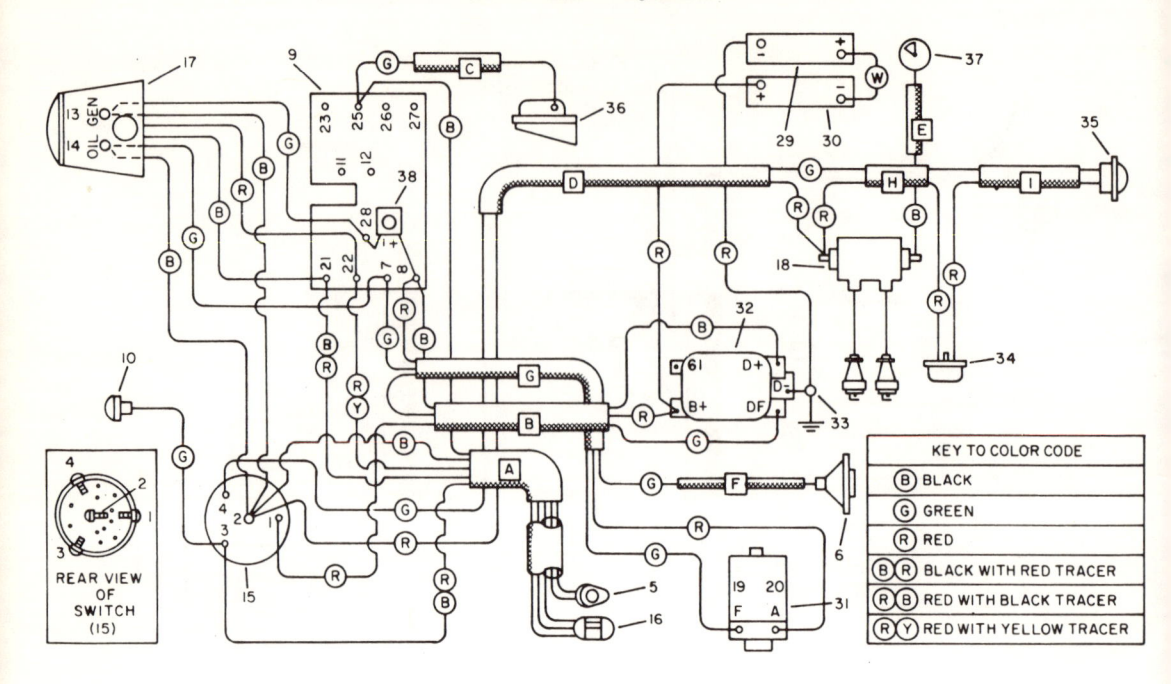

1965–1966 Sportster H wiring diagram.

A. Handlebar—Red wire with black tracer, black wire with red tracer, red wire with yellow tracer, 2 black wires
B. Conduit (three wires)—Green, red and black
C. Conduit—Green wire
D. Conduit (two wires)—Red and green
E. Conduit (one wire)—Black
F. Conduit (one wire)—Green
G. Conduit (three wires)—Red and 2 green
H. Conduit (two wires)—Black and red

5. Horn switch—2 black wires
6. Oil signal light switch—Green wire
7. Terminal—2 green wires
8. Terminal—Black, red, and rectifier positive terminal
9. Terminal plate
10. Speedometer light—Green wire
11. Terminal—Not used with standard wiring
12. Terminal—Not used with standard wiring
13. Generator signal light—Green and black wires
14. Oil signal light—Green and black wires
15. Ignition—Light switch—Terminal No. 1 red wire; terminal No. 2 red wire and 3 black wires; terminal No. 3 green wire, and red wire with black tracer; and terminal No. 4 green wire
16. Headlamp switch—Red wire with black tracer, black wire with red tracer, and red wire with yellow tracer
17. Headlamp—Black and red wires
18. Ignition coil—3 red wires and black wire
19. Generator "F" terminal—Green wire
20. Generator "A" terminal—Red wire
21. Terminal—Black wire with red tracer and black wire
22. Terminal—Red wire with yellow tracer and red wire
23. Terminal—Not used with standard wiring
25. Terminal—Black wire and green wire
26. Terminal—Not used with standard wiring
27. Terminal—Not used with standard wiring
28. Terminal—Green wire and rectifier negative terminal
29. Front battery—
    Negative terminal—Black wire
    Positive terminal—White wire
30. Rear battery—
    Positive terminal—Red wire
    Negative terminal—White wire
31. Generator—See terminals 19 and 20
32. Regulator—
    B+ terminal—2 red wires
    DF terminal—Green wire
    D+ terminal—Black wire
    Gnd. terminal—Black wire
    G1 terminal—Not used with standard wiring
33. Terminal, frame screw—2 black wires
34. Stoplight switch—2 red wires
35. Tail lamp—Red and green wires
36. Horn—Green wire
37. Circuit breaker—2 black wires
38. Rectifier—
    Positive terminal (painted red) to terminal No. 8
    Negative terminal to terminal No. 28.

Disassembly and Reassembly

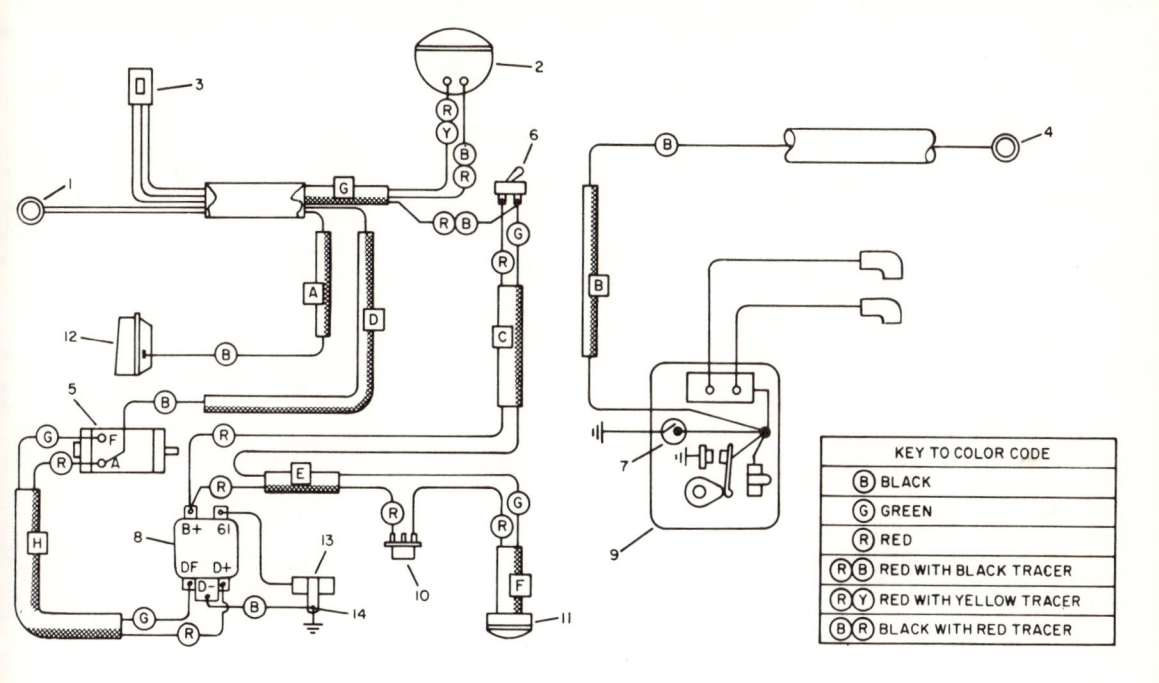

1965 Sportster CH wiring diagram.

	KEY TO COLOR CODE
Ⓑ	BLACK
Ⓖ	GREEN
Ⓡ	RED
ⓇⒷ	RED WITH BLACK TRACER
ⓇⓎ	RED WITH YELLOW TRACER
ⒷⓇ	BLACK WITH RED TRACER

A. Conduit (one wire)—Black
B. Conduit (one wire)—Black
C. Conduit (two wires)—Red and green
D. Conduit (one wire)—Black
E. Conduit (two wires)—Red and green
F. Conduit (two wires)—Red and green
G. Conduit (three wires)—Red wire with black tracer, red wire with yellow tracer, black wire with red tracer
H. Conduit (two wires)—Green and red

1. Horn switch—2 black wires
2. Headlamp—Black wire with red tracer and red wire with yellow tracer
3. Dimmer switch—Red wire with black tracer, red wire with yellow tracer, black wire with red tracer
4. Ignition cutout switch—Black wire
5. Generator—
   "F" terminal—Green wire
   "A" terminal—Red and black wires
6. Light switch (three wires)—Red, green and red with black tracer
7. Ignition ground switch lock
8. Voltage regulator—
   "61" terminal—Condenser black wire
   DF terminal—Green wire
   D+ terminal—Red wire and condenser wire
   B+ terminal—2 red wires
   Gnd. terminal—Black wire
9. Magneto—Black wire
10. Stoplight switch—2 red wires
11. Tail and stop lamp—Red and green wires
12. Horn—Black wire
13. Capacitor—Lead connected to regulator 61 terminal
14. Grounding screw—Black wire and condenser ground strap

Electrical Systems

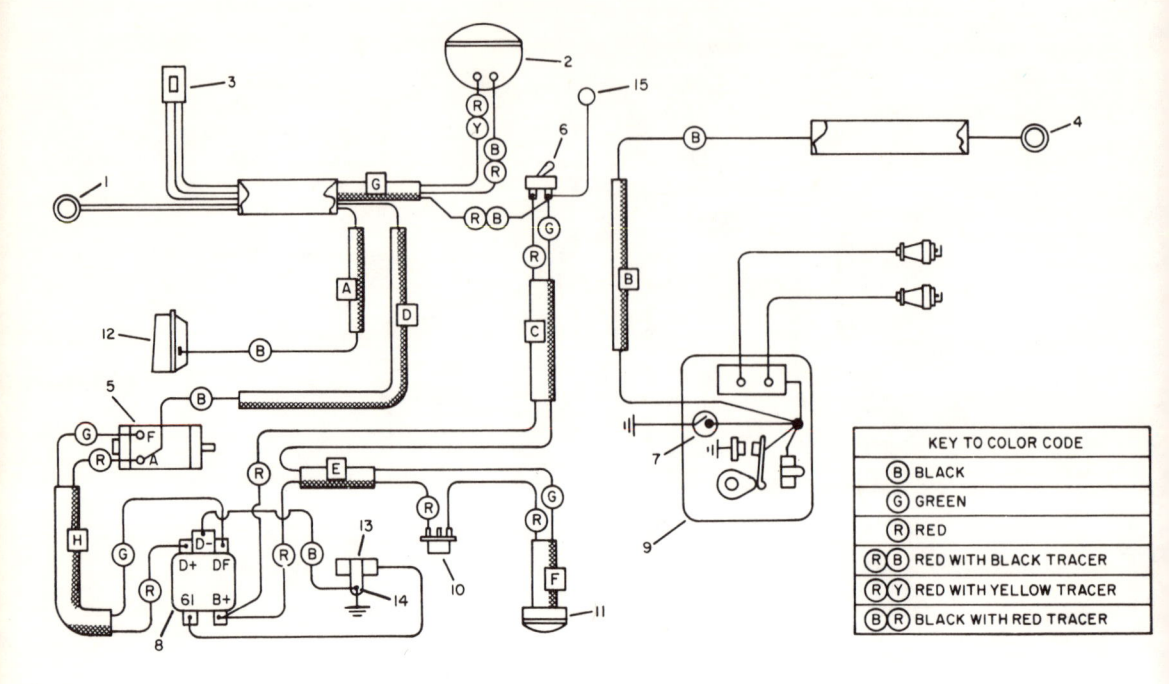

1966 Sportster CH wiring diagram.

A. Conduit (one wire)—Black
B. Conduit (one wire)—Black
C. Conduit (two wires)—Red and green
D. Conduit (one wire)—Black
E. Conduit (two wires)—Red and green
F. Conduit (two wires)—Red and green
G. Conduit (three wires)—Red wire with black tracer, red wire with yellow tracer, black wire with red tracer
H. Conduit (two wires)—Green and red

1. Horn switch—Two black wires
2. Headlamp—Black wire with red tracer and red wire with yellow tracer
3. Headlamp dimmer switch—Red wire with black tracer, red wire with yellow tracer, black wire with red tracer
4. Ignition cutout switch—Black wire
5. Generator—
   "F" terminal—Green wire
   "A" terminal—Black wire
6. Light switch—Red, green and red with black tracer wires
7. Ignition ground switch lock
8. Voltage regulator—
   "DF" terminal—Green wire
   "D+" terminal—Red wire and condenser wire
   "B+" terminal—2 red wires
   "61" terminal—Black wire
9. Magneto—Black wire
10. Stoplight switch—2 red wires
11. Tail and stop lamp—Red and green wires
12. Horn—Black wire
13. Capacitor—Center black wire connected to regulator "61" terminal
14. Grounding screw—Black wire
15. Speedometer lamp

KEY TO COLOR CODE
- (B) BLACK
- (G) GREEN
- (R) RED
- (R)(B) RED WITH BLACK TRACER
- (R)(Y) RED WITH YELLOW TRACER
- (B)(R) BLACK WITH RED TRACER

Disassembly and Reassembly

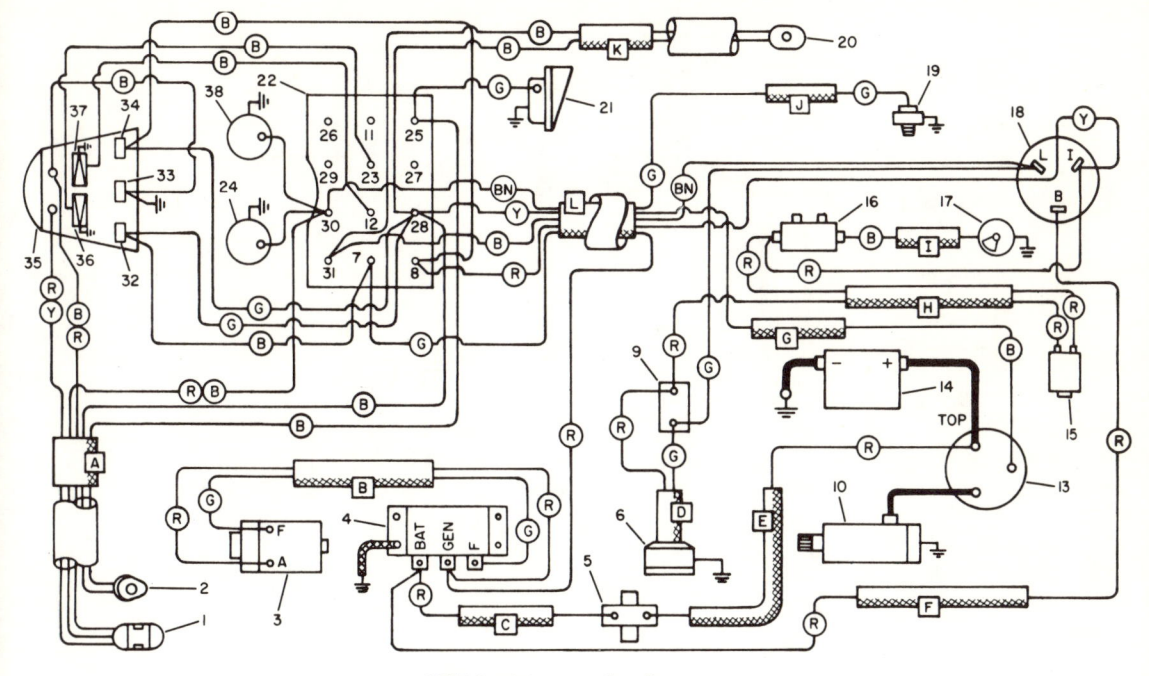

1967 Sportster H wiring diagram.

A. Handlebar (five wires)—Red wire with black tracer, black wire with red tracer, red wire with yellow tracer, and 2 black wires
B. Conduit (two wires)—Green and red
C. Conduit (one wire)—Red
D. Conduit (two wires)—Red and green
E. Conduit (one wire)—Red
F. Conduit (one wire)—Red
G. Conduit (one wire)—Black
H. Conduit (two wires)—Red
I. Conduit (one wire)—Black
J. Conduit (one wire)—Green
K. Conduit (two wires)—Black
L. Conduit (five wires)—Brown, yellow, black, red and green

1. Headlamp dimmer switch
2. Horn switch
3. Generator "F" and "A" terminals
4. Regulator—
   "BAT" terminal
   "GEN" terminal
   "F" terminal
5. Overload circuit breaker
6. Tail lamp
7. Terminal
8. Terminal
9. Junction terminal board
10. Starter motor
11. Terminal—Not used with standard wiring
12. Terminal
13. Starter solenoid
14. Battery
15. Stoplight switch
16. Ignition coil
17. Circuit breaker
18. Ignition—light switch
19. Oil signal light switch
20. Starter button
21. Horn
22. Terminal plate
23. Terminal
24. Speedometer light
25. Terminal
26. Terminal—Not used with standard wiring
27. Terminal—Not used with standard wiring
28. Terminal
29. Terminal—Not used with standard wiring
30. Terminal
31. Terminal
32. Oil signal light
33. High beam indicator light
34. Generator indicator light
35. Headlamp
36. Left direction signal pilot lamp
37. Right direction signal pilot lamp
38. Tachometer light

KEY TO COLOR CODE		
B		Black
Y		Yellow
BN		Brown
G		Green
R		Red
B	R	Black with red tracer
R	B	Red with black tracer
R	Y	Red with yellow tracer

Caution: Disconnect ground cable at battery (−) terminal to prevent accidental starter operation when servicing motorcycle.

Electrical Systems

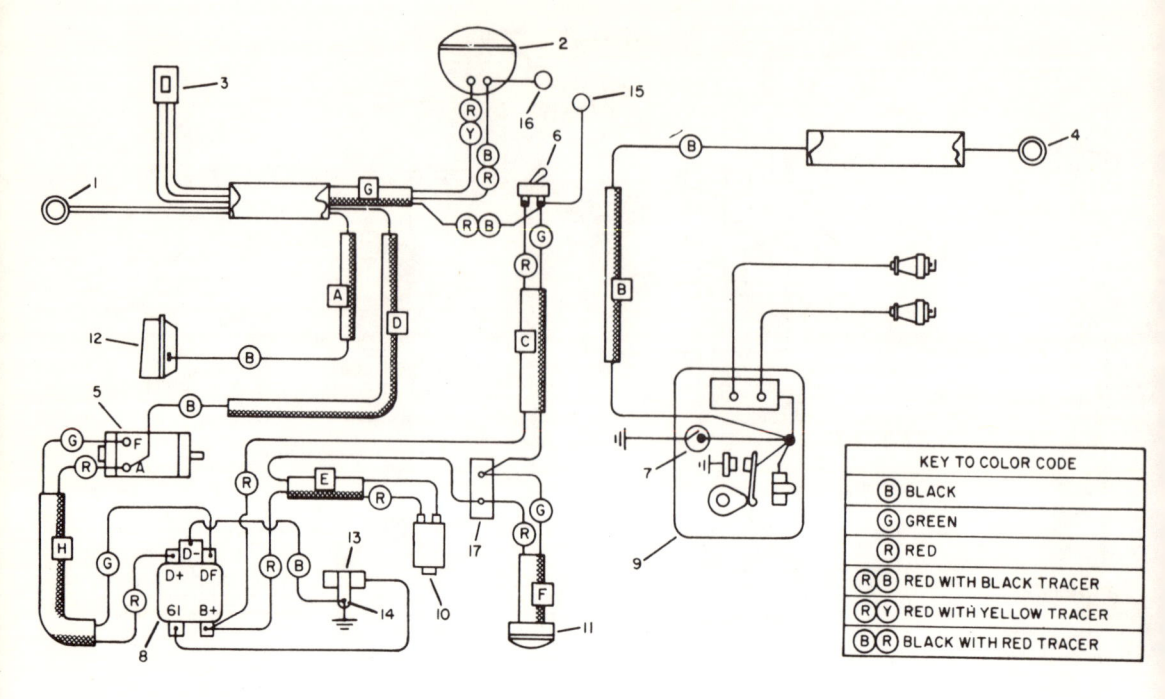

1967 Sportster CH wiring diagram.

A. Conduit (one wire)—Black
B. Conduit (one wire)—Black
C. Conduit (two wires)—Red and green
D. Conduit (one wire)—Black
E. Conduit (two wires)—Red
F. Conduit (two wires)—Red and green
G. Conduit (three wires)—Red wire with black tracer, red wire with yellow tracer, black wire with red tracer
H. Conduit (two wires)—Green and red

1. Horn switch—2 black wires
2. Headlamp—Black wire with red tracer and red wire with yellow tracer
3. Headlamp dimmer switch—Red wire with black tracer, red wire with yellow tracer, black wire with red tracer
4. Ignition cutout switch—Black wire
5. Generator—
   "F" terminal—Green wire
   "A" terminal—Black wire
6. Light switch—Red, green and red with black tracer wires
7. Ignition ground switch lock
8. Voltage regulator—
   "DF" terminal—Green wire
   "D+" terminal—Red wire and condenser wire
   "B+" terminal—2 red wires
   "D−" terminal—Black wire
9. Magneto—Black wire
10. Stoplight switch—2 red wires
11. Tail and stop lamp—Red and green wires
12. Horn—Black wire
13. Capacitor—Black wire connected to regulator "D−" terminal
14. Grounding screw—Black wire
15. Speedometer lamp
16. High beam indicator lamp
17. Terminal strip

CHAPTER 6

Carburetion

Harleys use a variety of carburetors, depending on age and size of bikes. The oldest and most familiar to veteran riders is the Schebler Model M. It is a good, simple carburetor but does not have the capacity of the later HD.

Note: Adjustment of carburetors is described in the MAINTENANCE AND TUNING chapter. Service of each type will be covered here.

Model M

Removal

① Remove air cleaner cover, element and back plate.
② Disconnect fuel line with strainer at carburetor.
③ Disconnect throttle control wire.
④ Remove carburetor support from top center crankcase bolt.
⑤ Remove intake (choke) lever stud nut and washer.
⑥ Twist intake lever off intake lever rod, and remove intake lever rod from carburetor.
⑦ Remove four carburetor fastening bolts and pull carburetor out to right.

Disassembly and reassembly

① Remove bowl lock nut, gasket, main nozzle retainer spring and main nozzle.
② Remove bowl and bowl cover gasket.
③ Take out float valve seat and gasket.
④ Turn out float lever pin.
⑤ Slip float, float lever and float valve out of bowl.
⑥ Loosen throttle stop lock screw and slide throttle lever off throttle shaft with throttle lever arm and throttle shaft spring.
⑦ Remove throttle shaft screws, pull throttle disc out of slot in throttle shaft and pull out throttle shaft.
⑧ Unscrew low-speed needle valve and high-speed needle valve.
⑨ Remove needle valve lever screw, needle valve lever, lever spring, and lever spring collar.
⑩ Remove air intake shaft nut and washer, air intake shaft stop, friction ball and friction spring.
⑪ Remove air intake disc screws, air intake disc and pull out air intake shaft.
⑫ Remove idle hole body plug, two idle passage plug screws, and carburetor fixed jet.

The carburetor is now completely disassembled and ready for inspection and cleaning. To reassemble, reverse the above process. Be sure the following items are correctly handled.

① Install venturi with choke end (small end) facing air intake opening.
② Install throttle shaft from bottom of carburetor so counterbored screw head notches are facing left side of carburetor when viewing carburetor from throttle shaft end. Notice that an edge of the disc has a flat on each side. Pass this edge of the disc through the throttle shaft, close throttle and insert throttle shaft screws, but do not tighten. Shift disc slightly until it seats all the way around the carburetor throat. Tighten screws. Work disc several times. If there is any bind, loosen screws and reposition disc.
③ Position both throttle disc and throttle lever in wide open position before tightening throttle stop lock screw.
④ Throttle lever and shaft should open and close with just a slight drag. If too loose, loosen stop lock screw and compress parts on throttle shaft with fingers while tightening.
⑤ Install only replacement throttle disc containing same identification number on face. With disc correctly installed and closed, the number will be on the right half of disc when viewed through manifold end of carburetor.
⑥ Always use new gaskets.

Cleaning and inspection

① Clean all parts except float and gaskets in Gunk Hydro-Seal or similar cleaner. Dry with compressed air and keep parts on clean shop towel.
② Assemble float, lever, valve and seat in bowl and turn upside down. Measure distance from lip of float bowl to top of float directly opposite float lever. This should be exactly ¼". *Do not bend the float lever while installed in bowl.* Adjusting in this manner develops lash or lost motion between float and needle. Float and lever assembly should be removed from bowl, and lever then bent as required.
③ Check needle head fit in float lever. It should be a free fit to about .003" clearance. To check clearance with float assembled, hold needle against seat with small screwdriver with-

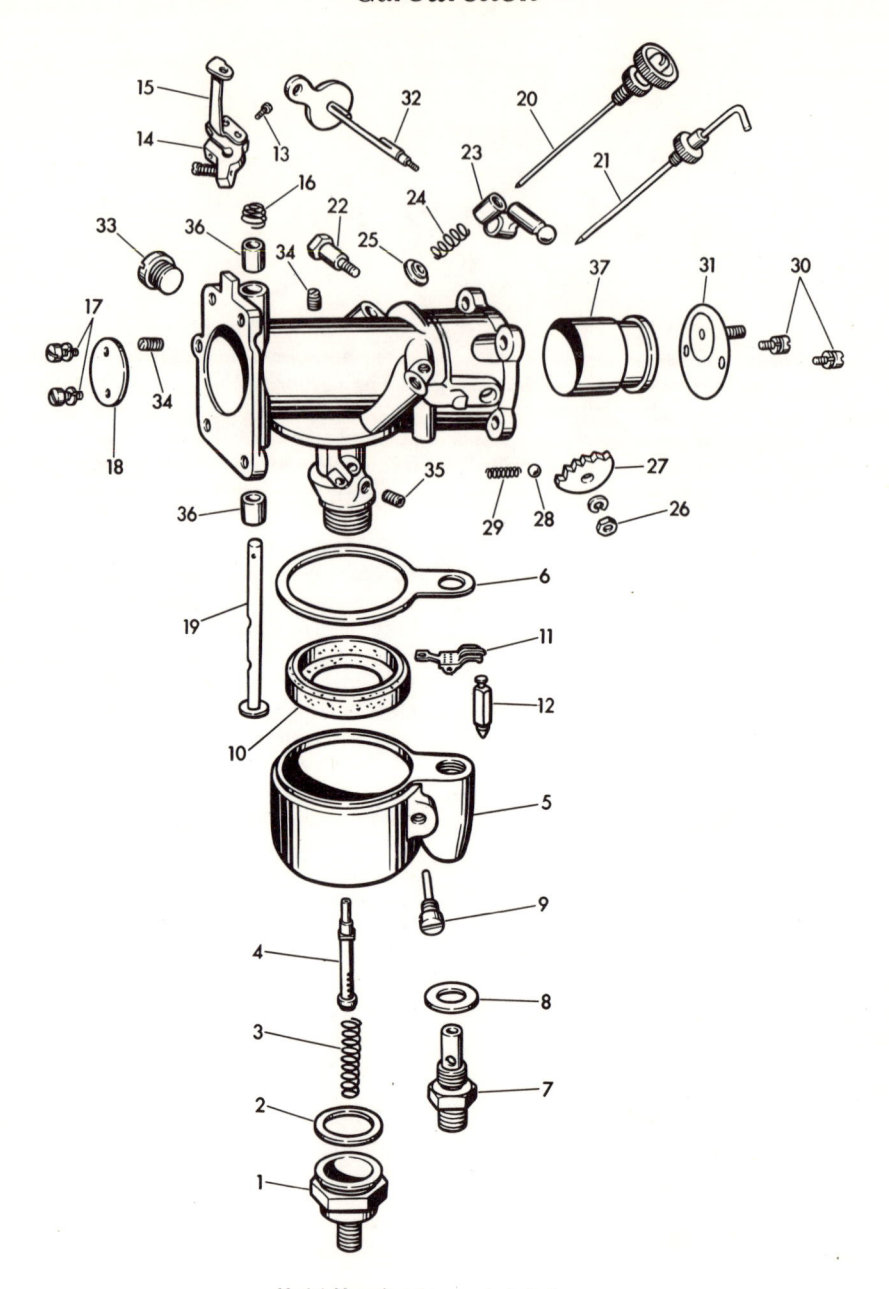

Model M carburetor, exploded view.

1. Bowl lock nut
2. Lock nut gasket
3. Main nozzle retainer spring
4. Main nozzle
5. Bowl
6. Bowl cover gasket
7. Float valve seat
8. Float valve seat gasket
9. Float lever pin
10. Float
11. Float lever
12. Float valve
13. Throttle stop lock screw
14. Throttle lever
15. Throttle lever arm
16. Throttle shaft spring
17. Throttle shaft screw (2)
18. Throttle disc
19. Throttle shaft
20. Low speed needle valve
21. High speed needle valve
22. Needle valve lever screw
23. Needle valve lever
24. Needle valve lever spring
25. Lever spring collar
26. Air intake shaft nut and washer
27. Air intake shaft stop
28. Friction ball
29. Friction spring
30. Air intake disc screw (2)
31. Air intake disc
32. Air intake shaft
33. Idle hole body plug
34. Idle passage plug screw (3)
35. Fixed jet
36. Throttle shaft bushing (2)
37. Venturi (1$\frac{5}{16}$")

Figure following name of part indicates quantity necessary for one complete assembly.

Model M

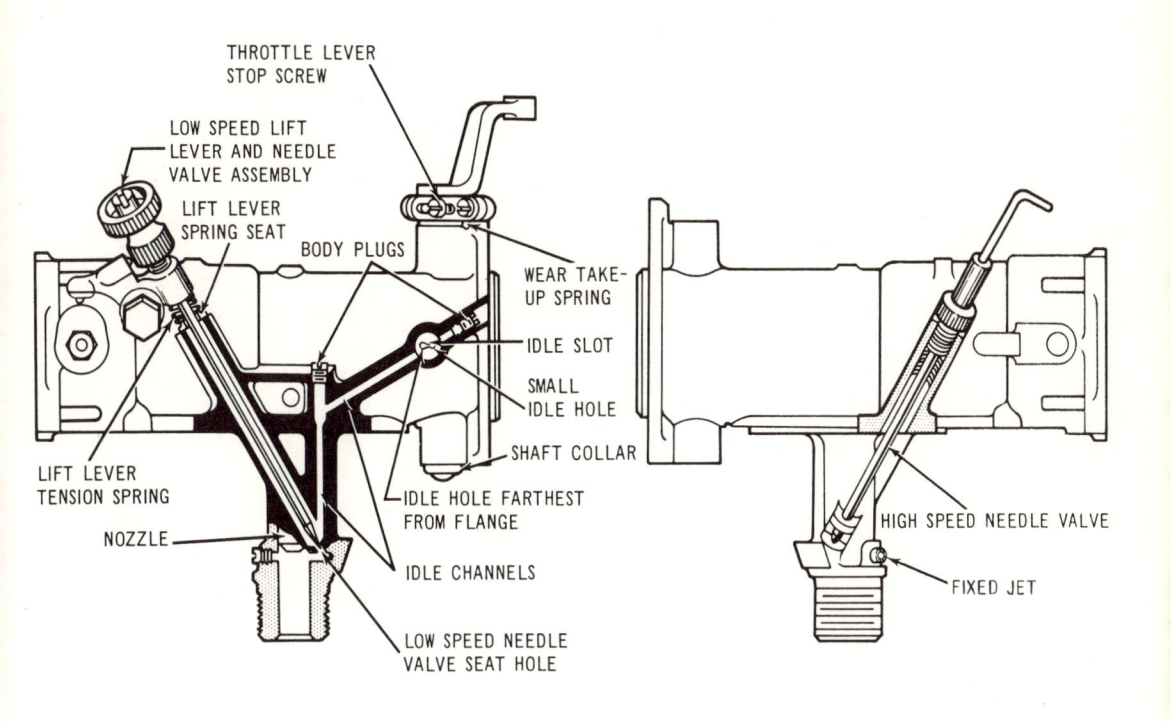

Model M carburetor passages and needle seats.

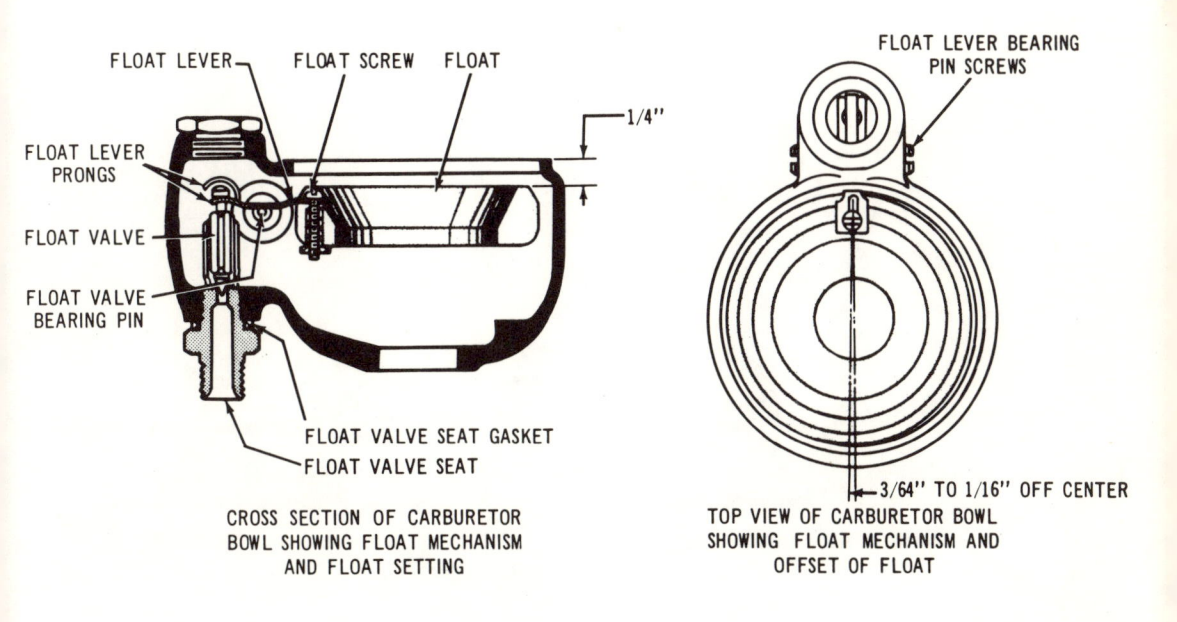

Adjusting Model M bowl float and needle.

Carburetion

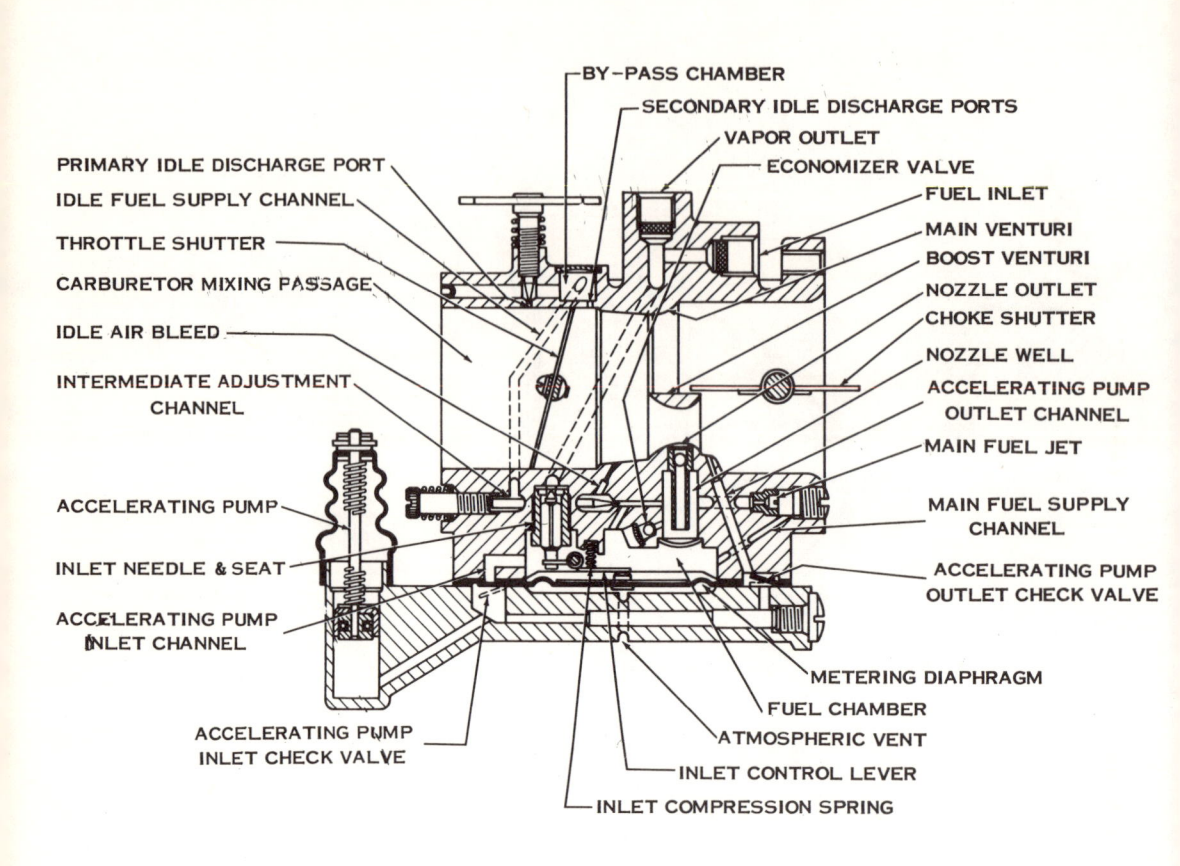

Carburetor cross section—Model HD.

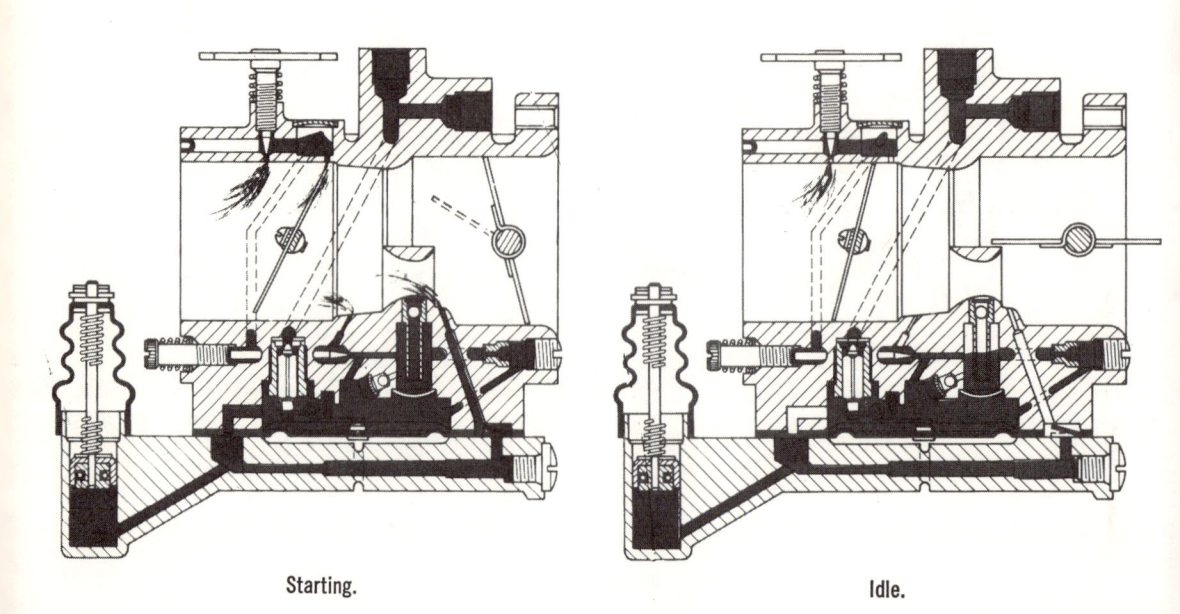

Starting.

Idle.

Model HD

Accelerating.

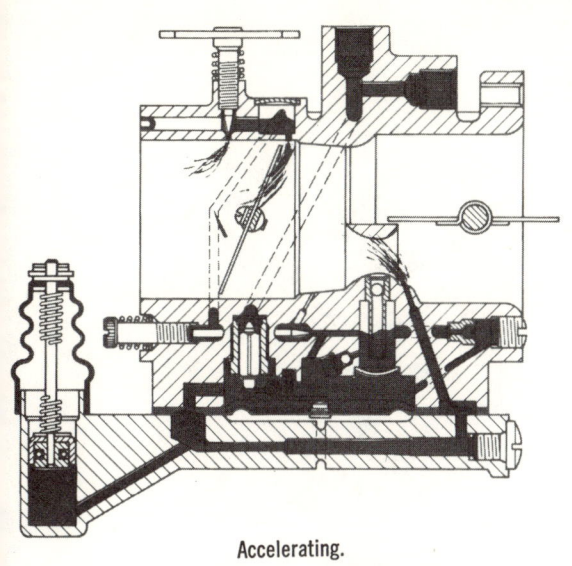

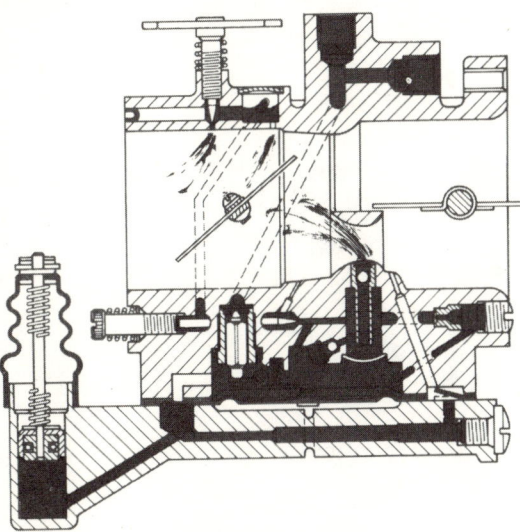

Intermediate speed.

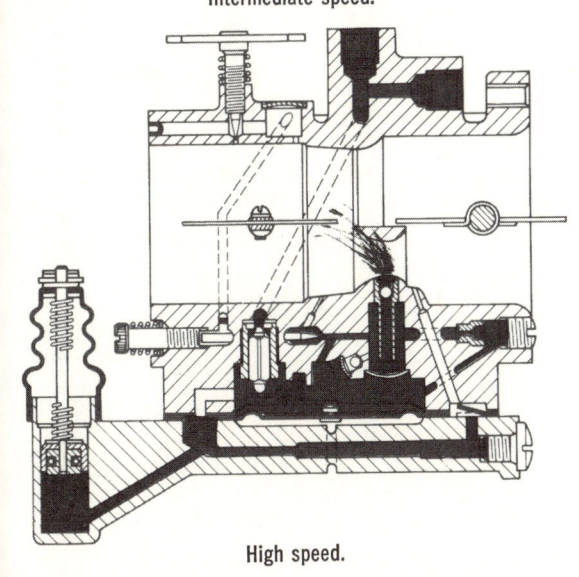

High speed.

out restricting float lever. Move float up and down and observe free play between needle head and float lever.

④ Hold bowl upside down so that float valve closes. Suck on bottom of float valve seat. If valve leaks, replace valve and seat.

Model HD

This is a sophisticated unit with a secondary venturi, accelerating pump and economizer.

An improved needle valve regulates fuel flow in any position and resists vibration.

In the accompanying diagrams, fuel flow under various engine operating conditions is shown. These will help the rider visualize the effects of maladjustments as well as contamination with dirt, gum varnish, etc. The troubleshooting guide is based on factory recommendations for locating the source of the problems and correcting it.

Note: To correct general richness or leanness, the following main jets are available: .053″, .055″, .057″, .059″, .061″ and .063″.

Disassembly and reassembly

With carburetor on the bench, remove the following in order:

① Idle and intermediate fuel adjustment screws.

② Throttle disc screws and the throttle disc. (The sides of the disc are tapered 15° to conform to the throttle bore. Observe the direction of this taper and the position of the disc so that it can be reassembled later in the correct position.)

③ Accelerating-pump-lever retaining screw.

④ Throttle-shaft assembly.

⑤ Compression spring washers and shaft dust seals.

⑥ Six screws and washers and the body cover.

⑦ Accelerating pump plunger assembly.

⑧ Channel plug screw.

⑨ Metering diaphragm.

⑩ Meter-diaphragm gasket. (Note that the gasket is assembled next to the body casting.)

⑪ Fulcrum-pin retaining screw, fulcrum pin, inlet control lever, and metering spring.

⑫ Inlet needle.

⑬ Inlet seat and cage assembly. (Use a ⅜″ thin-wall hex socket wrench. Note the position of the inlet seat insert with the contoured side toward the outside of the cage and the smooth side toward the inside of the cage.)

⑭ Inlet seat gasket. (Use a small tap or bent wire.)

⑮ Plug screw.

⑯ Fixed main jet and gasket.

⑰ If necessary, remove main-nozzle or idle port welch plug by drilling ⅛″ diameter hole off center and just breaking through the welch plug. Do not drill deeper than the welch plug,

Carburetion

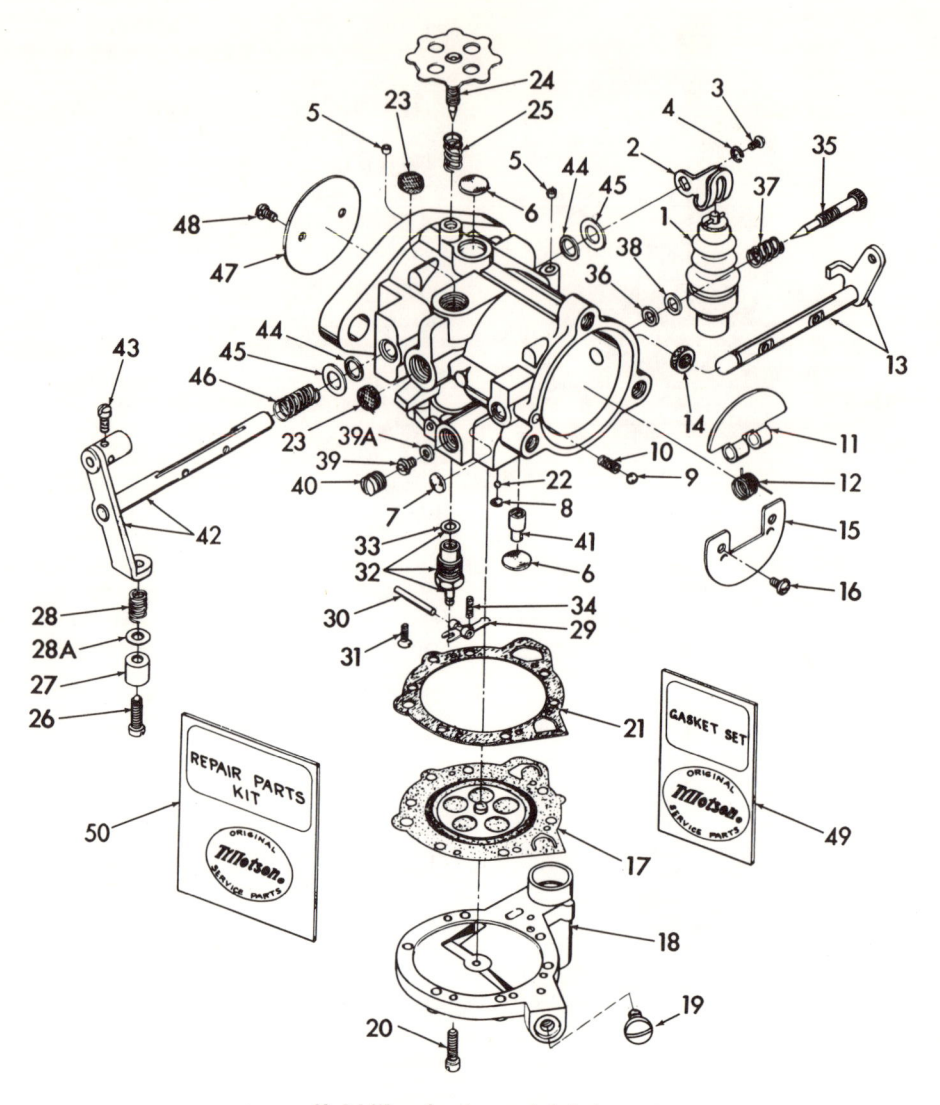

Model HD carburetor, exploded view.

1. Accelerating pump	20. Diaphragm cover screws (2)	36. Intermediate adjusting screw packing
2. Accelerating pump lever	21. Diaphragm cover gasket	37. Intermediate adjusting screw spring
3. Accelerating pump lever screw	22. Economizer check ball	38. Intermediate adjusting screw washer
4. Accelerating pump lever screw L.W.	23. Fuel filter screen (2)	39. Main jet
5. Channel plug (2)	24. Idle adjustment screw	39A. Main jet gasket
6. Welch plug	25. Idle adjustment screw spring	40. Main jet plug screw
7. Welch plug	26. Throttle stop screw	41. Main nozzle check valve
8. Welch plug	27. Throttle stop screw cup	42. Throttle shaft assembly
9. Choke shaft friction ball	28. Throttle stop screw spring	43. Throttle lever wire block screw
10. Choke shaft friction spring	28A. Throttle stop screw spring washer	44. Dust seal (2)
11. Choke shutter (top)	29. Inlet control lever	45. Washer (2)
12. Choke shutter spring	30. Inlet control lever pin	46. Throttle shaft spring
13. Choke shaft assembly	31. Inlet control lever screw	47. Throttle shutter
14. Choke shaft dust seal	32. Inlet needle and seat	48. Throttle shutter screws
15. Choke shutter (bottom)	33. Inlet needle seat gasket	49. Gasket overhaul set
16. Choke shutter screws	34. Inlet control lever tension spring	50. Overhaul repair kit
17. Diaphragm	35. Intermediate adjusting screw	
18. Cover		
19. Diaphragm cover plug screw		

Figure following name of part indicates quantity necessary for one complete assembly.

Model HD

HD Carburetor Troubleshooting

Problem	Possible Cause	Remedy
1. Idle operation too lean	(a) Dirt in idle fuel channels (b) Intermediate adjustment closed or adjusted too lean (c) Welch plug or channel plugs missing or not tightly sealed (d) Nozzle check valve not sealing	(a) Blow out with compressed air (b) Readjust (c) Reseat or replace plugs (d) Blow out with compressed air
2. Idle operation too rich	(a) Carburetor flooding (b) Idle adjustment screw point damaged (c) Idle adjustment hole damaged, forced oversize, or casting cracked in the idle port area	(a) See item 8 (b) Replace the adjustment screw (c) Replace carburetor
3. Lean operation at steady speeds between 15 and 65 mph	(a) Intermediate adjustment too lean (b) Dirt in intermediate fuel ports or supply channels (c) Welch plug or channel plugs not tightly sealed (d) Nozzle check valve not sealing (e) Intermediate adjustment packing missing or damaged (f) Economizer check ball stuck closed	(a) Readjust (b) Remove welch plug and channel plugs and blow out with compressed air (c) Reseat or replace plugs (d) Blow out with compressed air or replace (e) Replace (f) Remove welch plug and check ball and blow out channel with compressed air
4. Rich operation at steady speeds between 15 and 65 mph	(a) Intermediate adjustment adjusted too rich (b) Fixed main jet too large, not tightly in place or missing (c) Carburetor flooding (d) Nozzle check-valve welch plug not tightly sealed (e) Choke valve partially closed	(a) Readjust (b) Seat firmly or replace jet (c) See item 8 (d) Reseat or replace (e) See that choke friction spring and choke friction ball are correctly assembled
5. Lean operation at speeds above 60 mph	(a) Dirt in nozzle system (b) Main fuel jet too small or damaged (c) Main fuel jet plug screw not tightly sealed (d) Nozzle check valve damaged (e) Nozzle check valve not seated correctly in casting	(a) Remove main fuel jet plug screw and blow channels out with compressed air (b) Replace (c) Tighten to stop air leak (d) Replace (e) Reseat flush with nozzle-well surface
6. Rich operation at speeds above 60 mph	(a) Main jet too large, not tightly in place or missing (b) Carburetor flooding (c) Economizer check ball not seating	(a) Seat firmly or replace (b) See item 8 (c) Remove welch plug and check ball and blow channel out with compressed air
7. Lean acceleration	(a) Dirt in acceleration fuel channels (b) Incorrect carburetion adjustment (c) Accelerator pump assembly damaged or worn (d) Diaphragm cover plug screw loose or missing (e) Diaphragm flap check valves damaged or worn (f) Economizer check ball stuck closed	(a) Blow out all channels in diaphragm cover and the accelerating pump discharge channel in the body casting (b) Readjust idle and intermediate adjustments (c) Replace assembly (d) Tighten or replace (e) Replace diaphragm (f) Remove welch plug and check ball and blow channel clean with compressed air
8. Carburetor	(a) Dirt in inlet needle and seat assembly (b) Inlet seat gasket missing or damaged (c) Inlet control lever not correctly adjusted (d) Diaphragm incorrectly installed	(a) Remove and clean, or replace (b) Replace (c) Readjust lever flush with metering chamber wall (d) Replace or correct installation

HD Carburetor Troubleshooting—*Continued*

Problem	Possible Cause	Remedy
	(e) Inlet control lever pin loose or not correctly installed	(e) Tighten retaining screw and correct installation
	(f) Inlet control lever tight on lever pin	(f) Replace damaged part, or clean dirt from these parts
	(g) Inlet needle or seat damaged or worn	(g) Replace the assembly
9. Lean operation in all speed ranges	(a) Filter screens plugged or dirty	(a) Clean or replace
	(b) Inlet control lever incorrectly adjusted	(b) Readjust lever flush with wall of metering chamber
	(c) Diaphragm cover plate loose	(c) Tighten screws
	(d) Air leak in metering system	(d) All channel plugs, plug screws and lead plugs to be tightly sealed.
	(e) Inlet tension spring stretched or damaged	(e) Replace
10. Rich operation in all speed ranges	(a) Carburetor flooding	(a) See item 8
	(b) Choke valve not staying fully open	(b) See that choke friction spring and friction ball are assembled correctly
	(c) Inlet control lever incorrectly adjusted	(c) Readjust lever flush with metering chamber wall
11. No fuel supply	(a) Tank valve closed or defective	(a) Check operation with hose disconnected
	(b) Vent hose from carburetor blocked off	(b) Blow through hose
	(c) Inlet needle stuck in seat	(c) Replace seat and needle. For temporary correction, blow into fuel supply hose to force needle from seat. On 1967 model having inlet lever connected to inlet needle, insert a small wire through diaphragm cover center hole and push lightly against center of diaphragm. This will pull inlet needle off seat.

Checking inlet control lever setting.

because this would probably damage the nozzle assembly. Pry out the welch plug with a small punch, being careful not to damage the casting counterbore edges around the plug.

⑱ Welch plug and economizer check ball. (Pry out the welch plug carefully, using a small punch.)

⑲ Two choke-disc screws and the bottom half of the choke disc.

⑳ Choke-shaft assembly out of the body. (This will release the top half of the choke disc, the spring, the choke friction ball and friction ball spring.)

㉑ Choke-shaft dust seal.

Reassemble in reverse, paying attention to the following:

Make certain that all parts are kept clean during reassembly. Lint or threads can easily block small orifices. Welch plugs should be seated with a flat-end punch of a slightly smaller diameter than the welch plug. The seated plug should be flat, not concave, to assure a tight fit around the circumference.

The metering spring should be seated into the counterbore in the body casting, and located on the protrusion on the inlet control lever. The

Model DC

lever should be adjusted flush with the floor of the metering chamber by bending the diaphragm end of lever as necessary.

Caution: Bend lever at diaphragm end only, being careful to hold other end away from needle. If needle is forced into seat it may be damaged and cause sticking. Check setting as shown in the illustration. Important: This setting is critical, since it controls the correct amount of fuel to the entire metering system.

Two torque values are important: the inlet seat assembly should be tightened to 40–45 lb./in., and the accelerating-pump channel plug should be tightened to 23–28 lb./in.

Model DC

This carburetor is much like the M and has only two variable orifices—low speed and high speed needle valves. It is made in three sections: throttle body, carburetor body and float bowl.

Disassembly and reassembly

A. Float bowl

① Remove four bowl attaching screws and washers.
② Tap bowl lightly to break free from carburetor body.
③ Remove gasket.
④ Unscrew flat speed nut from float rod and free float.
⑤ Remove matched float valve and seat assembly.
⑥ Remove float lever screw, lock washer and float washer to free float lever and bracket assembly.

B. Throttle body

① Remove three throttle body screws and lock washers, body gasket, idle hole body plug, low-speed needle valve, washer and needle valve spring.
② Take out throttle shaft screws and lock washers and free throttle disc from shaft.
③ Loosen throttle lever clamping screw from lever and free spring, washer and shaft from throttle body. If necessary, remove stop screw and spring from throttle lever.

C. Carburetor body

① Remove support bracket nut and lock washer, and support bracket, if used.
② Remove bowl nut and gasket. *Note:* The idle tube extends up through the nozzle and venturi into the upper wall of the body. Ordinarily, it will remain in the body when the bowl nut is removed. If for any reason it should stick in the bowl nut, do not attempt to remove it from the nut.

If the tube remains in the body when the bowl nut is removed, remove it gently by moving the plug end of the tube back and forth, and pulling at the same time.

The nozzle is screwed into the body and shoulders against the casting at the top. Use a good screwdriver for removing and replacing nozzle. Preferably grind a pilot on the end of a special screwdriver to fit the inside of the nozzle and grind the sides to clear the ⅜-24 thread hole. At the same time, grind the blade to fit the nozzle slot. The slot is .051″ wide.

③ Remove the high-speed needle valve extension housing to free the high-speed needle valve, packing nut and packing.
④ Remove the high-speed metering plug or fixed jet located directly opposite the high-speed needle valve hole.
⑤ Remove drain plug and gasket and free the idle passage tube.
⑥ Remove screws and clamp to free vent housing assembly, vent gasket, and idle bleed tube from carburetor body.

Reassemble in reverse order, paying attention to these points:

Clean all metal parts in Gunk Hydro-Seal or equivalent; blow dry with compressed air; keep parts on clean shop rags.

If necessary, clean out orifices and passages with appropriate-sized drills, being careful not to enlarge them.

Throttle body
1. IDLE PORT HOLES

Model (marked on carburetor)	Drill Sizes
DC-1, 1L, 1M, 10	70 (.028″)
DC-2	56 (.0465″)

2. LOW-SPEED NEEDLE HOLE

Model	Drill Size
All	57 (.043″)

3. ANGULAR HOLE IN BARREL

Model	Drill Size
All	52 (.0635″)

Carburetor body
1. NOZZLE BLEED HOLES

Model	Drill Size
All	54 (.055″)

2. NOZZLE MAIN PASSAGE

Model	Drill Size
All	17 (.173″)

3. HIGH SPEED NEEDLE HOLE

Model	Drill Sizes
DC-1, 1L, 1M, 10, 6, 7, 12	55 (.052″)
DC-2	70 (.028″)

Do not use a drill or wire in the idle tube or idle feed hole. Just blow through them after cleaning in solvent.

Setting float level

① Assemble float valve and seat assembly.
② Install float lever bracket screw loosely so that bracket can be adjusted if necessary.
③ Insert float valve and seat about halfway into bowl.
④ Position float rod at the same time for

90 Carburetion

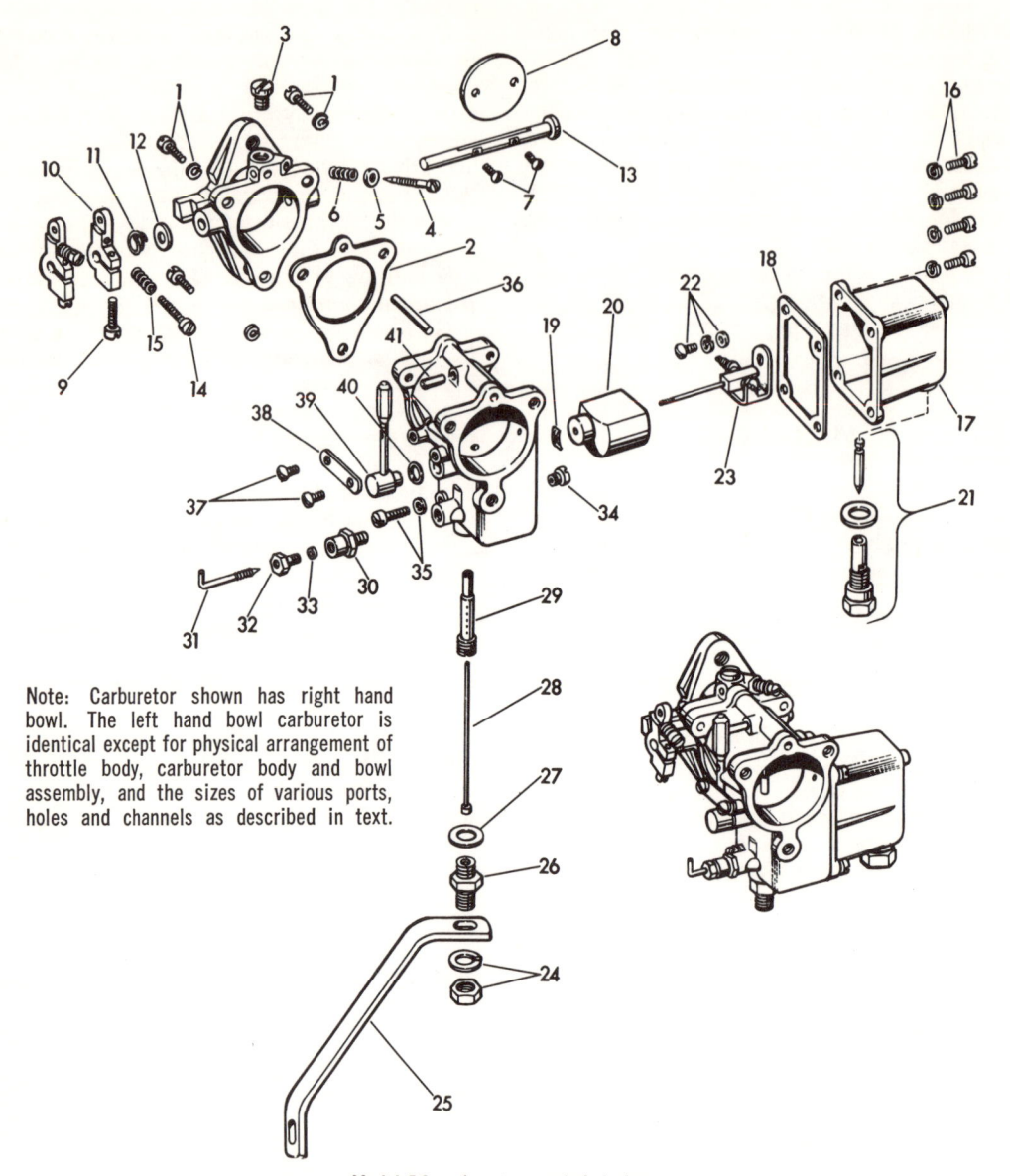

Note: Carburetor shown has right hand bowl. The left hand bowl carburetor is identical except for physical arrangement of throttle body, carburetor body and bowl assembly, and the sizes of various ports, holes and channels as described in text.

Model DC carburetor, exploded view.

1. Throttle body screw and washer (3)
2. Body gasket
3. Idle hole body plug
4. Low-speed needle valve
5. Low-speed needle valve washer
6. Low-speed needle valve spring
7. Throttle shaft screw (2)
8. Throttle disc
9. Throttle lever clamping screw
10. Throttle lever
11. Throttle shaft spring
12. Throttle shaft washer
13. Throttle shaft
14. Throttle lever stop screw
15. Throttle lever stop screw spring
16. Bowl mounting screw (4)
17. Bowl
18. Bowl gasket
19. Float nut
20. Float
21. Float valve and seat
22. Float lever screw and washers
23. Float lever and bracket assembly
24. Support bracket nut and lock washer
25. Support bracket
26. Bowl nut
27. Bowl nut gasket
28. Idle tube assembly
29. Main nozzle
30. High-speed needle valve extension housing
31. High-speed needle valve
32. High-speed needle valve packing nut
33. High-speed needle valve packing
34. Carburetor jet
35. Drain plug and gasket
36. Idle passage tube
37. Throttle shaft screw (2)
38. Vent clamp
39. Vent housing
40. Vent gasket
41. Idle bleed tube

Figure following name of part indicates quantity necessary for one complete assembly.

Model DC

easy engagement of nylon lever fingers in float valve stem groove.

⑤ Turn float valve into bowl and tighten against gasket.

Note: Do not screw valve seat fitting with valve into bowl without first removing bowl from carburetor body, because fingers of nylon lever will be damaged if not properly engaged.

⑥ Check float lever setting with carburetor bowl held upside down, measuring the distance from top of float rod to outer edge of bowl flange opposite fuel inlet fitting as shown in the illustration. This measurement should be taken when the lever is at the point where the float valve seats lightly. Move float lever up and down to determine seating point. Note that measurement is taken from outer edge of bowl opposite the fuel inlet fitting. Float rod position from edge should be 1″, plus or minus 1/64″. If setting is not 1″ with float valve closed, adjust slotted float lever bracket.

⑦ When correct position of float rod is obtained, tighten bracket screw securely and recheck setting of float rod. Install float on rod, flat side up, fastening with speed nut.

Carburetor body assembly

① Install vent housing assembly first with gasket, idle bleed tube, clamp and screws. Start tube into holes first, then tap housing into place.

② Pull clamp just tight enough so that outer ends of clamp touch body bosses.

③ Install drain plug and gasket and high-speed fixed jet.

④ Position high-speed needle valve housing in body, with needle valve, packing nut and packing assembled in housing.

Note: When installing this set of parts in the main body, *always back out* the needle valve so that the point will not enter the valve hole in the main body when the housing is pulled up tight. Pull up the packing nut just enough to prevent the needle valve from turning too freely. Be very careful not to jam the needle valve into the seat hole and deform the hole entrance.

⑤ Assemble the nozzle in place, using the ground-down screwdriver described previously.

⑥ Turn the entire body upside down, drop in the idle tube, small end first, jiggle the body, and the tube will locate itself in the body hole. Do not bend, twist or damage the idle tube. Press on plug end of tube until tube is seated and the bottom of the plug extends approximately 1/32″ out of the nozzle passage. When installing bowl nut and gasket, spring tension will hold the idle tube firmly in place.

Throttle body assembly

① The throttle shaft counterbored screw head notches face toward carburetor main body.

② Position throttle disc in shaft, milled side up, and facing carburetor body.

③ Insert and tighten shaft screws.

④ Work disc several times. If there is any binding, loosen screws and reposition disc.

Note: Install only a replacement throttle disc containing the same identification number on face. With disc correctly installed and closed, the number will be on top half of disc facing carburetor main body.

The Model DC carburetor is attached to the manifold flange with a certain thickness gasket and certain length cap screws. If for any reason the overall gasket thickness is reduced and no change is made in the cap screw length, the cap screw may bottom in the head of the lower throttle body screw. If it does bottom, a broken throttle body will result.

Engaging Model DC float lever in valve stem groove.

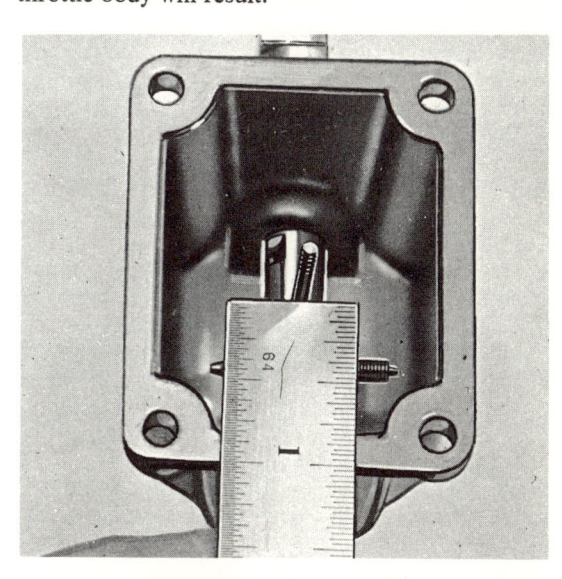

Checking Model DC float setting.

CHAPTER 7

Frame and Running Gear

The Harley-Davidson factory workshop manual places proper emphasis on the handling of the motorcycle. This highly important attribute is greatly influenced (almost totally) by tires. The factory has some excellent hints for the rider who wants to preserve the good handling characteristics of his machine.

Here is a list of possible causes of poor handling:

1. Loose wheel axle nuts.
2. Excessive wheel hub bearing play.
3. Loosened spokes.
4. Rear wheel out of alignment with frame and front wheel.
5. Rims and tires out-of-true sideways (tire run-out should not be more than 3/64").
6. Rims and tires out-of-round or eccentric with hub (tire run-out should not be more than 3/32").
7. Irregular or peaked front tire tread wear. Determine mileage since tires were last transposed. If mileage is found to be 2500 or more, transpose front and rear wheels and tires even though irregular wear or peaking of front tread is not noticeable.
8. Tires over-inflated.
9. Tire and wheel unbalanced. Static balancing alone may be satisfactory if dynamic balancing facilities are not at hand, however both are recommended.
10. Steering head bearings loose. Correct adjustment and replace pitted or worn bearings and races.
11. Shock absorber not functioning properly. Check possible causes.
12. Rear fork bearings loose. Check possible causes.
13. Heavy front end loading. Non-standard equipment on the front end such as heavy radio receivers, extra lighting equipment or luggage, tends to cause unstable handling. Extra equipment on front end should be held down to a minimum.

The larger the tire size and higher the average road speed, the more essential it is that wheels and tires be given proper attention. A front tire kept in continuous solo service long enough to allow tread to become irregular and peaked may cause high speed weave, especially if over-inflated.

Switching wheels and tires approximately every 5000 miles and inflating to recommended pressure are of major importance. In many cases, this attention alone applied to a solo motorcycle will remedy faulty handling at higher speeds.

WHEELS AND TIRES

Glide models (front)

Front and rear wheels may be removed as necessary for wheel or tire service. When removing a wheel, apply brake to hold drum securely while pulling wheel from drum. When

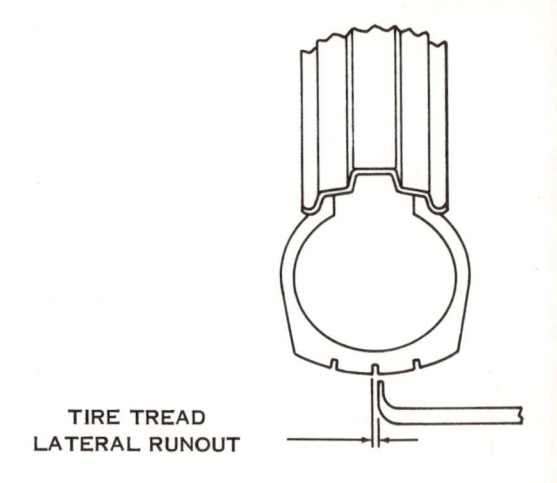

TIRE TREAD
LATERAL RUNOUT

Checking the tire lateral runout.

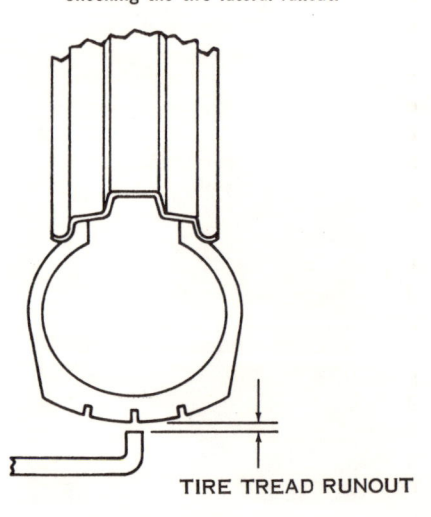

TIRE TREAD RUNOUT

Checking tire radial runout.

92

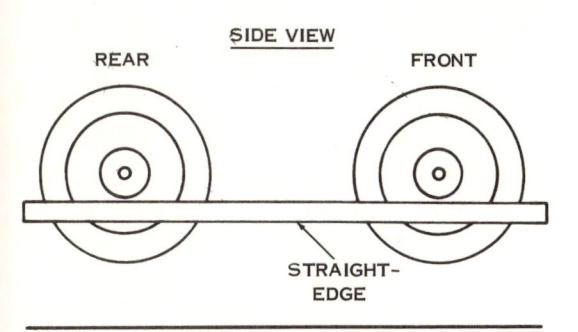

Wheels and Tires

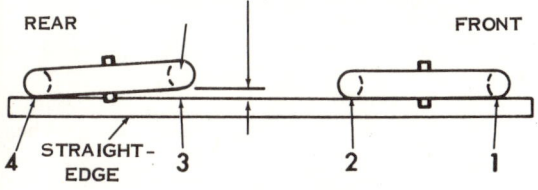

Wheel alignment diagram.

detached from drums, Duo-Glide and Electra-Glide wheels are interchangeable.

① Block motorcycle under frame until front wheel is off ground.

② Remove the cotter pin, axle nut and flat washer.

③ Remove the five wheel mounting socket screws.

④ Loosen the two right slider cap nuts and remove axle.

⑤ Remove front wheel, leaving the brake drum in its place over the brake shoes.

When replacing the wheel, assemble in reverse order.

Note: Clamping faces on wheel hub and brake drum must be clean so that wheel will be true and tight against brake drum when socket screws are tightened. Tighten wheel mounting socket screws and axle nut, and then tighten the two right slider cap nuts. This will insure correct alignment of fork sides.

Glide models (rear)

① Elevate motorcycle rear end with service stand, or suitable blocking under frame so rear wheel is off the ground.

② Remove two rear screws from fender support and raise end of fender.

③ Remove the five socket screws that secure wheel to brake drum. The socket screw wrench can be inserted only at the rear of axle; turn wheel to bring each screw into this position.

④ Remove axle nut and axle nut lock washer.

⑤ Remove axle from brake drum side of motorcycle and then remove spacer from be-

Removing front wheel, Glide models.

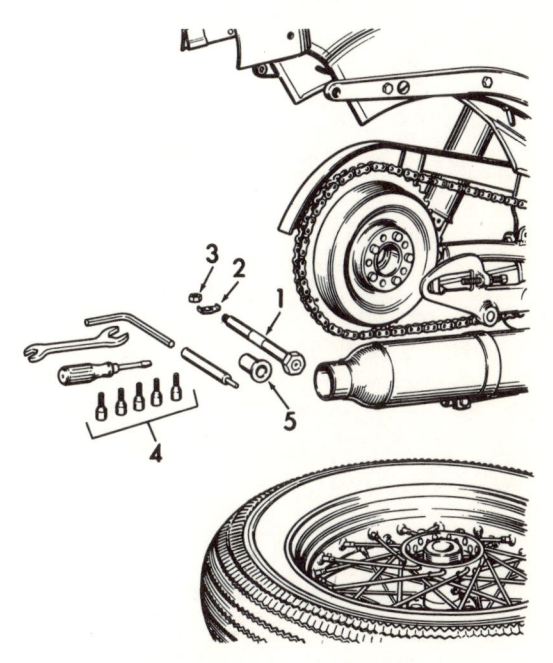

Removing rear wheel, Glide models.

1. Axle
2. Axle nut lock washer
3. Axle nut
4. Wheel mounting socket screws
5. Spacer

Frame and Running Gear

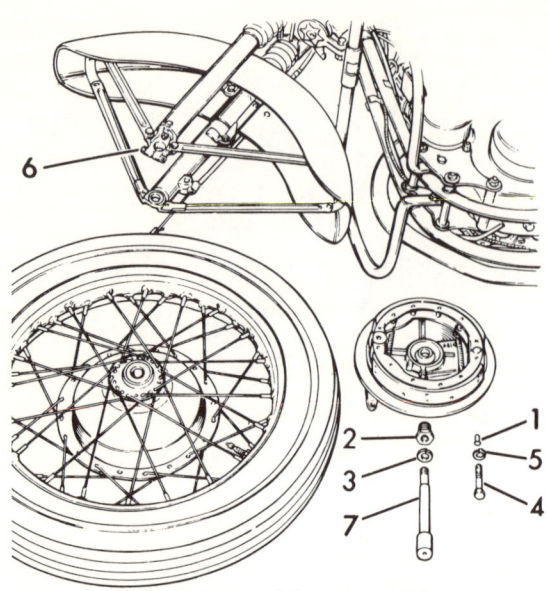

Front wheel removal, Sportster models.

1. Brake clevis pin
2. Axle nut
3. Axle nut lock washer
4. Brake anchor and centering bolt
5. Lock washer
6. Front axle pinch bolt
7. Front wheel axle

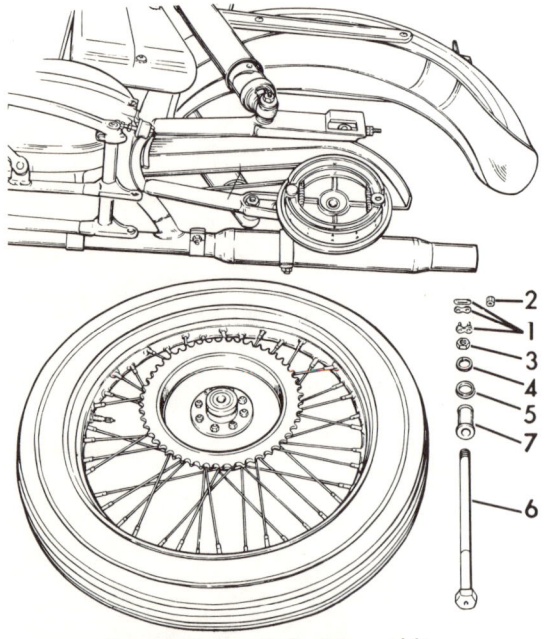

Rear wheel removal, Sportster models.

1. Chain connecting link
2. Rear brake rod adjusting nut
3. Axle nut
4. Axle nut lock washer
5. Axle centering collar, right side
6. Rear axle
7. Axle spacer, left side

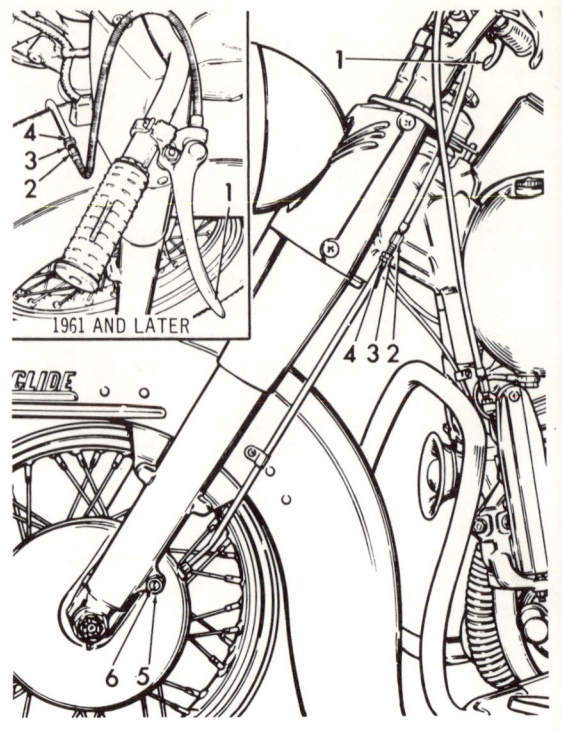

Adjusting front brake, Glide models.

1. Front wheel brake hand lever
2. Brake adjusting sleeve
3. Adjusting sleeve lock nut
4. Adjusting sleeve nut
5. Brake shoe pivot stud nut
6. Brake shoe pivot stud

tween wheel hub and right axle clip.

⑥ Apply rear brake and remove wheel.

When installing wheel, reverse the removal procedure.

Note: Tighten the five wheel socket screws before tightening the axle nut. To avoid possibility of wheel working loose and damaging clamping flange, it is important that socket screws be pulled very tight.

Sportster models (front)

① Block up frame and raise front end of motorcycle high enough to permit revolving wheel.

② Disconnect brake control by removing brake clevis pin.

③ Remove axle nut and axle nut lock washer.

④ Remove brake anchor, shoe centering bolt, and lock washer.

⑤ Loosen axle pinch bolt.

⑥ With a soft hammer loosen axle and remove from hub and fork assembly.

⑦ Remove front wheel and brake assembly complete.

To reinstall front wheel and brake assembly, reverse the disassembly procedure. Be sure to

Front Brake Adjustment

center brake shoes as described in FRONT BRAKE ADJUSTMENT. Inject one ounce of "Grease-All" grease into the wheel hub and spin wheel to make sure it has free movement.

Sportster models (rear)

① Raise rear end of motorcycle high enough to permit removing wheel; support motorcycle by suitable blocking underneath frame.
② Locate and remove chain connecting link.
③ Disengage chain from rear sprocket.
④ Remove brake adjusting nut from brake rod.
⑤ Remove axle nut, axle nut washer and centering collar.
⑥ With a soft hammer tap right end of axle to loosen from left side of frame.
⑦ Remove axle from hub and frame assembly.
⑧ Remove axle spacer from left side.
⑨ Slide wheel and brake assembly to extreme rear end of frame.
⑩ Lift wheel up to pass brake drum over brake shoes.
⑪ Remove wheel from motorcycle.

To reinstall rear wheel, reverse the disassembly procedure. Center brake shoes as described in REAR BRAKE ADJUSTMENT. Inject one ounce of "Grease-All" grease into the wheel hub and spin wheel to make sure it turns free.

FRONT BRAKE ADJUSTMENT

Glide models

The front brake cable may be adjusted as follows: Loosen adjusting sleeve lock nut and turn adjusting sleeve nut to obtain desired amount of hand lever free movement; clockwise for less movement and counterclockwise for more movement. About 3/16" of brake cable movement should be free, or about 1/4 of the full lever movement. Retighten adjusting sleeve lock nut.

Front brake shoes may be adjusted as follows:
① Raise front wheel off ground so it may be rotated.
② Loosen brake shoe pivot stud nut.
③ Loosen axle sleeve nut.
④ Apply brake.
⑤ With brake pressure applied, tighten axle sleeve nut and pivot stud nut. This procedure centers shoes against drum so full lining length contacts drum on brake application.

Sportster models

① Loosen lock nut on adjusting sleeve and turn sleeve nut in toward the cable support tube to decrease the free movement of hand lever and tighten the brake.

② Turn sleeve nut away from the cable support tube to increase the free movement of hand lever and loosen the brake.

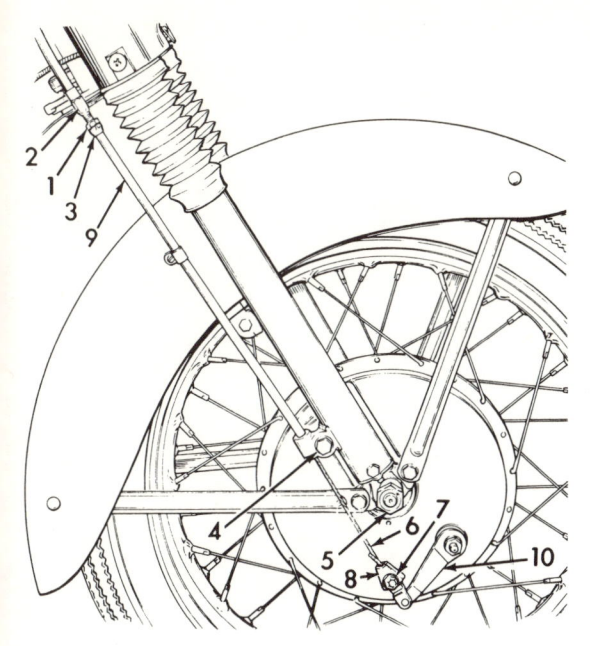

Front wheel brake, Sportster models.

1. Adjusting sleeve lock nut
2. Front brake adjusting sleeve
3. Adjusting sleeve nut
4. Brake shoe pivot stud
5. Front wheel axle nut
6. Brake cable
7. Brake cable clevis clamp nut
8. Brake cable clevis clamp
9. Brake cable support tube
10. Brake lever

Adjusting rear brake, Glide models.

1. Front brake shoe adjusting cam nut
2. Rear brake shoe adjusting cam nut

③ When free movement of the hand lever is about ¼ of its full movement, tighten lock nut against adjusting sleeve nut.

④ Rotate the wheel to make sure brake is not too tight and dragging.

If brake should drag with correct free movement in hand lever, recenter brake shoes in brake drum as follows:

① Loosen, but do not remove, front brake shoe pivot stud and axle nut.

② Spin front wheel.

③ While wheel is turning apply brake and tighten pivot stud and then axle nut.

④ Recheck brake for correct adjustment as described above.

REAR BRAKE ADJUSTMENT

Glide models

① Raise rear wheel so it can be turned freely by hand.

② Turn front adjusting cam nut counterclockwise until wheel has noticeable drag.

③ Spin wheel forward and backward to center shoes.

④ Slowly turn cam nut clockwise until wheel turns freely.

⑤ Repeat process on rear cam nut which spreads shoes with a clockwise rotation and retracts shoes with a counterclockwise rotation.

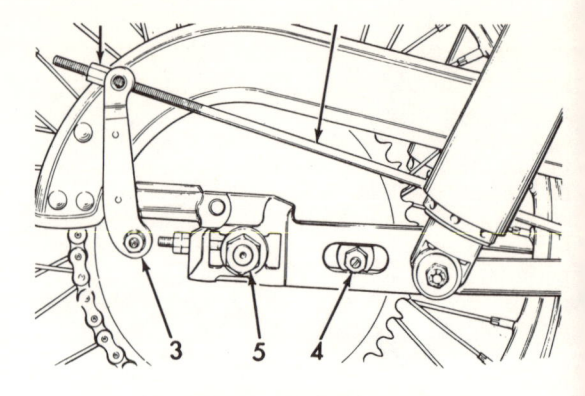

Rear wheel brake, Sportster models.

1. Brake rod adjusting nut
2. Brake rod
3. Operating lever
4. Brake shoe pivot stud nut
5. Rear wheel axle nut

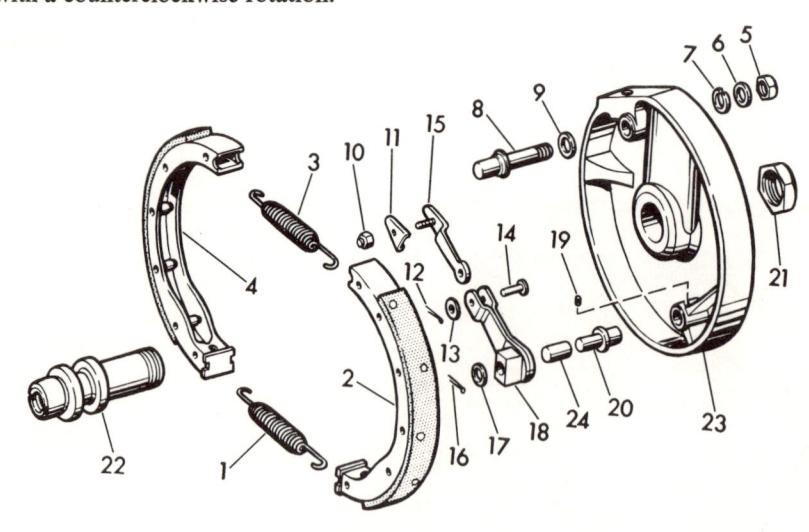

Front wheel brake, exploded view, Glide models.

1. Brake shoe spring (2)
2. Brake shoe and lining (2)
3. Brake shoe spring (see item 1)
4. Brake shoe and lining (see item 2)
5. Brake shoe pivot stud nut
6. Pivot stud flat washer
7. Pivot stud lock washer
8. Pivot stud
9. Pivot stud washer
10. Clevis clamp nut
11. Cable clevis clamp
12. Cotter pin
13. Flat washer
14. Cam lever clevis pin
15. Cable clevis
16. Cotter pin
17. Cam lever washer
18. Cam lever
19. Set screw
20. Cam lever stud
21. Axle sleeve nut
22. Front axle sleeve
23. Brake side cover
24. Cam lever bushing

Figure following name of part indicates quantity necessary for one complete assembly.

Sportster models

① Turn adjusting nut to change the effective length of the brake rod. The adjusting nut has a notch which fits against the clevis pin in the operating lever. Thus, it is locked in place on the rod, but may be turned down or backed off the rod by half turns as required.

② Set the adjusting nut so that the brake begins to take effect when the foot lever is pushed downward about 1¼".

③ Turn the nut onto the rod to tighten the brake; back it off to loosen the brake.

④ Turn the wheel to be sure the brake is not too tight and dragging.

If the brake should drag with correct free movement in the foot pedal, recenter brake shoes in brake drum as follows:

① Loosen but do not remove rear brake pivot stud nut and axle nut.

② Spin rear wheel.

③ While wheel is turning, apply brake and tighten pivot stud nut and then the axle nut.

④ Re-check brake for correct adjustment, as previously described.

BRAKE SHOE REPLACEMENT

Glide models (front)

① Remove wheel as described previously.

② Spring brake shoes out and away from side cover at top to free shoes and springs from pivot stud and cam lever.

③ Remove cotter key and cam lever washer from cam lever stud.

④ Disconnect control coil ferrule by loosening clamp nut and depressing brake hand lever.

⑤ Slip cam lever assembly off stud.

Replace in reverse order of disassembly, except (for ease of assembly) connect two shoes with top return spring. Position unit on pivot stud and cam lever. Insert lower spring. Spring hooks must be in shoe spacer notch nearest side cover. Reassemble wheel.

Glide models (rear)

① Remove rear wheel from motorcycle as described previously.

② Disconnect shoe return spring and slip shoes and anchor (lower) spring away from side cover.

③ Remove hold-down springs from side cover.

④ If necessary, remove wheel cylinder by turning out the two cylinder screws on outside of side cover.

Note: Do not depress rear wheel brake pedal with shoe assemblies disassembled.

If faulty wheel cylinder unit is found, install a repair kit. Remove old boots, pistons, cups and spring. Be sure cylinder wall and pistons are free from burrs. Dip replacement parts in brake fluid and assemble. Never dip or wash hydraulic brake cylinder parts in gasoline, kerosene or oil. If necessary to clean parts, use denatured alcohol.

Note: Front shoe and rear shoe are of different widths on 1963 and later models. Narrow shoe must be in rear position and wide shoe in front position.

To replace:

① Assemble shoes to lower return spring.

② Position shoe assembly on plate anchor block at bottom of side cover and install top spring.

③ Short hook is inserted in elongated hole on front shoe.

④ Reassemble wheel.

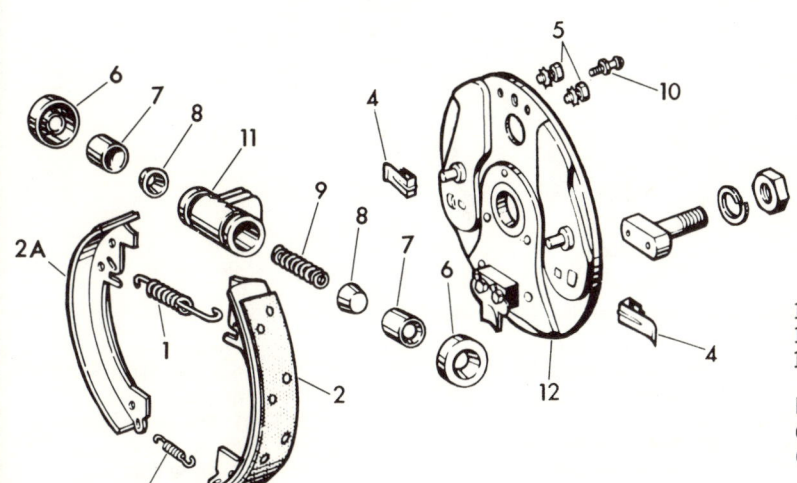

1. Shoe return spring
2. Front brake shoe
2A. Rear brake shoe
3. Brake shoe spring
4. Hold-down spring (2)
5. Cylinder screw and lock washer (2 each)
6. Boot (2)
7. Piston (2)
8. Cup (2)
9. Spring
10. Bleeder nipple
11. Wheel cylinder
12. Brake side cover

Figure following name of part indicates quantity necessary for one complete assembly.

Rear wheel brake, exploded view, Glide models.

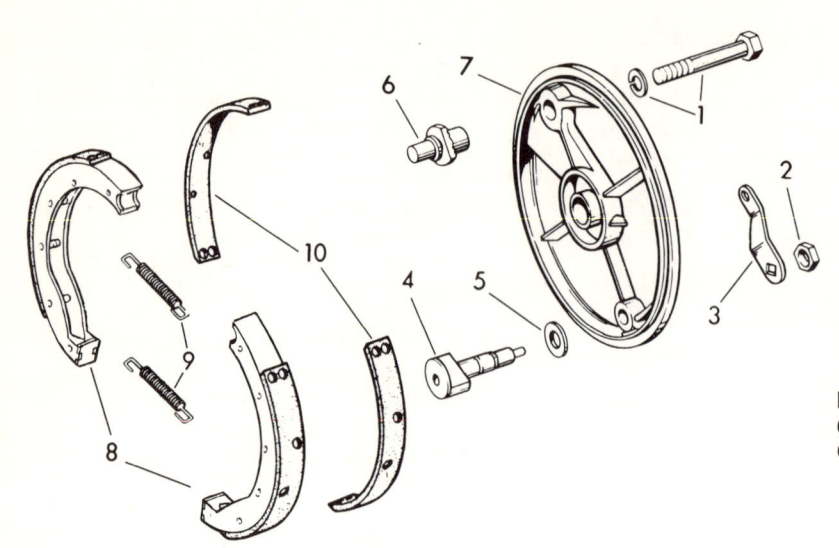

Frame and Running Gear

1. Pivot stud screw and washer
2. Operating shaft nut
3. Operating lever
4. Operating shaft
5. Operating shaft washer
6. Shoe pivot stud
7. Brake side plate
8. Brake shoe and lining (2)
9. Brake shoe spring (2)
10. Brake lining (2)

Figure following name of part indicates quantity necessary for one complete assembly.

Front wheel brake, exploded view, Sportster models.

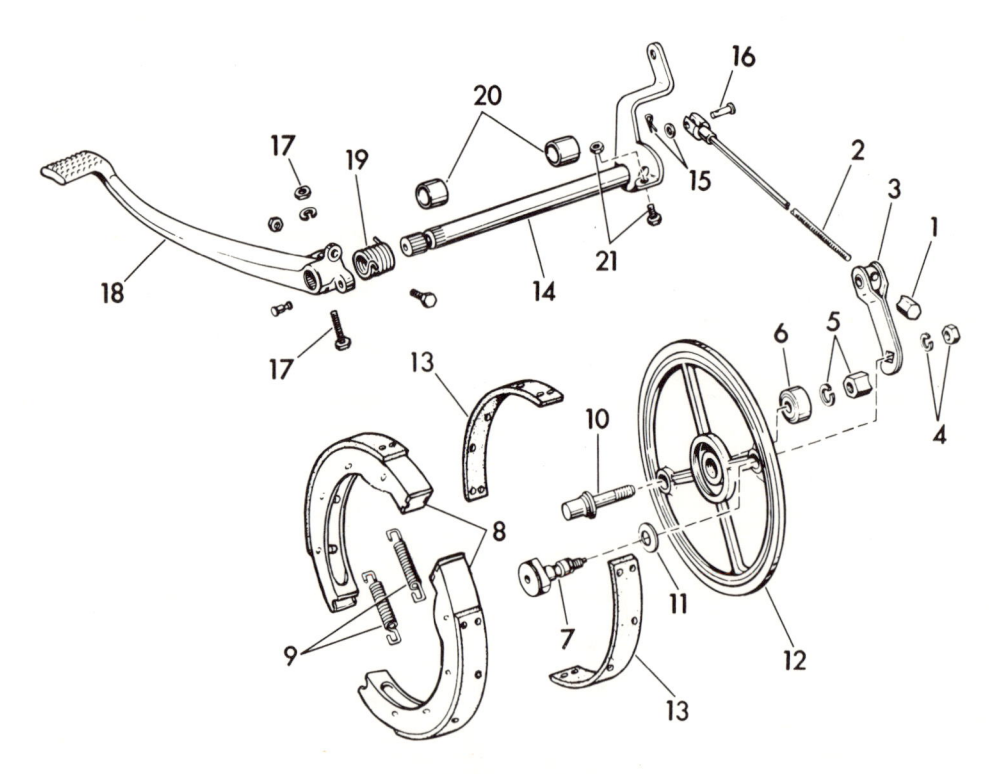

Rear wheel brake, exploded view, Sportster models.

1. Brake rod adjusting nut
2. Brake rod
3. Brake operating lever
4. Operating shaft nut and lock washer
5. Pivot stud nut and lock washer
6. Locating block
7. Operating shaft
8. Shoe and lining (2)
9. Shoe spring (2)
10. Pivot stud
11. Operating shaft washer
12. Brake side plate
13. Brake lining (2)
14. Cross shaft
15. Rod clevis cotter pin and washer
16. Rod clevis pin
17. Foot lever bolt and nut
18. Foot lever
19. Lever torsion spring
20. Frame brake shaft tube bushing (2)
21. Cross shaft adjusting screw and nut

Figure following name of part indicates quantity necessary for one complete assembly.

Front Forks

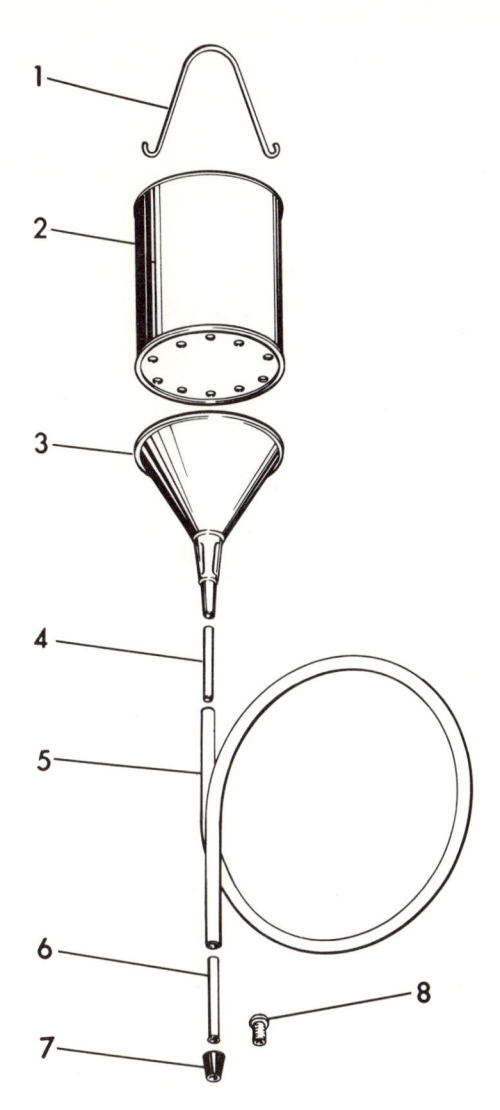

Fork filler can components, Glide models.

1. Bail
2. Filler can
3. Tin funnel
4. Metal tubing
5. Flexible tubing
6. Metal tubing
7. Rubber plug
8. Fork tube cap

Sportster models (front)

① Remove front wheel and brake assembly from motorcycle as described.
② Remove operating shaft nut and operating lever.
③ Lightly tap operating shaft to remove brake shoes, springs, operating shaft, washer and pivot stud as a unit from brake side plate.
④ Remove shoes from operating shaft and pivot stud.

Reassembly is essentially the reverse order of disassembly.

① Assemble brake shoes on operating shaft and pivot stud with one spring.
② Secure spring in groove that is nearest brake side plate.
③ Position washer.
④ Assemble unit to brake side plate.
⑤ Make sure flat side of pivot stud registers in recess of brake side plate.
⑥ Install operating lever and nut.
⑦ Attach second spring in place with pliers.
⑧ Install front wheel and brake assembly as described earlier. Adjust brakes and center brake shoes.

Sportster models (rear)

① Remove rear wheel from motorcycle.
② Remove rear brake rod adjusting nut and free brake rod from operating lever.
③ Remove brake assembly.
④ Remove operating shaft nut and washer, operating lever, pivot stud nut and lock washer, and locating block.
⑤ Lightly tap operating shaft to remove brake shoes, springs, pivot stud, operating shaft and washer as a unit from brake side plate.
⑥ Remove shoes from operating shaft and pivot stud.

To reassemble:

① Assemble brake shoes on operating shaft and pivot stud with one spring.
② Secure spring in groove nearest brake side plate.
③ Position washer on shaft.
④ Assemble unit on brake side plate.
⑤ Install locating block, nut and lock washer, operating lever and nut and lock washer.
⑥ Attach second spring in place with pliers.
⑦ Position brake assembly in rear wheel brake drum and install wheel assembly in frame.
⑧ Insert brake rod through lever.
⑨ Assemble adjusting nut loosely on rod.
⑩ Adjust brakes and center brake shoes.

FRONT FORKS

GLIDE MODELS

The Hydra-Glide fork is comprised of two sets of telescoping tubes that work against springs, with an oil-filled (hydraulic) dampening mechanism to control the action. The unit is engineered to give long service with a minimum of repair. Oil change is not necessary unless oil has been contaminated or leakage has occurred.

The non-adjustable Duo-Glide fork is for use on a solo motorcycle. The fork "trail" is set and cannot be adjusted. This fork may be recognized by the two hexagon head upper bracket bolts in the slider tube tops.

The adjustable Duo-Glide fork is for use on a motorcycle which operates with and without a sidecar. It is essentially the same as the non-adjustable fork except that it has a two-position bracket that allows the trail to be changed for

100   *Frame and Running Gear*

1. Fork stem nut
1A. Nut lock (1963 models)
2. Fork upper bracket bolt and valve (2)
3. Tube plug oil seal (2)
4. Fork upper bracket cover
5. Handlebar and fork bracket
6. Head bearing nut
7. Head bearing (2)
8. Fork bracket clamping stud (2)
9. Fork bracket with stem
10. Fork slider cover (2)
11. Slider tube plug (2)
12. Fork spring (2)
12A. Spring spacer (1965 and later) (2)
13. Damper valve stud lock nut (2)
14. Fork slider tube (2)
15. Slider tube snap ring (2)
16. Damper tube bushing gasket (2)
17. Damper tube lower bushing (2)
18. Damper valve stud gasket (2)
19. Damper tube valve (2)
20. Spring ring (2)
21. Spring ring washer (2)
22. Upper oil seal felt washer (2)
23. Upper oil seal (2)
24. Slider (2)
25. Slider upper and lower bushing (2 each)
26. Head bearing (see item 7)
27. Lower head bearing guard

Figure following name of part indicates quantity necessary for one complete assembly.

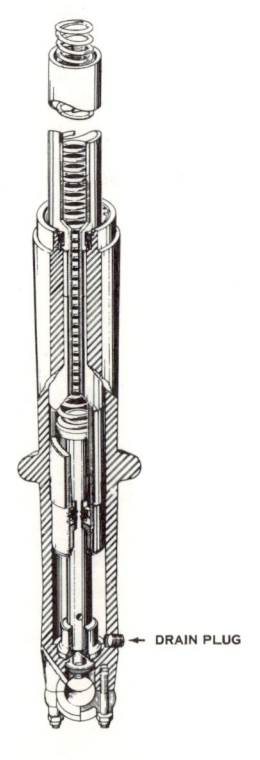

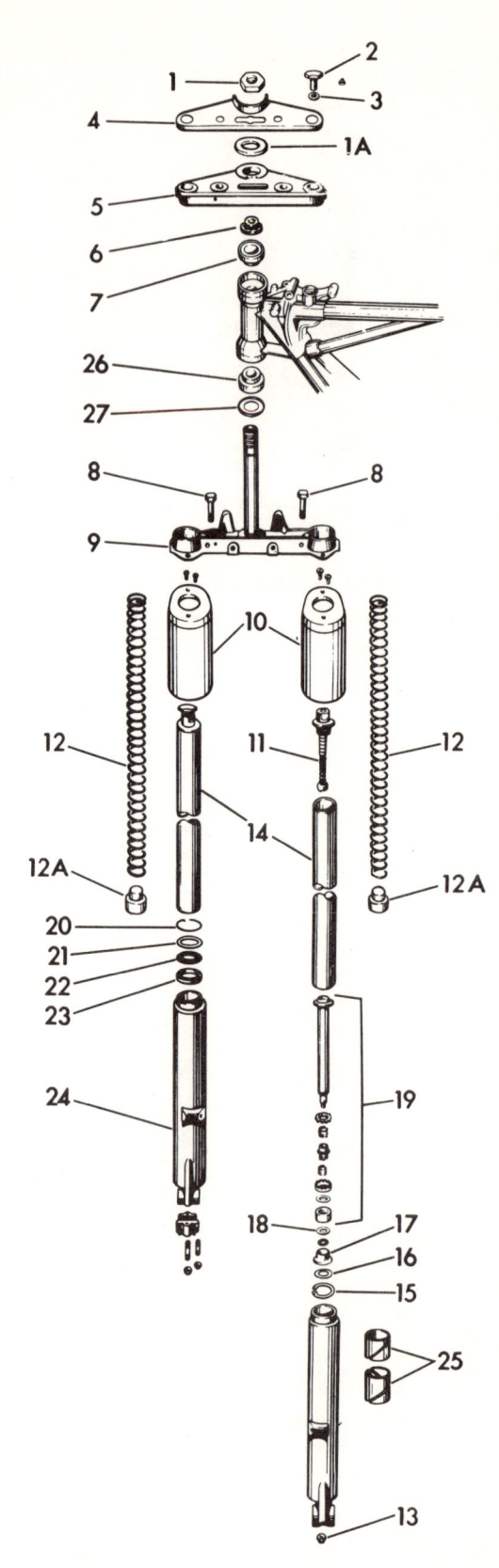

DRAIN PLUG

Hydra-Glide fork, exploded view.

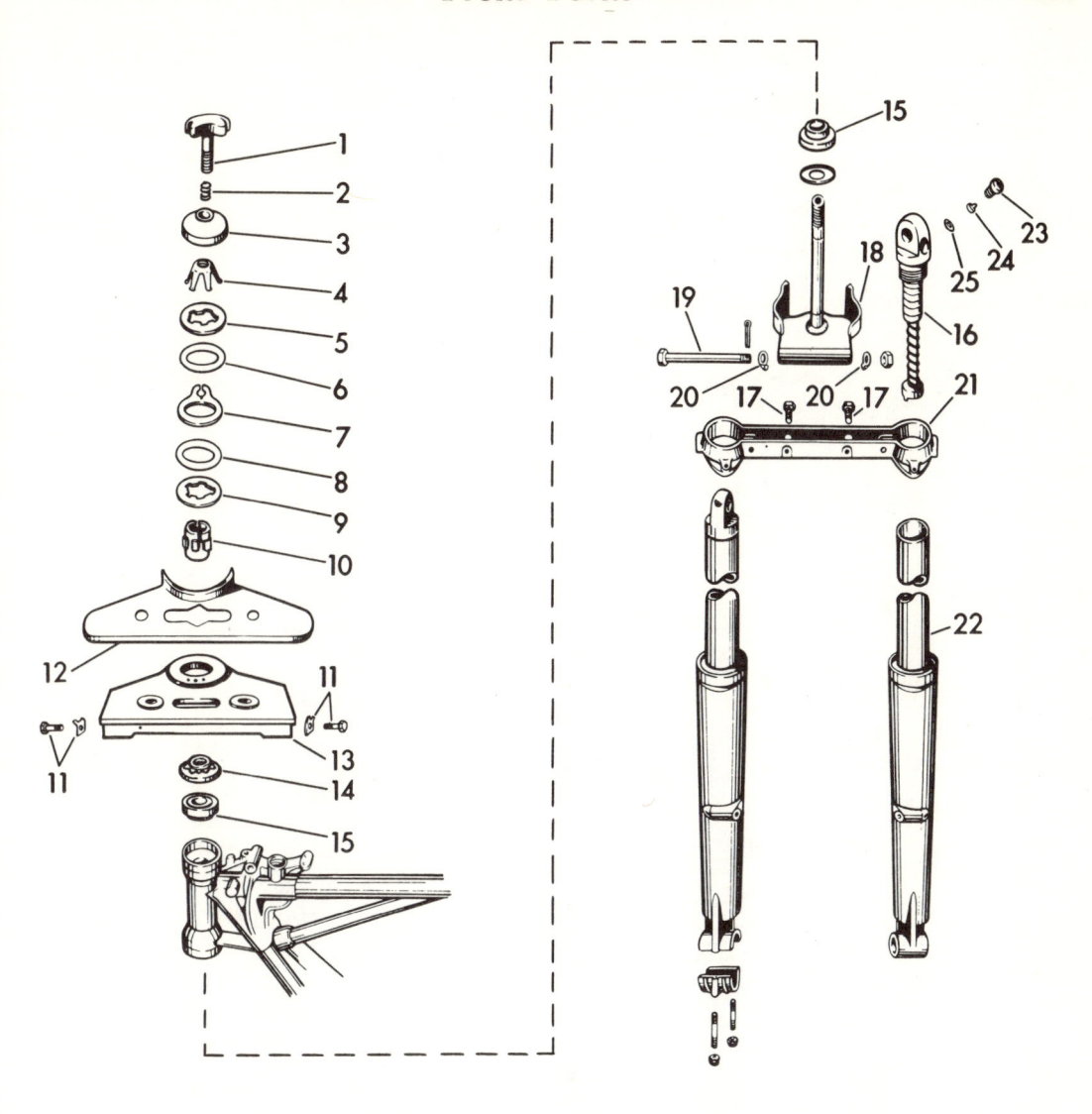

Front Forks

Adjustable fork, exploded view, Glide models.

1. Steering damper adjusting screw
2. Spring
3. Spider spring cover
4. Spider spring
5. Pressure disc (2)
6. Friction washer (2)
7. Anchor plate
8. Friction washer (see item 6)
9. Pressure disc (see item 5)
10. Fork stem nut
11. Upper bracket bolt and washer (2 each)
12. Upper bracket cover
13. Upper bracket
14. Head bearing nut
15. Head bearing (2)
16. Slider tube plug (2)
17. Bracket clamping stud (2)
18. Bracket with stem
19. Bracket bolt with nut and cotter pin
20. Bracket bolt washer (2)
21. Bracket
22. Fork tube and slider assembly (2)
23. Filler screw (2)
24. Filler screw valve (2)
25. Filler screw washer (2)

Figure following name of part indicates quantity necessary for one complete assembly.

102 Frame and Running Gear

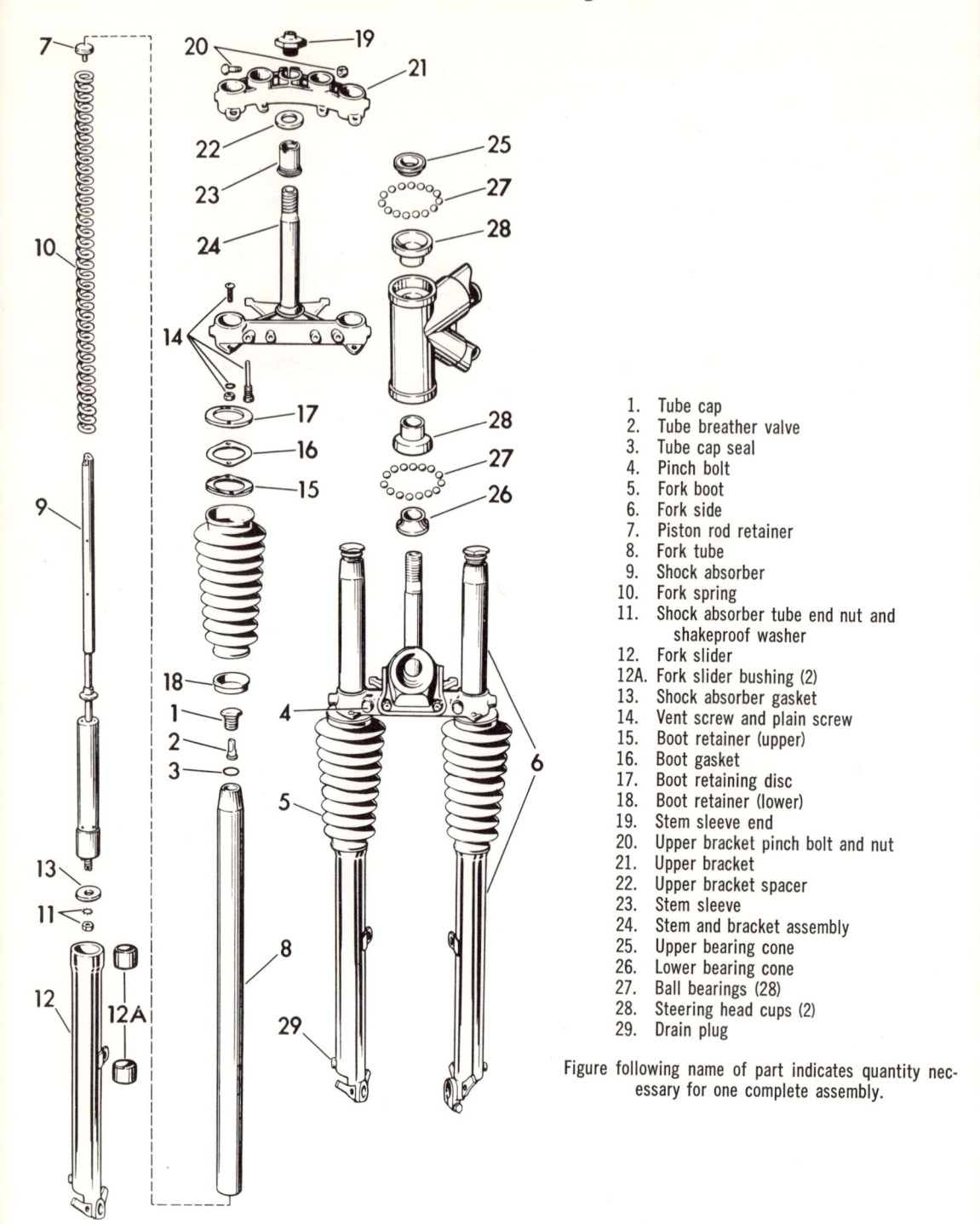

1. Tube cap
2. Tube breather valve
3. Tube cap seal
4. Pinch bolt
5. Fork boot
6. Fork side
7. Piston rod retainer
8. Fork tube
9. Shock absorber
10. Fork spring
11. Shock absorber tube end nut and shakeproof washer
12. Fork slider
12A. Fork slider bushing (2)
13. Shock absorber gasket
14. Vent screw and plain screw
15. Boot retainer (upper)
16. Boot gasket
17. Boot retaining disc
18. Boot retainer (lower)
19. Stem sleeve end
20. Upper bracket pinch bolt and nut
21. Upper bracket
22. Upper bracket spacer
23. Stem sleeve
24. Stem and bracket assembly
25. Upper bearing cone
26. Lower bearing cone
27. Ball bearings (28)
28. Steering head cups (2)
29. Drain plug

Figure following name of part indicates quantity necessary for one complete assembly.

Front fork and steering head, exploded view, Sportster models.

best solo or sidecar equipped operation, also a steering damper adjusting mechanism which dampens the steering head to suit conditions and rider preference. This fork may be recognized by the reversible bracket bolt washers, bolt and stem design.

Changing oil

① Remove drain plug at the outside bottom of each slider tube with a 3/16" Allen wrench and drain.
② Draining speed will be increased by gently flexing the fork as it empties.
③ Replace drain plugs and pour 6–12 oz. of Harley-Davidson Hydra-Glide Fork Oil into each tube (7 oz. if fork has been disassembled and washed).
④ Measure amount very carefully.
⑤ Flow of oil into tubes will be increased if fork is worked up and down during filling operation.
⑥ Replace upper bracket bolts and tighten securely.

SPORTSTER MODELS

Follow same procedure as for bigger models, noting the following:

1. Insufficient oil in either fork side will result in faulty recoil action, and excess oil will cause leakage from the top of the fork tubes. When checking oil level in each fork side, also check for water in fork oil which will cause leakage from fork tube cap or oil to bypass fork slider bushings. Oil will appear emulsified, aerated or light brown in color.
2. If the fork does not function correctly after eliminating the possibility of water contamination of fork oil and incorrect oil level in fork sides, inspect the fork tube breather valve for defective condition. Remove fork tube cap, submerge in water and blow compressed air through cap vent hole. Breather valve should not leak below 15 lbs. air pressure. If breather valve is faulty, renew valve.
3. If snubbing action of the front fork remains unsatisfactory, bottoms on compression, stops suddenly on recoil and does not operate smoothly after checking above conditions, the bike is best referred to your Harley-Davidson dealer for disassembling of the shock absorber.

Replacing breather valve

① Take headlight housing from motorcycle and remove fork tube cap.
② Place in vise and break the three stake locks that secure breather valve.
③ Free valve from cap.

When reassembling, coat breather valve seat with DuPont Pliobond or a similar sealing agent. Seat rubber valve in cap and stake lock in three places.

Replacing boots

To replace fork boot parts that are damaged or worn, or to remove boot parts for straightening or replacement of fork stem and bracket assembly:

① Free front fork sides from motorcycle.
② Remove fork boot plain screw and vent screw.
③ Free retainer, gasket and retaining disc.
④ Lower retainer is a light press fit in fork slider. Remove from slider by prying on retainer lip.

Assembly is the reverse order of disassembly.

① Start fork boot retainer by hand into the counterbore in upper end of fork slider.
② Insert the pilot end of oil seal driver, part No. 96310-55, through fork boot retainer and into the upper fork slider bushing.
③ With a soft hammer, use very light blows to drive fork boot retainer to bottom against the end of fork slider.

Note: If fork tube slider bushings are being replaced, install them before replacing lower fork boot retainer.

CHAPTER 8

Maintenance and Tuning

The Harley-Davidson factory recommends a thorough inspection of its machines after the first 500 and 1000 miles. The check list is complete and the procedure is worthwhile. Even if your Harley-Davidson is not new, we suggest that you perform the following before riding it any great distance. Then carry out the regular servicing as noted. The result will be a much better-performing, cheaper-to-maintain, and safer mount.

Glide and Sportster Models

Check list

⓵ Drain oil tank through drain plug, flush with kerosene and refill with fresh oil.

② Clean oil filter (if applicable). Clean overhead valve and tappet oil supply screen.

③ Drain transmission through drain plug and refill to level of filler opening with fresh oil. Use same grade oil used in engine.

④ Lubricate all points indicated for 2000 mile attention in the Regular Service chart.

⑤ Aim headlight.

⑥ Inspect and service air cleaner if needed.

⑦ Check chains and adjust if necessary.

⑧ Check lubrication of front chain and readjust chain oiler adjusting screw if necessary (1964 and earlier models).

⑨ Check lubrication of rear chain and adjust chain oiler (if provided).

⑩ Check wheel mounting bolts and tighten if needed. These bolts must be kept very tight.

⑪ Check level of solution in battery and add distilled water if needed. See that terminals are clean and connections tight.

⑫ Check tightness of all cylinder head bolts and all cylinder base nuts, and tighten where necessary.

⑬ Check brake adjustment and hydraulic fluid level.

⑭ Check tire pressure and inspect tread.

⑮ Check front fork bearing adjustment.

⑯ Clean carburetor gas strainer.

⑰ Clean chain housing magnetic plug (if applicable).

⑱ Inspect and clean spark plugs.

⑲ Check ignition timing and circuit breaker point gap.

⑳ Check all nuts, bolts and screws and tighten any found loose.

㉑ Check and tighten wheel spokes.

㉒ Check clutch adjustment.

㉓ Road test.

Regular service

Check tires and battery weekly.

Every 1000 miles:

① Oil rear chain (14).
② Clean air cleaner (24).
③ Check battery (25).
④ Check rear chain adjustment (26).
⑤ Check hydraulic brake fluid (33).

Every 2000 miles

① Grease: Saddle post (10)
  Saddle bar bearing (9)
  Rear brake pedal bearing (8)
  Foot shift lever bearing (11)
  Hand clutch booster bearing (1)
  Front wheel hub thrust bearing (1966 and earlier) (17)
  Rear wheel hub thrust bearing (1966 and earlier) (18)
  Foot clutch pedal bearing
  Rear fork pivot bearing (1962 model) (22A)

② Oil: Clutch and brake levers (15, 5)
  Clutch control cable, front brake cable, throttle cable, spark control cable (1964 and earlier) (23, 20, 7, 12)
  Clutch lever rod clevis (21)
  Shifter control joints
  Generator bearing (1960 and earlier) (4)
  Saddle post roller and bolt

③ Clean/Check: Oil filter (27)
  Fuel strainer (28)
  Tappet oil screen (if applicable) (29)
  Front chain adjustment (1965 and later) (34)
  Front chain oiler (30)
  Rear chain oiler
  Circuit breaker points (31)
  Clutch adjustment
  Brake adjustment

Every 5000 miles or one year (whichever comes first)

① Grease: Throttle control spiral (7)
  Spark control spiral (1964 and earlier) (6)
  Front wheel hub (center) (1966 and earlier) (2)

Engine Lubrication

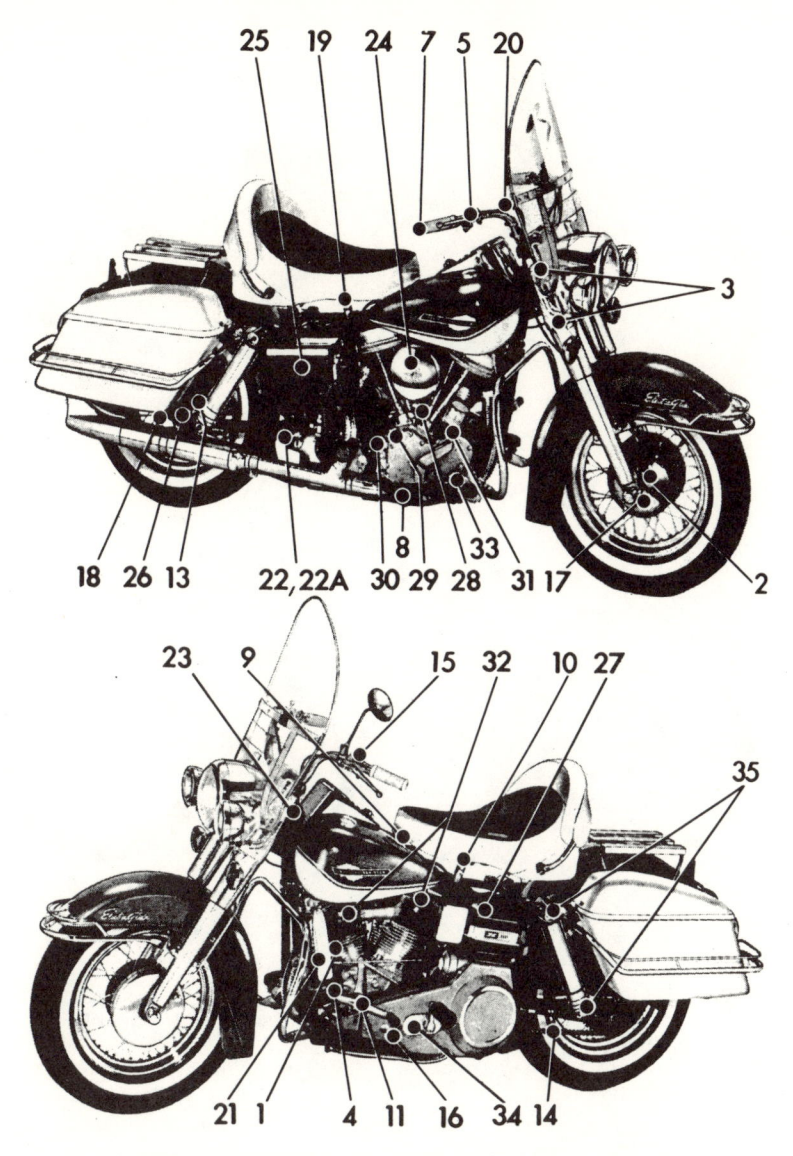

Lubrication and service chart (1965 and later Glide models).

    Rear wheel hub (center) (1966 and earlier) (13)
    Compensating engine sprocket (1964 and earlier) (16)
    Circuit breaker camshaft (31)
    Speedometer and tachometer cables
② Replace: Spark plugs (32)
    Oil filter element
③ Check/Service: Time ignition (31)
    Switch tires
    Check generator brushes (4)
    Check shock rubber bushings (35)

Every 10,000 miles or as required
① Grease generator bearing (1961 and later) (4)
② Repack rear fork pivot bearings (1959 to 1961 models) (22)
③ Repack steering head bearings (3)

ENGINE LUBRICATION

GLIDE MODELS

The engine is lubricated by a pressure system circulating oil from the tank through the moving parts and back to the tank. Oil consumption varies from 250 to 500 miles per quart, depending on the nature of service.

Remove tank cap and check oil supply at not more than 300 miles after each complete refill. If level is down near "Refill" mark on gauge rod, add oil. When level is down to "Refill" mark, add *two* quarts. Engine will run cooler and usage will be less with oil level well up in tank.

Maintenance and Tuning

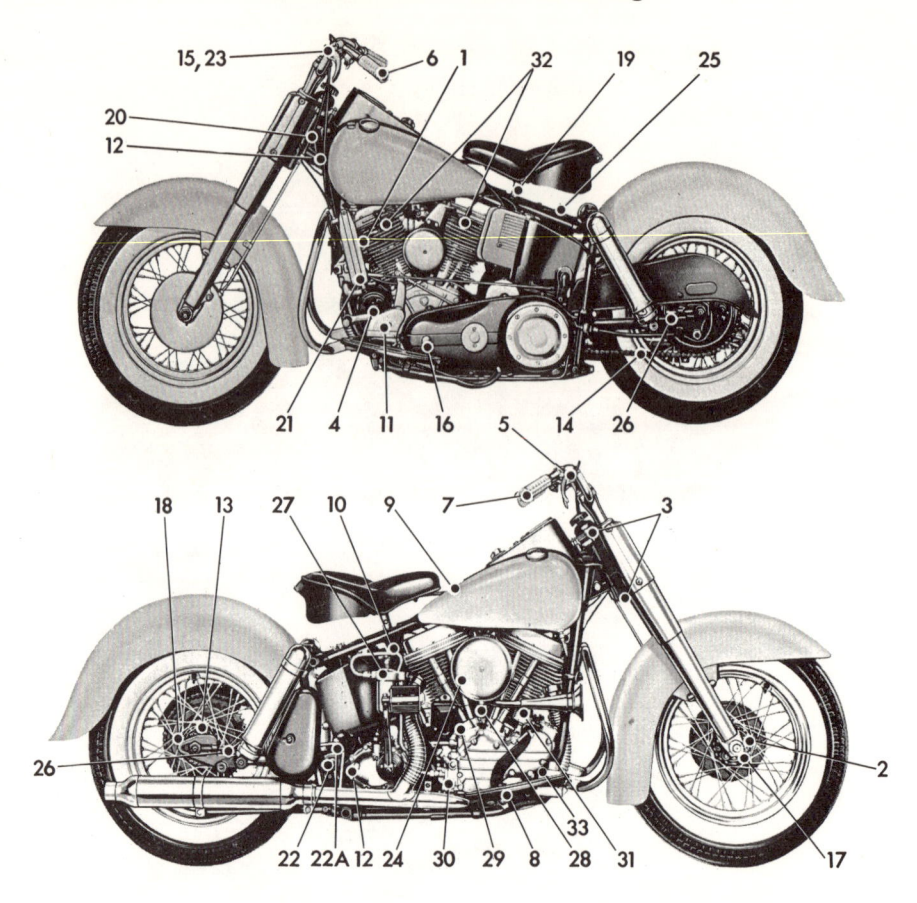

Lubrication and service chart (1964 and earlier Glide models).

The oil tank capacity is one gallon. The tank is full when the oil level is about one inch from top. Do not fill above this level. The tank needs some air space. Tighten the cap securely to prevent leakage.

Change oil in the new engine after the first 500 and 1000 miles and at about 2000-mile intervals thereafter. Completely drain the oil tank of used oil and refill with fresh oil. If service is extremely hard, hot, on dusty roads or in competition, drain and refill at shorter intervals. Draining should be done while oil is hot. It is not necessary to drain the crankcase, for it does not accumulate more than about 5 oz. of oil at any time. At the time of the first oil change, and along with at least every second oil change thereafter, thoroughly flush and clean out tank with flushing oil to remove any sediment and sludge that may have accumulated.

Here is the circulation scheme: (Numbers refer to locations on factory cutaway drawings.)

1. Gravity feed from tank to feed pump.
2. Feed (pressure) section of oil pump.
3. Check valve prevents gravity oil drainage from tank to engine. Builds up oil pressure to operate oil signal switch.
4. Oil pressure regulating valve limits maximum pressure. Surplus oil is dumped back into gearcase.
5. Oil is forced through pinion gear shaft to lubricate lower connecting rod bearings from which oil splashes to cylinder walls, piston, piston pin and main bearings.
6. Oil is forced through passages or external oil lines to lubricate rocker arm bearings and rods, valve stems, valve springs and pushrod sockets. A branch passage supplies oil to the hydraulic lifters. On some models, oil supply is filtered through oil screen (6a).
7. Front chain oil. Oil is bled from bypass oil for front chain lubrication. On 1964 and earlier models, chain oiler screw on pump is adjustable.
8. Oil drains from cylinder rocker housing through passage in each cylinder, then flows through hole in the base of each cylinder, lubricating cylinder walls, piston, piston rings and main bearings.
9. Oil flows from the rocker arm bearings through pushrod covers into the gearcase compartment, lubricating pushrods and tappets.
10. Rotary breather valve is timed to open

Engine Lubrication 107

Lubrication and service chart (XLH model shown), Sportster models.

on the downward stroke of pistons, allowing crankcase exhaust air pressure to expel scavenge oil from crankcase breather oil trap into gearcase. Breather valve closes on upward stroke of pistons, creating vacuum in crankcase.

During this interval, the small ports in the breather valve line up with the passage in the crankcase. Oil is then retrieved through the passage by vacuum from the breather oil trap in crankcase and (on 1965 model) from front chain compartment.

11. Oil blown and drained into timing gearcase (steps 4, 8 and 9) lubricates generator drive gear, timing gears and gear shaft bearings.

12. Gearcase oil settles in gearcase sump from which it returns to pump.

13. Scavenge (return) section of oil pump.

14. Engine oil return to tank.

15. Exhaust air baffle and transfer passage to breather oil trap.

16. Breather oil trap with screen.

17. Oil transfer passage to breather valve.

18. Crankcase exhaust air escapes from gearcase through outside breather tube on 1965 and later models. Air exhausts to front chain guard on earlier models.

19. Return line from chain housing (1965 and later).

20. Vent line to oil tank and chain housing.

To change the oil:

① Run engine until it is fully warm.
② Block machine upright or tilted to right at slight angle.
③ Remove oil tank plug from bottom of tank at right rear corner.
④ Allow all oil to drain.
⑤ Replace plug.
⑥ Pour a quart of kerosene into tank and agitate by rocking motorcycle from side to side.
⑦ Remove plug and drain.
⑧ Replace plug and fill with recommended grade of oil.

Note: Old oil may be removed using a suction gun through filler hole and flushed by squirt-

Maintenance and Tuning

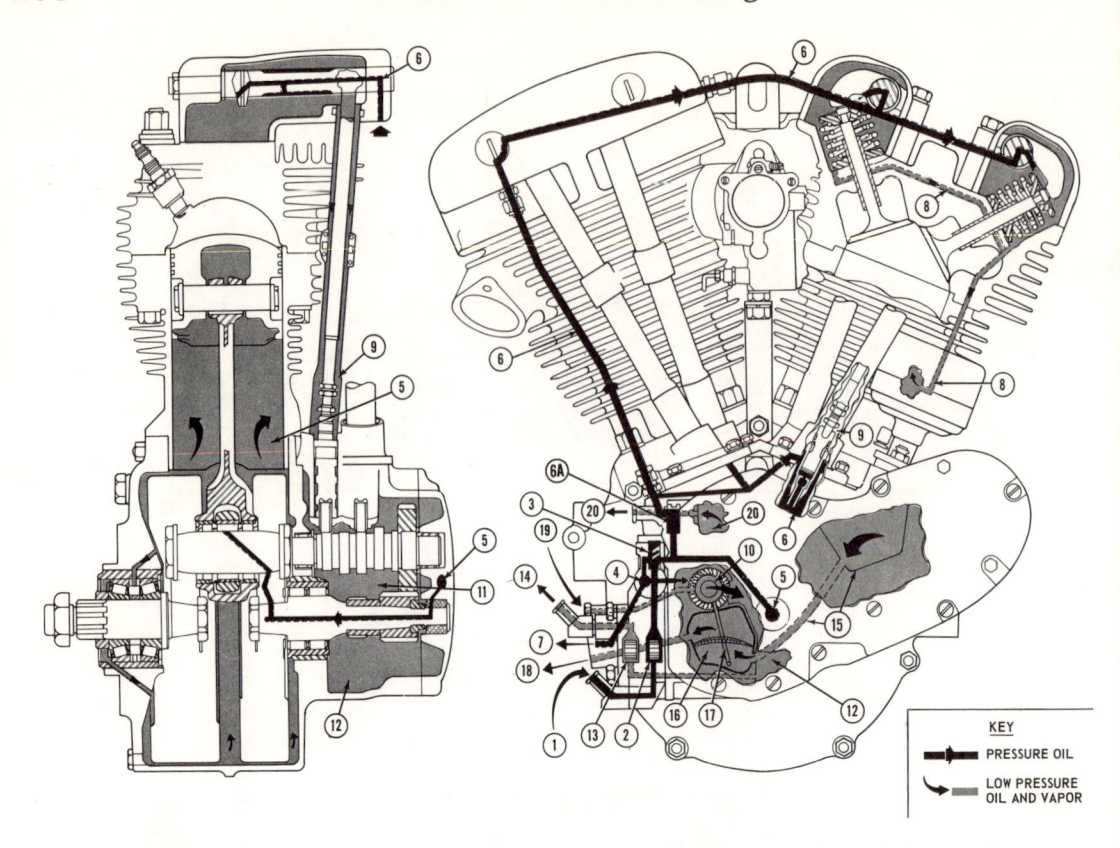

1966 Electra-Glide lubrication system. Oil flow is from tank supply through pump which pressurizes mainshaft (5), and rocker feed (6). Gravity flow and vapor lubricates cylinder walls, followers (9) etc. Scavenger pump (13) returns oil to tank.

ing kerosene into tank from a gun.

Use Harley-Davidson 105 (regular heavy) oil when predominating temperature is 75°F or above. Use Harley-Davidson 75 (medium heavy) oil when predominating temperature is 32°F to 75°F. Use Harley-Davidson 58 (light) oil when predominating temperature is 32°F or below.

If cycle is equipped with an oil filter, wash the filter element in clean gasoline or solvent at least once every 2000 miles when the engine oil is changed. Blow out element with compressed air before installing.

Replace filter element every 5000 miles.

Oil pressure

With engine completely warmed, pressure should be 25 to 28 pounds per square inch at 20 mph. At 30 mph and over, pressure should be steady at 35 to 38 pounds.

SPORTSTER MODELS

The Sportster engine has a force-feed (pressure) type oiling system incorporating oil feed and return in one pump body, with one check valve on the oil feed side.

Here is the oil routing scheme: (Numbers refer to locations on drawing.)

1. Gravity feed to oil pump.
2. Feed section of oil pump.
3. Check valve prevents gravity oil drainage from tank to engine. Builds up pressure to operate oil signal switch.
4. Oil is forced through pinion gear shaft to lubricate lower connecting rod bearings from which oil splashes to cylinder walls, piston, piston pin and main bearings.
5. Oil is forced through oil lines to lubricate rocker arm bearings and rods, valve stems, valve springs and pushrod sockets.
6. Oil drains from cylinder head through passages in each cylinder, then flows through two holes in the base of each cylinder, lubricating cylinder walls, piston, piston rings and main bearings.
7. Oil flows from the rocker arm boxes into the gearcase compartment, lubricating pushrods, tappets, tappet-guides and tappet rollers.
8. Oil accumulated in crankcase base is scavenged by the flywheels to the breather oil trap.
9. The rotary breather valve is timed to open on the downward stroke of pistons, allowing the crankcase exhaust air pressure to expel scavenge oil from the crankcase breather oil trap into the timing gearcase. Breather valve closes on the upward stroke of the pistons, creating vacuum in the crankcase.

Engine Lubrication

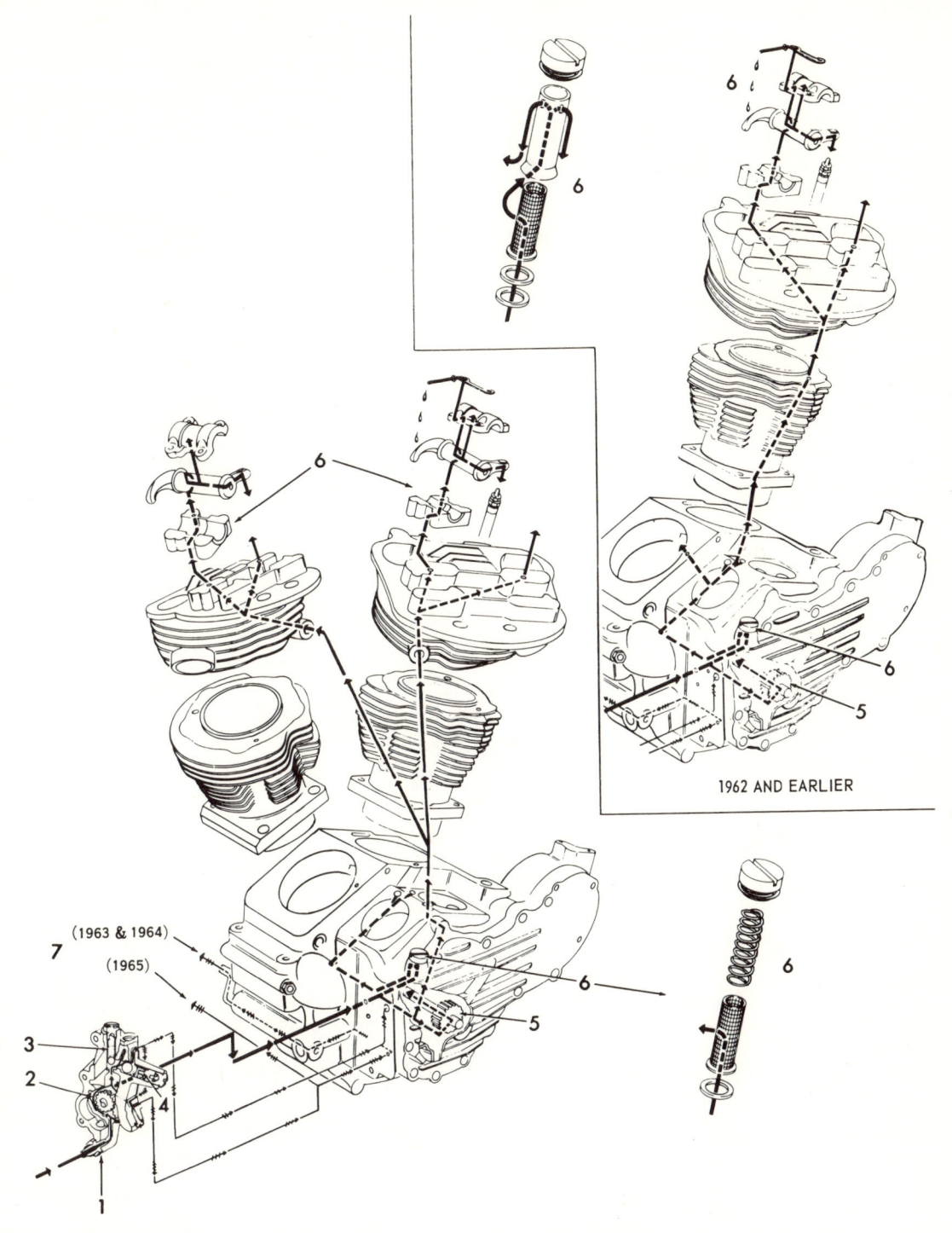

109

1963 to 1965 Glide model oil feed pressure system. Various oil routings were used on 1962, 1963, 1964 and 1965 models so replacement of correct head is important.

110   *Maintenance and Tuning*

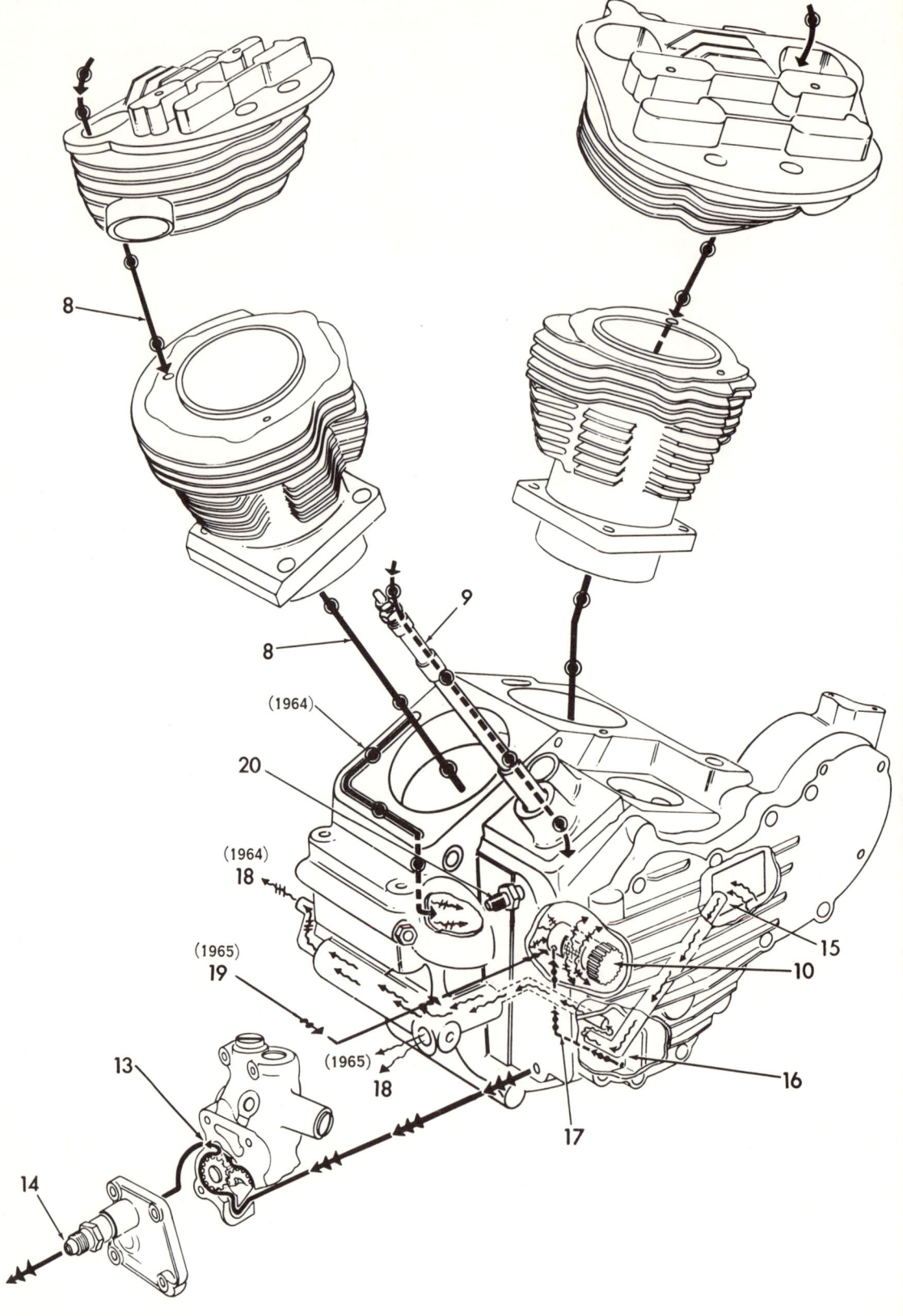

1965 and earlier Glide model oil scavenger system. Pre-1966 models used a variety of return points for low-pressure, or scavenged oil. Note different outlets (18) and drillings between block and case.

Engine Lubrication

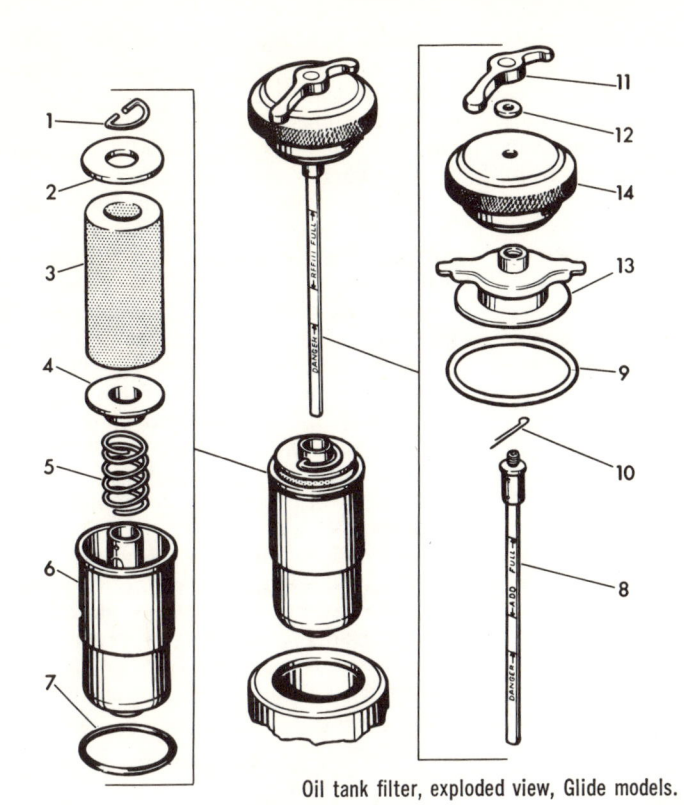

111

1. Filter clip
2. Cap plain washer
3. Filter element
4. Filter lower retainer
5. Cup spring
6. Cup
7. "O" ring
8. Dipstick and valve assembly
9. Cap gasket
10. Cap cotter pin
11. Cap screw
12. Cap washer
13. Cap nut
14. Cap top

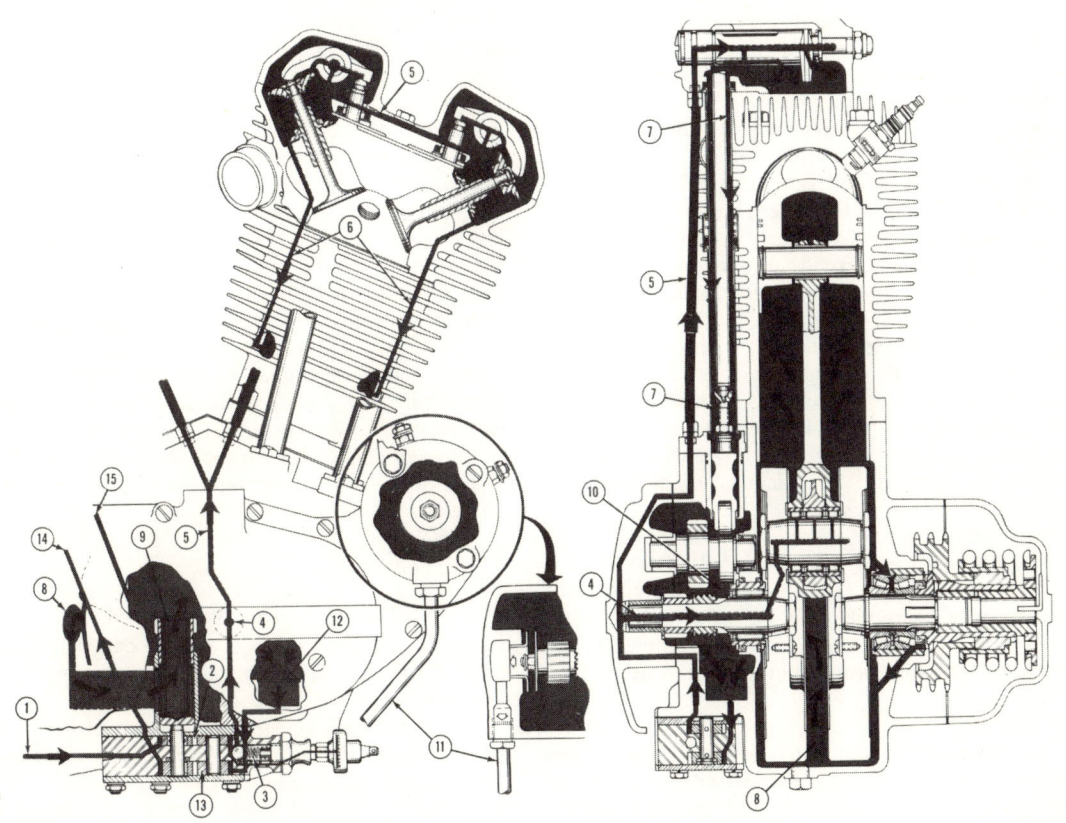

Oil tank filter, exploded view, Glide models.

Oiling system, Sportster models. Sportster engine is well lubricated through pressurized oil flow and vapor-phase mist as indicated by black areas.

10. Oil blown and drained into timing gearcase (steps 7 and 9) lubricates generator drive gear, timing gears and gear shaft bearings.

11. Crankcase exhaust air escapes from timing gearcase through outside breather tube. Any oil still carried by exhaust air is separated from the air by an oil slinger on the generator drive gear.

12. Gearcase oil flows through fine mesh oil strainer preventing foreign particles from entering scavenge section of pump.

13. Scavenge (return) section of oil pump.

14. Engine oil returns to tank and also supplies oil to the rear chain oiler.

15. Vent line from the oil tank.

Oil mileage normally varies from 250 to 500 miles per quart, depending on the nature of service.

Remove tank cap and dip stick and check oil supply at least every 300 miles after each complete refill, or more often depending on the condition of the engine. Tank capacity is three quarts ("Full" mark on dip stick). Do not fill above "Full" mark, for the tank needs some air space. When the oil is down to "Refill" mark on dip stick, *one* quart can be added. Never allow oil level to go down to "Danger" mark on dip stick. Tighten the cap securely to prevent leakage. Oil runs cooler and oil mileage is somewhat higher with oil level well up in the tank. Furthermore, unless oil tank is kept well filled, frequent checking of oil level will be necessary to avoid any chance of running dry.

After a new engine has run its first 500 and 1000 miles, and at 2000-mile intervals thereafter, completely drain the oil tank of used oil and refill with fresh oil. If the engine is driven extremely hard, or used on dusty roads or in competition, drain and refill at shorter intervals. Draining should be done while oil is hot. It is not necessary to drain the crankcase, because it does not accumulate used oil. At the time of the first 500-mile oil change, and at least every second oil change thereafter, thoroughly flush and clean out tank with kerosene to remove any sediment and sludge that may have accumulated. Refill with fresh oil as indicated under GLIDE MODELS.

In winter the oil change interval should be shorter than normal, and any engine used only for short runs must have oil drained frequently along with a thorough tank flush-out before new oil is put in tank. The lower the temperature, the shorter the oil change interval should be.

Oil pressure

The oil pressure signal light switch is an electrically operated diaphragm-type switch. The diaphragm is spring loaded and held against its contact point by spring tension when oil is not circulating through the system, closing the circuit (indicator light on). When engine is started, and as the engine speed is increased, oil pressure is raised sufficiently to counteract the diaphragm spring and open the circuit (indicator light off). Oil signal light switch cannot be repaired. Defective switches must be replaced.

The oil pump is non-regulatory and delivers its entire volume of oil under pressure to the engine. When a cold engine is started, engine oil will be thick or viscous, restricting circulation through the oiling system and causing high oil pressure; as the engine becomes hot and oil thins, pressure will correspondingly drop. Similarly, when an engine is operated at high speeds, the volume of oil circulated through the oiling system increases, resulting in higher oil pressure; as engine speed is reduced, volume of oil pumped is also reduced, resulting in lower oil pressure.

To check oil pressure, install an oil pressure gauge in oil switch connection of pump nipple. Run the engine until oil becomes hot. Under normal riding conditions oil pressure will vary from 10 to 14 pounds. Idle down, retard spark and check the gauge. Oil pressure will vary from 3 to 7 pounds.

CHAIN ADJUSTMENT

The Harley-Davidson factory recommends that chain adjustment be checked at regular intervals of 1000 miles for rear chain and 2000 miles for front chain, on larger models. For Sprint and smaller models, check every 500 to 1000 miles. As chains stretch and wear, they run tighter at one spot than another, so always adjust free movement at tightest spot in chain to allow specified play midway between sprockets. Running chains too tight will result in excessive wear, particularly on chain tensioner shoe of 1965 and later models.

Inspect chains frequently for cracked, broken or badly worn links. The rear chain may be taken apart for replacement or repair at the connecting, or master, link. The front chain does not have a connecting link. It is necessary to remove the engine sprocket before the chain is removed for replacement. Repair of the rear chain is not recommended.

Primary chain

GLIDE MODELS—1964 and Earlier

① Loosen four nuts and one cap screw that secure the transmission to its mounting plate and bracket on the right side frame tube.

② Move the transmission forward or backward by means of the adjusting screw at the rear of the transmission on the right side.

③ Turn the adjusting screw clockwise to tighten the chain and counterclockwise to loosen the chain.

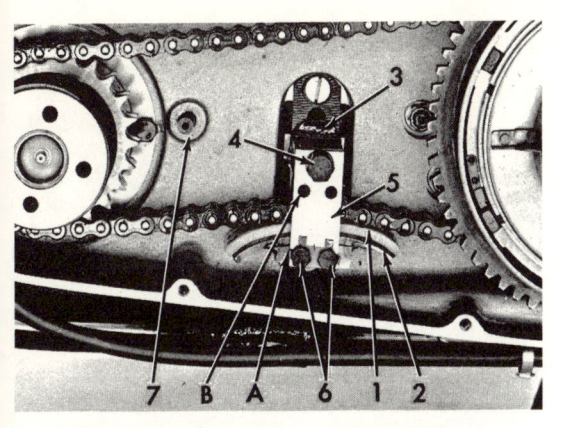

Chain Adjustment

④ Specified front chain play is ½".
⑤ When correctly adjusted, tighten the transmission plate securely to its mounting.
⑥ Check mounting plate bolts occasionally and keep them tight.

Note: Adjusting front chain requires adjustment of rear chain. Moving the transmission to adjust the front chain may require adjustment of gear shifter and clutch controls.

GLIDE MODELS—1965 and Later

① Remove rear pivot bolt from left footboard and swing rear end of footboard down, away from chain cover.
② Remove cover.
③ Front chain tension is adjusted by means of a shoe which is raised or lowered underneath the chain to tighten or loosen it. The shoe support bracket moves up or down in a slotted backplate.
④ After loosening center bolt in backplate nut, adjust shoe support as necessary to obtain specified up and down free movement in upper strand of chain, midway between sprockets, and retighten bolt securely.

Front chain adjustment:
⅝" to ⅞" chain slack with cold engine
⅜" to ⅝" chain slack with hot engine

Note: Shoe support bracket and outer plate have two sets of shoe attaching holes (A and B) so that entire assembly can be inverted to accommodate various sprocket sizes or chain lengths.

SPORTSTER MODELS

① Disconnect battery cable from starter motor.
② Remove left footrest and rear brake foot lever.
③ Place an oil drain pan under clutch.
④ Remove front chain cover and gasket.
Correct adjustment is ⅝" to ⅞" slack cold; ⅜" to ⅝" hot.
⑤ Loosen bolts and raise or lower chain adjuster.
⑥ When chain is correctly adjusted, tighten bolts securely and reassemble remaining parts.

Rear chain

GLIDE MODELS

① Remove the rear axle nut, lock washer and loosen the brake sleeve nut and brake anchor stud nut.
② Loosen the lock nuts on wheel adjusting screws.
③ Turn the adjusting screws as necessary to adjust the chain to ½" play. Turn each screw an equal number of turns in order to keep the wheel in alignment.
④ Check correct alignment of the wheel to see that the tire runs in center of rear fork and

Adjusting front chain (1965 and later Glide models).

Front chain tensioner adjustment, Sportster models.

1. Drive chain
2. Chain adjuster shoe
3. Support bracket
4. Support bracket bolts (2)
5. Support bracket brace (XLH)
6. Brace bolt (XLH)

Figure following name of part indicates quantity necessary for one complete assembly.

Adjusting rear chain, Glide models.

Maintenance and Tuning

also that the rear sprocket runs centrally in the chain.

⑤ Tighten the sleeve nut, anchor stud nut, axle nut and adjusting screw lock nuts in that order.

SPORTSTER MODELS

① Loosen axle nut on right side of motorcycle.

② Loosen lock nut on both sides of motorcycle.

③ Turn adjusting nut clockwise to tighten chain; turn counterclockwise and at the same time tap each end of the axle to loosen the chain.

④ Turn adjusting nut on either side exactly the same number of turns to maintain alignment of wheel.

⑤ Obtain ½″ free play at midpoint.

⑥ With lock nut tight against adjusting nut, the distance from lock nut to outer end of adjusting stud should be the same on both sides. Check correct alignment of wheel by observing that tire runs about midway between rear frame tubes and rear wheel sprocket runs centrally in the chain.

⑦ When readjustment is completed, be sure to tighten rear axle nut and rear wheel adjusting stud lock nut securely.

⑧ After adjusting rear chain, the rear brake may be too tight. Readjust brake rod, if necessary.

FRONT CHAIN OILING

A well lubricated chain has an oily surface and is clean and free of discoloration. If chain has a brownish hue and a rusty appearance at the side and center plates, it is under-lubricated, even though the surface may be oily.

GLIDE MODELS—1964 and Earlier

The adjusting screw of the primary chain oiler fits into an orifice through which engine oil bleeds to the chain. Since very little oil is needed to lubricate the chain, the orifice is very small. Sediment and gummy matter accumulate in the oil supply and form deposits in and around this orifice, gradually decreasing the oil supplied to the chain. A chain that has been lubricated perfectly the first 2000 miles may run short of oil the second 2000 miles. Even though inspection indicates the chain is amply lubricated, it is advisable to flush away accumulated sediment and restore the orifice to its original size at intervals of approximately 2000 miles.

① Loosen the chain oiler adjusting screw and back it out exactly two full turns.

② Tighten lock nut.

③ Operate this way for a few miles and then reset screw to its established setting.

④ To reset adjusting screw to its established setting, turn adjusting screw inward exactly two

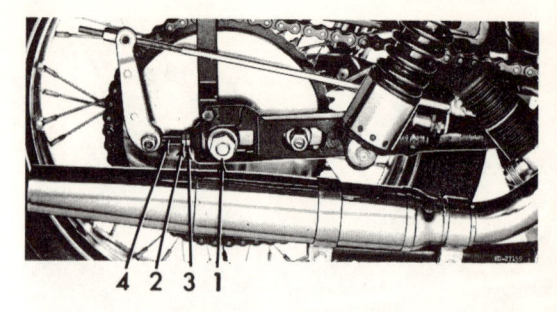

Right side rear wheel (XLH model shown), Sportster series.

1. Rear axle nut
2. Adjusting stud lock nut
3. Adjusting stud nut
4. Adjusting stud

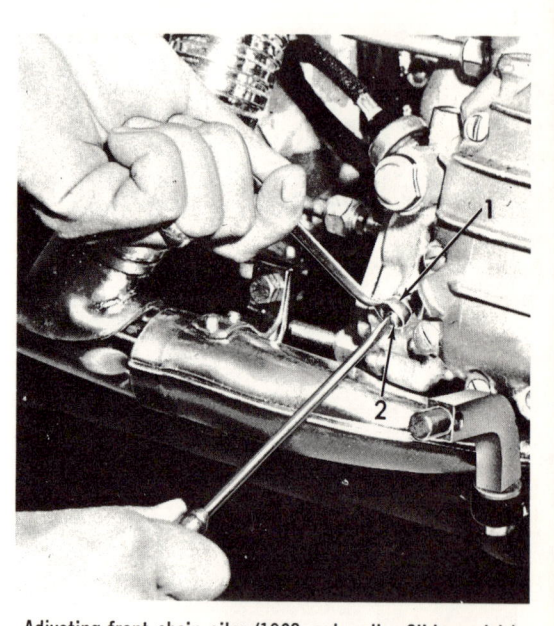

Adjusting front chain oiler (1963 and earlier Glide models).

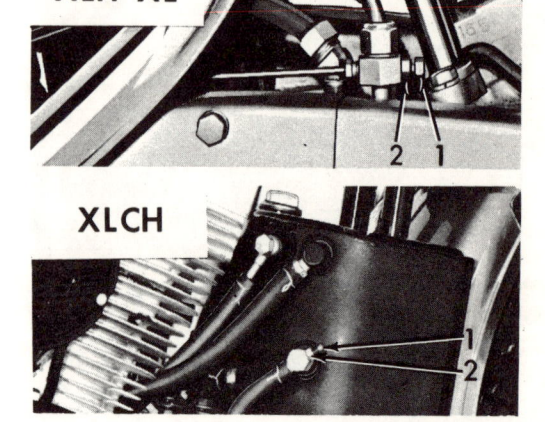

XLH-XL

XLCH

Rear chain oiler (1966 models shown), Sportster series.

1. Adjusting screw
2. Adjusting screw lock nut

Rear Chain Oiling

Specific Gravity Conversion Chart

Temperature	−10° C (14° F)	0° C (32° F)	10° C (50° F)	20° C (68° F)	30° C (86° F)	40° C (104° F)
Specific gravity	1.321	1.314	1.307	1.300	1.293	1.286
	1.311	1.304	1.297	1.290	1.283	1.276
	1.301	1.294	1.287	1.280	1.273	1.266
	1.291	1.284	1.277	1.270	1.263	1.256
	1.281	1.274	1.267	1.260	1.253	1.246
	1.271	1.264	1.257	1.250	1.243	1.236
	1.261	1.254	1.247	1.240	1.233	1.226
	1.251	1.244	1.237	1.230	1.223	1:216
	1.241	1.234	1.227	1.220	1.213	1.206
	1.231	1.224	1.217	1.210	1.203	1.196
	1.221	1.214	1.207	1.200	1.193	1.186
	1.211	1.204	1.197	1.190	1.183	1.176
	1.201	1.194	1.187	1.180	1.173	1.166

Specific gravity-temperature chart.

full turns and lock it in place with lock nut.

If established setting of adjusting screw should become completely lost while making readjustment or flushing orifice, back up lock nut and turn the screw inward until its point bottoms lightly but firmly against its seat. Then back screw out about 1¼ turns and establish this setting with the lock nut. This is the approximate original factory setting.

GLIDE MODELS—1965 and Later

A fixed amount of oil is supplied to the primary chain through an oil line from a metering orifice in the oil pump. Oil drops on the front chain from the oiler outlet tube. Excess oil collects at rear of chain compartment and is drawn back into the engine gearcase breather.

When the chain adjustment is checked at 2000 mile intervals, also check to see that oil comes out of the oiler tube when the engine is running, when viewing through cover inspection hole. If oil does not come from oiler, the supply orifice at pump is probably blocked due to accumulation of dirt and requires cleaning. To do this, remove orifice screw and washer from oil pump and blow out passage to chain compartment with compressed air.

SPORTSTER MODELS

There is an opening between the front chain and the transmission compartments, and the same oil supply automatically lubricates moving parts in both compartments.

REAR CHAIN OILING

Under normal operating conditions, brush the dirt off and lubricate the rear chain at 1000-mile intervals. Lubricate with Harley-Davidson "Chain Saver" if available; if not, use lightest engine oil available.

If motorcycle is equipped with rear chain oiler, disregard above instructions and proceed as follows: At regular 2000-mile intervals, make a close inspection of rear chain. If rear chain does not appear to be getting sufficient lubrication, or if there is evidence of an over-supply of oil, proceed as follows:

On 1964 models equipped with front chain guard oiler, the rear chain receives its lubrication from the rear chain oiler outlet tube located at the rear of the front chain guard back. A shelf inside the front chain guard picks up oil thrown off by the front chain. This oil drains out through a small tube onto the rear chain.

Check the front chain oiler adjustment as explained previously under FRONT CHAIN OILING. Normally, if the front chain oiler is adjusted for correct front chain lubrication, the rear chain will be adequately lubricated.

If the rear chain is dry, the oiler outlet tube may have become blocked with dirt. This may occur when the motorcycle is operated under extremely dusty or dirty conditions. Check to see that the oiler outlet tube is open by inserting a ⅛"-diameter wire into the tube behind the chain guard.

The oil return line bleed type oiler is located on the oil return line at the oil pump. To adjust the chain oiler, follow the same procedure explained in adjusting the front chain oiler (1964 and earlier Glide models).

If the motorcycle is operated under extremely dusty or dirty conditions, whether equipped with a rear chain oiler or not, additional lubrication of the rear chain may be advisable. Remove chain from motorcycle. Soak and wash thoroughly in a pan of kerosene. Remove chain from kerosene and hang so kerosene will drain off. Immerse in a pan of grease heated to consistency of light engine oil, or use light engine oil. While immersed, move chain around to be sure that hot grease or oil works through all inside parts. After removing, allow chain to drain and wipe surplus grease or oil from surface of chain. Install chain on motorcycle. Inspect connecting link and spring clip closely for bad condition. Replace if at all questionable. Be sure spring clip is properly and securely locked on pin ends with open end trailing direction of chain travel.

When chain has been removed for cleaning, check it for elongation caused by wear as follows:

① Lay chain on a flat surface.

② Take up the play in the links by pushing the chain ends toward each other, a few links at a time.

③ When the chain is fully compressed, measure its length. Stretch the chain to its full length and measure again. Replace rear chain if play exceeds one inch; replace front chain if play exceeds one inch.

Note: Front chain is not equipped with a connecting link, so it may be checked only if it has been opened for repair. Front chain of models with tensioner shoe should not be opened. Replace chain when you run out of shoe adjustment.

BATTERY

It is the care given the battery rather than time and miles of service which is most important in determining its life.

At least once every month, or even more often in hot weather or when motorcycle is used very much, the battery should be removed from its holder and serviced as follows:

Unscrew filler plugs from the cells and add distilled water to the cells to upper level marked on side of battery jar or slightly above plate separators. Be careful not to overfill. Overfilling will result in some of the electrolyte being forced out through the cap vent holes, diluting or weakening the solution strength. An overflow of battery solution will cause cables to corrode and motorcycle parts near the battery to be damaged. Electrolyte should not be allowed to go below lower level, or below plate separators, while in service.

Clean battery and terminals when necessary with a baking soda-water solution. Be careful to avoid getting any of the solution into the cap vent holes. When solution stops bubbling, flush off battery with clean water.

Charging

The small storage batteries in motorcycles are of low ampere/hour capacity and like all batteries, are self-discharging in storage. Most manufacturers advise that stored batteries be charged once a month. Since many bikes are not used for several months at a time during the winter, this factor accounts for lots of complaints. Others are caused by carelessness in leaving lights on where this can be done with key removed, direct shorts in wiring or faulty voltage regulator.

Do not, repeat *not,* have a motorcycle battery re-charged on a quick charger at your neighborhood service station. The charging rate is too high and the battery will be ruined.

Trickle-charge only, and then at a low rate such as 1.5 to 2 ampere/hours. You can go as high as 4 a/h for short periods. The battery will get pretty warm, but as long as it stays below 110°, it will not be damaged.

Fill the battery to the specified level with water before re-charging.

After charging, check the specific gravity of the electrolyte. A 12-volt battery should register above 1.250 at temperature of 68°. A 6-volt unit should be above 1.230. Specific gravity will be lower at higher temperatures, higher at lower temperatures, so allowance can be made if temperature is drastically different from 68°. (See accompanying chart.)

TUNING

Most motorcycle engine troubles stem from inept tuning. Because the cycle engine is so simple in format and so accessible, nearly every rider at one time or another undertakes to "tune it up".

This isn't bad; in fact, it is commendable. But too few of them attempt to find out anything about the process before they begin. No good mechanic ever picks up a screwdriver unless he has access to the right information about the machine he is approaching. Amateurs should be as conscientious.

Tuning consists of adjusting the variables so that they meet factory specifications, as far as street bikes are concerned.

The four-stroke variables are (1) valve timing, (2) valve clearance, (3) fuel/air ratio, (4) spark timing, (5) point and plug gap.

① Set the valve/tappet (rocker arm, lifter, etc.) clearance. This is specified with engine cold. "Cold" simply means that the engine should be approximately the same temperature as the rest of the bike, the frame, etc. In other words, don't adjust the valves if the engine, or the oil in the engine, is warmer to the touch than any other part.

Letting it sit overnight is the rule followed by most shops, but whatever time it takes to cool down is the amount to allow.

The best way to gauge the clearance is by "go" and "no-go". If clearance is specified as .008", don't check it with a .008" feeler gauge. Use a .007", which should slide (go) through the space, and a .009", which should not. The most important thing is to be sure you have the tappet on the heel of the cam, and not slightly onto the quieting ramp or the lobe itself. This means

Ignition Timing

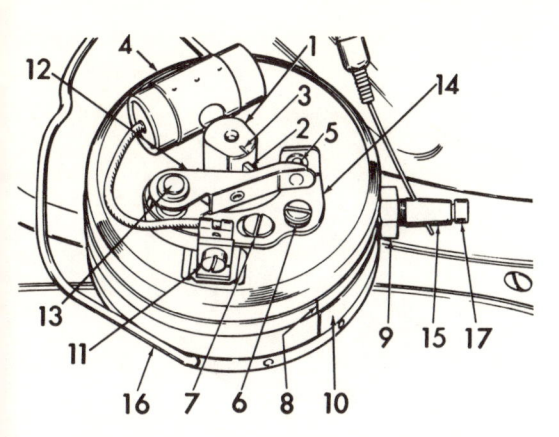

Single contact point distributor—manual advance.

1. Breaker cam
2. Fiber cam follower
3. Cam timing mark
4. Condenser
5. Contact points
6. Lock screw
7. Eccentric adjusting screw
8. Timing mark
9. Adjusting stud lock nut
10. Timing adjusting stud plate
11. Wire stud screw
12. Circuit breaker lever
13. Pivot stud
14. Contact point and support
15. Timing adjusting stud
16. Cover retainer
17. Control wire lock screw

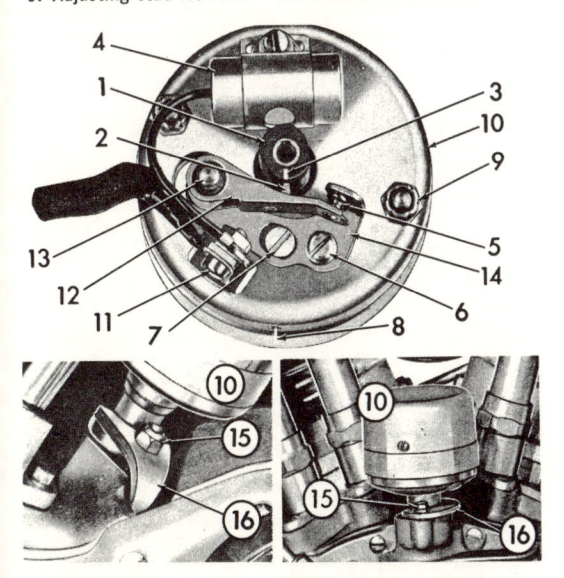

1966 Electra-Glide   1966 Sportster and Servi-car

Single contact point distributor—automatic advance.

1. Breaker cam
2. Fiber cam follower
3. Cam timing mark
4. Condenser
5. Contact points
6. Adjustable point lock screw
7. Eccentric adjusting screw
8. Timing marks (1965 model)
9. Circuit breaker head nut (2)
10. Circuit breaker head
11. Wire stud screw
12. Circuit breaker lever
13. Pivot stud
14. Contact point and support
15. Stem clamp nut
16. Stem clamp

Figure following name of part indicates quantity necessary for one complete assembly.

that you should have the piston at top dead center on the compression stroke, not the exhaust stroke. At this point, you can set both inlet and exhaust valve clearances.

② Adjust the point gap. Use a pair of feeler gauges in the same way as for the valves. Points are on spring tension and they can easily be forced open with the gauge.

③ Set the ignition static timing.

④ Re-check the point gap, just to be sure.

⑤ Check the automatic advance with a timing light, or by spreading the governor weights.

⑥ Clean, adjust, or replace the spark plug.

⑦ Make sure the throttle is opening fully when the twistgrip is wide open.

⑧ Start the engine, warm it up, adjust the idle mixture and speed.

IGNITION TIMING

GLIDE AND SPORTSTER

Two types of distributors are used: single-point and dual-point. In addition, both manual and automatic advance spark control systems will be found. They all perform essentially the same function, i.e., to deliver high-tension electrical impulse to the spark plug at the proper time to ignite the fuel/air charge in the cylinder.

In the single-point distributor, the breaker points are operated by a cam with one narrow and one wide lobe. The narrow lobe times the front cylinder and the wide lobe times the rear cylinder. A single ignition coil fires both spark plugs at the same time. One spark occurs in the exhaust stroke of one cylinder, and the other spark fires the combustible gases in the other cylinder.

In the dual-point distributor, ignition spark is produced by operation of separate circuit breaker contact points and ignition coils for each spark plug. The breaking of each set of breaker points by a single-lobe cam on the timer shaft determines the spark timing. The single-lobe cam opens the breaker points, individually firing alternate cylinders at every crankshaft revolution.

The condition and alignment of the point contacts are highly important to best performance. Points should be free from pits and mated as shown in the illustrations. Worn ones can be cleaned and trued with point file or oilstone. However, the small investment in new points is well repaid.

After dressing or replacing points, proceed with setting gap as follows:

Single-point distributor

① Check the gap between the contact points with a feeler gauge. (Point gap should be exactly .022″ when the fiber lever is on the highest point of the cam. Incorrect point gap spacing affects ignition timing.)

Maintenance and Tuning

② Adjust the points by loosening the lock screw and moving the eccentric adjusting screw to provide correct gap.

③ Retighten lock screw and again check the gap.

Dual-point distributor

① Adjust front cylinder contact points (marked "F" on base) to .022" gap according to above procedure.

② Adjust rear cylinder contact points to .022" gap in similar manner.

Note: Always check ignition timing whenever dual points are adjusted, since any change in rear contact point gap affects ignition timing.

With point gap correctly set, time the ignition according to whether a manual or an automatic advance distributor is fitted. First remove spark plugs so engine can be rotated easily, and take the inspection plug out of the left side of the crankcase. Telescope a front cylinder pushrod cover so you can determine when the valve is fully closed. Then proceed as follows:

Manual advance distributor

① Rotate engine until front piston is on compression stroke (just after front intake valve closes), and continue turning engine slowly (less than ½ revolution) until timing mark for front cylinder on flywheel is aligned in inspection hole as shown in the illustration of your model.

② Make sure timing mark on distributor base aligns with end of timing adjusting plate.

③ Rotate distributor head counterclockwise against stop (fully advanced position).

④ Timing mark on cam lobe should now align with breaker arm fiber cam follower. If it does not, but is only slightly out of alignment, loosen timing adjusting stud lock nut and shift distributor head to attain alignment. Timing mark will no longer line up exactly with edge of plate.

⑤ Retighten lock nut.

Note: Distributor must be fully advanced when checking alignment of timing mark with fiber cam follower.

To check that points break at the proper time, use a static timing light, as follows:

Single-point distributor

① Connect one test lamp wire to coil wire at distributor.

② Ground the other test lamp wire to the engine and turn ignition switch on. With points open, the lamp will light, and with points closed, the lamp will be out.

③ With distributor fully advanced against its stop and flywheel marks correctly positioned as noted, contact points should just begin to open. The instant that direction is reversed (spark retarded) from full advance stop position, points

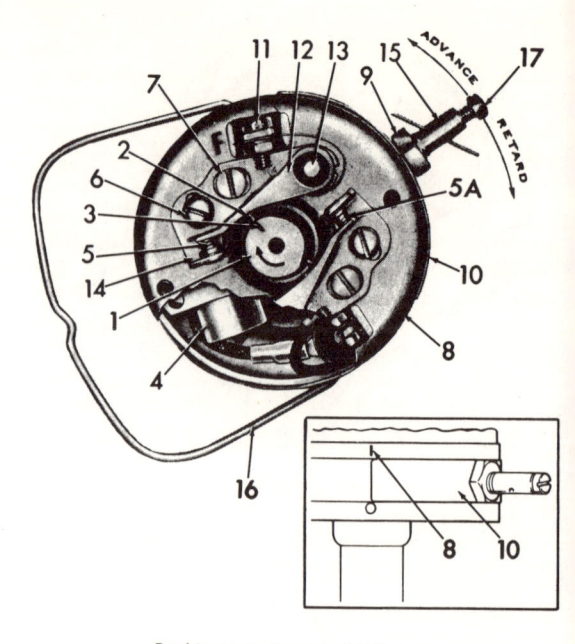

Double contact point distributor.

1. Cam
2. Fiber cam follower
3. Cam timing mark
4. Condenser
5. Front cylinder contact points
5A. Rear cylinder contact points
6. Lock screw
7. Adjusting screw
8. Timing mark
9. Adjusting stud lock nut
10. Timing adjusting plate
11. Wire stud screw
12. Circuit breaker lever
13. Pivot stud
14. Contact point and support
15. Timing adjusting stud
16. Cover retainer
17. Control wire lock screw

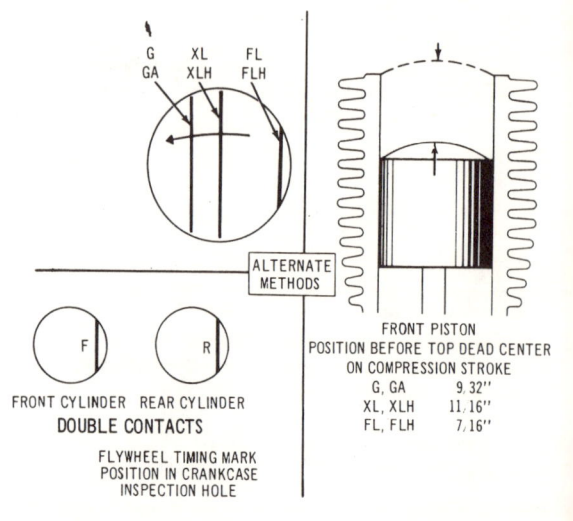

ALTERNATE METHODS

FRONT CYLINDER   REAR CYLINDER
DOUBLE CONTACTS
FLYWHEEL TIMING MARK POSITION IN CRANKCASE INSPECTION HOLE

FRONT PISTON POSITION BEFORE TOP DEAD CENTER ON COMPRESSION STROKE
G, GA   9/32"
XL, XLH   11/16"
FL, FLH   7/16"

Ignition timing schematic, manual advance distributor.

should begin to close and the light will go off.

④ If the contact points remain closed (light off) in the fully advanced position, timing is late. Loosen adjusting stud lock nut and shift base counterclockwise until contact points just begin to open (timing light just flickers or goes on) in fully advanced position.

⑤ If the contact points begin to open before circuit breaker is in fully advanced position, timing is early. Loosen adjusting stud lock nut and shift breaker base clockwise until contact points just begin to open in fully advanced position.

⑥ Retighten lock nut.

⑦ Move distributor from retard to advance to see that points will just open when the circuit breaker reaches the advance stop. Be sure to keep flywheel mark correctly positioned during the entire procedure.

Note: Timing the front cylinder automatically times the rear cylinder.

Dual-point distributor

Timing of dual-point distributors is carried out by setting the point gap and timing the front cylinder as for the single-point distributor. (Points are marked "F" on plate.) Then hook up the test lamp lead to the rear coil terminal (black wire).

① Turn distributor to fully advanced.

② Rotate engine slowly until breaker cam approaches the fiber rubbing block of the rear points and watch for timing mark for rear cylinder "R" on flywheel to appear.

③ Align "R" mark as shown in illustration.

④ Points should just open to light test lamp.

⑤ If points stay closed, adjust point gap so they just open to make light flicker.

Note: On earlier Duo-Glides (prior to engine No. 61FLH7987), there is no rear "R" mark on the flywheel. If necessary to check timing, use an accurate steel rule or dial indicator to find 7/16" BTDC for rear piston.

Automatic advance distributors

Refer to the accompanying diagram for flywheel timing marks on various models. Then follow same procedure as given for setting manual advance distributors by aligning the "retard" marks.

On 1965 distributor having adjustable base, see that timing marks are in alignment. This is original factory timing in retarded position.

Dual-point models have timing mark on top edge of cam which aligns perfectly with breaker arm fiber cam follower. If it does not, shift distributor head to attain alignment. Distributor must be fully retarded counterclockwise against stop when checking alignment of mark with fiber cam follower.

To check operation of automatic advance, use

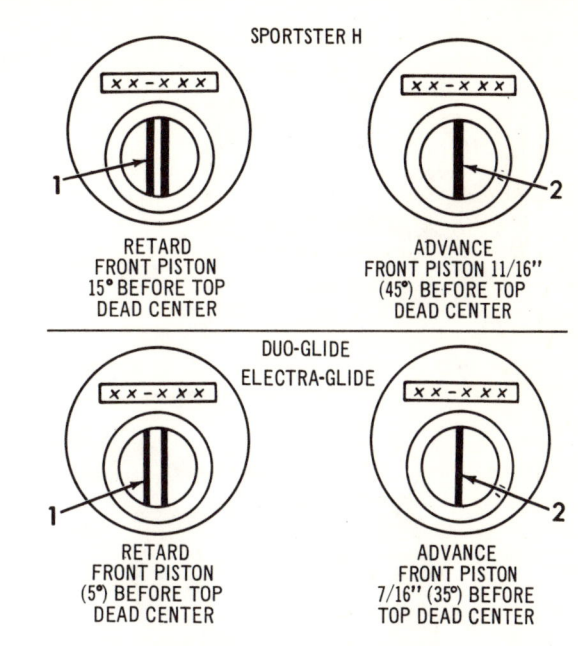

SPORTSTER H

RETARD FRONT PISTON 15° BEFORE TOP DEAD CENTER

ADVANCE FRONT PISTON 11/16" (45°) BEFORE TOP DEAD CENTER

DUO-GLIDE ELECTRA-GLIDE

RETARD FRONT PISTON (5°) BEFORE TOP DEAD CENTER

ADVANCE FRONT PISTON 7/16" (35°) BEFORE TOP DEAD CENTER

Ignition timing schematic, automatic advance distributor.

a strobe light aimed at inspection hole with leads connected to front spark plug, ground and battery positive terminal. Run engine at 1500–2000 rpm. A clear plastic plug for the inspection hole is available under part No. 96296-65.

MAGNETO

Timing of mag ignition is basically the same as with single-point coil ignition. First set the point gap (to .015") and then check timing with test lamp or strobe. On early models having safety gap, be careful not to bend points, since they are positioned to give correct safety gap of 3/8" with magneto cover installed. Use a spare cover with a 1½" by 1¼" opening and a 3/8"-diameter rod to set safety gap.

Note the factory timing marks on fixed position type. Harley-Davidson advises that if points cannot be opened by shifting the magneto housing within limits of slots in magneto mounting base, or if point opening occurs after magneto housing has turned to a position where it will interfere with the carburetor air cleaner, it is probable that timing according to original factory marks has been lost. This would occur if magneto were loosened and lifted far enough so its drive gears become unmeshed, or if the case were opened and gears removed and installed, or if magneto circuit breaker parts were removed and replaced for any reason. In this case, unbolt magneto from case and lift far enough to bring its driving gears out of mesh. Turn cam approximately as much as cam appears to be out of required position, and push assembly back down into gearcase, re-engaging its drive gears.

Maintenance and Tuning

MANUAL CONTROL TYPE

FIXED POSITION TYPE

FACTORY TIMING MARKS

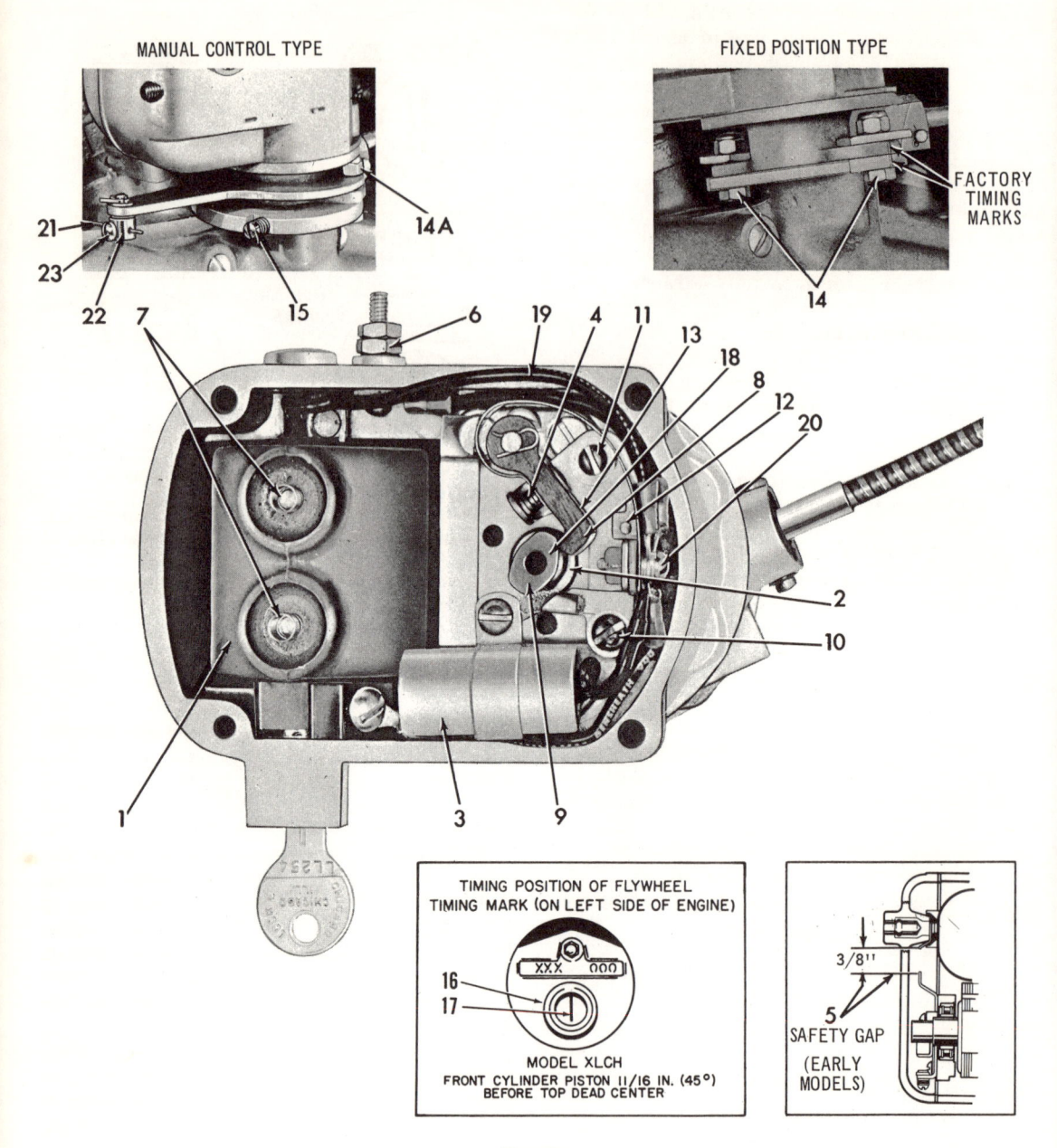

TIMING POSITION OF FLYWHEEL TIMING MARK (ON LEFT SIDE OF ENGINE)

MODEL XLCH
FRONT CYLINDER PISTON 11/16 IN. (45°) BEFORE TOP DEAD CENTER

3/8"
SAFETY GAP (EARLY MODELS)

Magneto.

1. Induction coil
2. Rotor
3. Condenser
4. Circuit breaker points
5. Safety gap points (1964 and earlier)
6. Ignition cutout terminal post
7. Coil secondary terminal spring
8. Cam follower
9. Cam
10. Pivot screw
11. Adjustment screw
12. Adjustment pry location
13. Cam oiler felt
14. Magneto mounting bolts and nuts (1964 and earlier)
14A. Magneto mounting bolts (1965)
15. Magneto advance stop screw (1965 to early 1967)
16. Timing inspection hole
17. Timing mark
18. Narrow cam lobe
19. Coil lead wire
20. Breaker point terminal post
21. Control wire (1965)
22. Swivel block (1965)
23. Control wire set screw (1965)

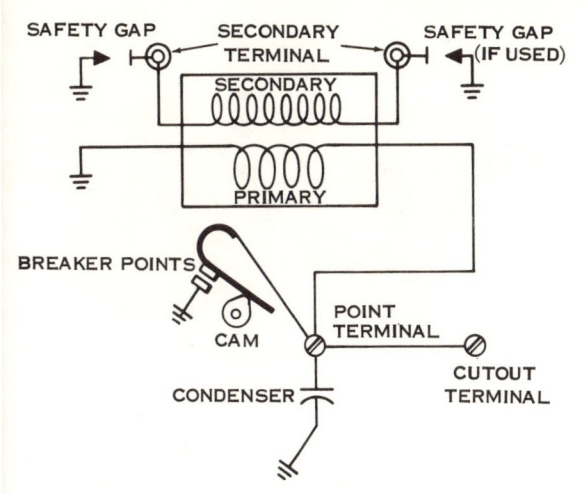

Carburetor Adjustments

Internal connections of magneto, Sportster models.

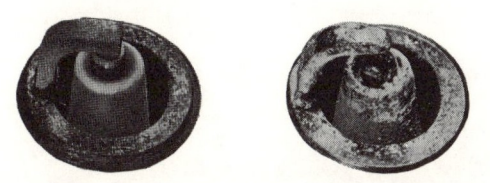

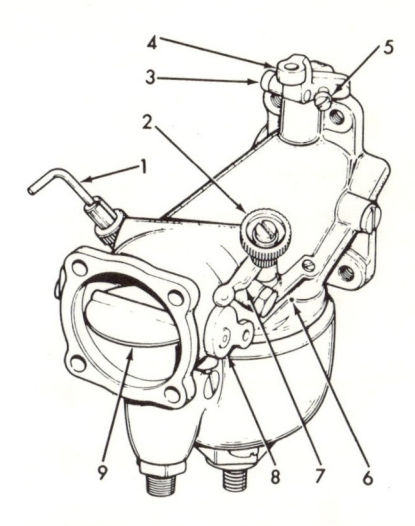

Model M carburetor controls and adjustments.

1. High-speed needle
2. Low-speed needle
3. Throttle lever lock screw
4. Throttle lever
5. Throttle stop screw
6. Carburetor bowl vent
7. Low-speed needle lift lever
8. Choke lever
9. Choke disc

Appearance of normal plug (left); plug too hot, mixture too lean (right).

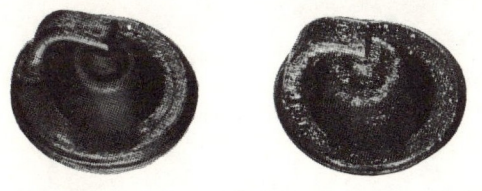

Plug too cold, mixture too rich (left); oil fouled spark plug (right).

If circuit breaker still cannot be shifted far enough to obtain point opening, repeat operation of lifting magneto and changing engagement of driving gears until proper point timing is obtained.

After correct timing is obtained, secure magneto base mounting bolts and recheck ignition timing as follows:

Turn engine in direction in which it runs until just after front intake valve closes and piston is coming up on compression stroke. Continue turning engine very slowly until timing light goes out, then see if flywheel timing mark is in center of hole. If timing mark is not in center of hole, loosen mounting bolts or turn adjusting screw to shift magneto as required. When rechecking, always turn the engine in the direction it runs. When correct timing is obtained, retighten the magneto base mounting bolts, reconnect coil lead wire to point terminal post and replace cover.

SPARK PLUGS

Plugs generally fail because of imposed operating conditions. Carbon formation, lead fouling from gasoline additives, and other destructive forces cause the electrodes to cease being the easiest path for current to follow.

Best advice about plugs is *replace rather than repair*. The accompanying illustrations disclose various plug conditions and causes. A study of them and a comparison between the photos and your bike's plugs will do much to educate you on engine operating conditions.

Always use the plug recommended by the manufacturer for normal conditions. If the recommended plug is clearly too hot or too cold for the conditions your cycle encounters, go to the next step in heat range. Set the gap right, keep it clean, and you'll have a spark if the rest of the ignition system is working.

CARBURETOR ADJUSTMENTS

In routine tune-up, only idle mixture strength and curb idle speed settings are involved. But high-speed adjustments can also be necessary or valuable. If the mixture is too rich or too lean, power is lost, plugs foul or burn, etc.

Two clues as to settings are:
    (a) Visual evidence of mixture strength
    (b) Performance

Under (a), we find the condition of exhaust pipe (sooty, gray or white), color of exhaust smoke, and condition of spark plugs.

Under (b), we go by experience.

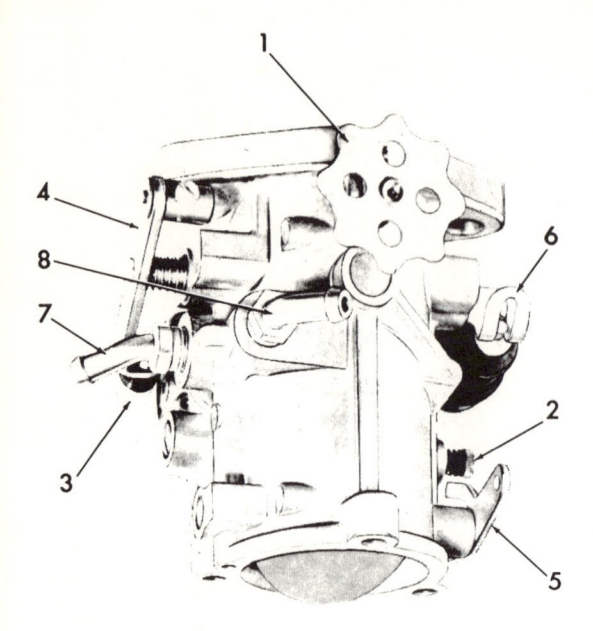

Maintenance and Tuning

Model HD carburetor adjustments.

1. Low-speed needle
2. Intermediate-speed needle
3. Throttle stop screw
4. Throttle lever
5. Choke lever
6. Accelerating pump
7. Inlet fitting
8. Vent fitting

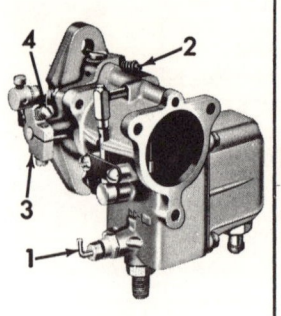

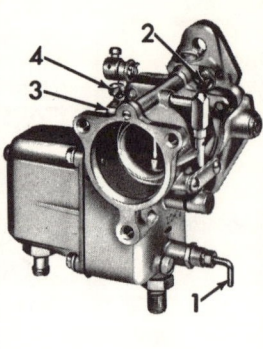

SPORTSTER AND ELECTRA-GLIDE   SERVI-CAR

Model DC carburetor.

1. High-speed needle
2. Low-speed needle
3. Throttle lever
4. Throttle stop screw

Model M carburetor (1965 model).

1. Choke
2. Idle speed stop screw
3. Carburetor control coil adjusting nut
4. Air cleaner silencer
5. Screw

"M"-type carburetor

Refer to drawing for parts identification and follow the Harley factory's advice:

① With the engine warmed up and idling, turn both low and high-speed needles all the way in (clockwise).

② Back out the low speed needle five turns.

③ Back out the high-speed needle two turns. With needles in these positions, the engine will start, but the mixture will be too rich.

④ Advance spark all the way or nearly all the way, whichever is best.

⑤ Turn low-speed needle in, one notch at a time, until the mixture becomes so lean that the engine misses and acts starved.

⑥ Back out the needle five to ten notches, or until engine hits regularly with spark advanced and throttle closed, or as nearly closed as it can be set and still have the engine run at idling speed.

⑦ Adjust throttle lever stop screw (5) to make engine idle at desired speed with throttle fully closed. Turning screw clockwise makes engine idle faster. Never set idle adjustment to slowest possible speed. An extremely slow idle causes bearing wear, oil consumption and slow speed accelerating difficulties.

⑧ Make final readjustment on low-speed needle. Try one notch at a time, first in and then out, to see if engine picks up speed or runs more smoothly. Starting and all-around carburetion will be better with low speed adjustment set slightly rich rather than lean.

⑨ If necessary, make further adjustment on idle stop screw to obtain desired idling engine speed. Retard spark completely. If carburetor is properly adjusted, engine will continue to run evenly and smoothly, though more slowly.

The high-speed adjustment should be carried out with the engine under load, but it can be made on the stand where the engine's ability to respond to sudden increase in throttle opening is the test.

① Set the spark to advanced position and blip the throttle, opening it up suddenly, accelerating to high speed and closing it abruptly.

② Screw the high-speed jet needle in until the

Setting Valve Lash

engine hesitates and dies or backfires.

③ Screw the control out gradually, blipping the throttle until the condition clears up. This is ordinarily about ¼ turn, but in old carburetors, it could be anything.

After adjusting the high-speed jet, it will probably be necessary to reset the idle to desired speed.

On-the-road adjustment is made by turning the high-speed needle control back and forth until the best acceleration characteristics from about 30 mph up to 50 mph are found.

The big problem with many of these carburetors is warpage of the flange caused by improper bolt tightening in the hands of past owners or mechanics. Air leakage is the result, and all the twiddling in the world won't bring them into adjustment. Check with an oil can filled with gasoline, i.e., squirt fuel at the flange base with the engine idling. If the engine speeds up, you've got an air leak.

Model HD carburetor

The same procedure is followed as for the "M" carburetor, but start with both low (1) and intermediate speed (2) needles at ⅞ of a turn back from bottoming. This is too rich, but it is the starting place. About ¾ of a turn on both needles seems to work at most altitudes.

Model DC carburetor

With this carburetor, we start with both needles backed off 1½ turns from fully screwed home. Follow procedure under "M" for idling and road adjustment. Best results will generally be found with high-speed needle about ¾ to 1¼ turns open. Keep this on the lean side is the advice of veteran riders.

SETTING VALVE LASH

GLIDE MODELS

Flywheel rotation is clockwise (viewing engine from right side). Using the front cylinder firing position as a starting point, the rear cylinder fires at 315 degrees rotation (360 degrees minus the 45 degrees between cylinders). The front fires in an additional 405 degrees (360 degrees plus the 45 degrees between cylinders), completing the 720 degrees of flywheel rotation necessary for the four piston strokes.

A single cam shaft with four cam lobes is gear driven. The engine valves are opened and closed through the mechanical linkage of tappets, pushrods and rocker arms. Tappets serve to transmit the cam action to the valve linkage. Hydraulic lifters installed in the tappets automatically compensate for heat expansion to maintain a no-lash fit of parts. Valve and breather timing are obtained by meshing gearcase gears with timing marks aligned.

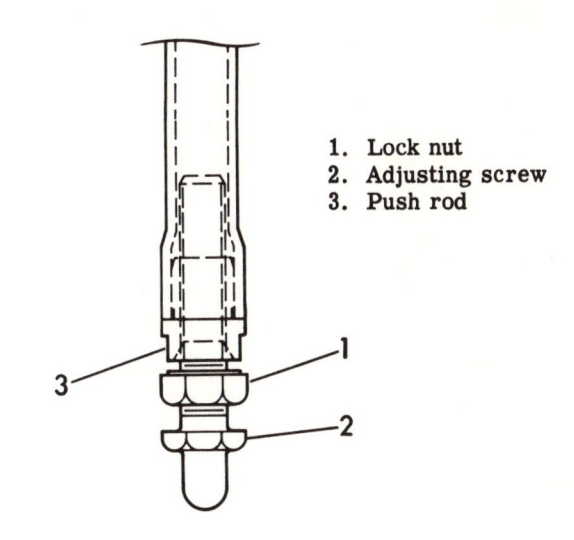

1. Lock nut
2. Adjusting screw
3. Push rod

Adjusting tappets, Glide models.

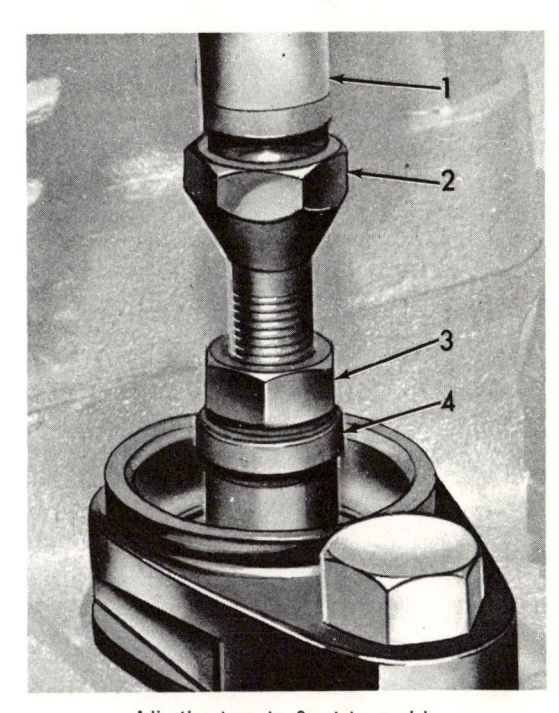

Adjusting tappets, Sportster models.

1. Push rod
2. Tappet adjusting screw
3. Tappet adjusting screw lock nut
4. Tappet body

With engine cold (air temperature, preferably several hours after operating):

① Loosen tappet adjusting lock nut. *Note:* Always adjust tappets with pushrod at its lowest position. Lowest position may be found by rotating engine until like tappet (intake or exhaust) in other cylinder is at highest point (valve fully open).

② Turn adjusting screw upward, shortening pushrod until pushrod has noticeable shake.

③ Keep pushrod from turning by holding with wrench on flats provided at base of pushrod.

④ Slowly turn pushrod adjusting screw downward, lengthening rod, until all shake has been taken up.

⑤ Mark adjusting screw with chalk and turn it downward exactly four full turns.

⑥ Lock adjustment by tightening tappet adjusting lock nut.

SPORTSTER MODELS

Flywheel rotation is clockwise (viewing engine from right side). Using the front cylinder firing position as a starting point, the rear cylinder fires at 315 degrees rotation (360 degrees minus the 45 degrees between cylinders). The front fires at an additional 405 degrees (360 degrees plus the 45 degrees between cylinders), completing the 720 degrees of flywheel rotation necessary for the four piston strokes.

① Press down on pushrod cover spring retainer and remove keeper at upper end. Cover then telescopes.

② Loosen tappet adjusting screw lock nut.

③ Turn adjusting screw downward (into tappet body) until pushrod is just free and has noticeable shake. When checking for pushrod shake, grasp pushrod with fingertips just below cylinder head and shake toward front and rear of engine.

④ Slowly turn adjusting screw upward (toward pushrod) until nearly all play is removed.

⑤ At this point, lock tappet screw lock nut against tappet body and recheck for correct tappet adjustment. Tappet is correctly adjusted when pushrod has slight amount of play or shake and can be turned completely around freely with fingertips without a trace of bind.

⑥ When reassembling pushrod covers, make sure that both ends of covers are properly seated against cork washers.

CHAPTER 9
Specifications

Glide Models

Dimensions
Wheel base .... 60"
Overall length .... 92"
Overall width .... 35"

Capacities
Fuel tanks .... 3½ gallons (U.S.)
                    1965—5 gallons (U.S.)
Oil tank .... 1 gallon (U.S.)
Transmission .... 1½ pints

Engine
Model designation letters .... FL - FLH
Number of cylinders 2
Type .... 45 degree V type
Horsepower ..... FLH..60.0 hp at 5400 rpm
               FL ..55.0 hp at 5400 rpm
Taxable horsepower 9.44
Bore .... (87.3mm) 3⁷⁄₁₆"
Stroke .... (100.8mm) 3³¹⁄₃₂"
Piston displacement ... (1207cc.) 73.66 cu. in.
Torque .... FLH..65 lb./ft. at 3200 rpm
               FL ..62 lb./ft. at 3200 rpm
Compression ratio .... FLH..8 to 1
                            FL ..7.25 to 1
Spark plug (heat range for
   average use) .... No. 3–4
Connecting rod—fit on
   crankpin ...001–.015" loose (1959 & earlier)
            .0006–.001" loose (1960 & later)
Cam gear end play .... .001–.005"
Sprocket shaft bearing
   end play .... .0001–.010" (below 63FL5076)
               .0005–.006" (above 63FL5076)
Pinion shaft roller bearing
   fit .... .0004–.0008" loose
Pinion shaft/cover bushing
   fit .... .0005–.0012" loose

Transmission
Type .... Constant mesh
Speeds—foot shift .... 4 forward
       hand shift .... 4 forward
            (optional) 3 forward and 1 reverse

Note: The engine (serial) number is stamped on the left side of the engine crankcase. Always give this number when ordering parts or making an inquiry.

Sportster Models

Dimensions

	XL, XLH	XLCH
Wheel base		
(to 1966)	56½ in.	57 in.
(1967)	58½ in.	
Overall length		
(to 1966)	87 in.	83¼ in.
(1967)	89 in.	
Overall width	34 in. (to 1966)	29½ in.
	(1967)	34 in.
Overall height	40½ in.	42 in.
Road clearance		
(1966 & earlier)	2½ in. min.	4⅛ in. min.
(1967)	4⅛ in. min.	

Capacities

	XL, XLH	XLCH
Gasoline tank (U.S. gallons)	4.0	2.2
Oil tank (quarts)	3	3
Transmission (pints)	1½	1½

Engine
Model designation letters ... XL, XLH, XLCH
Type of engine .... 4 cycle OHV
Number of cylinders 2
Placement of cylinders ..... 45 degree, V type
Horsepower .... XL 42 hp at 5500 rpm
              XLCH, XLH 55 hp at 6300 rpm
Taxable horsepower 7.2
Weight .... XLCH ...... 188 lbs.
                  XL, XLH .... 204 lbs.
Bore .... (76.2 mm.)..3.000 in.
Stroke .... (96.8 mm.) 3.8125 in.
Piston displacement .... (883 cc.) 53.9 cu. in.
Torque .... XL 48 lb.-ft. at 3600 rpm
           XLCH, XLH 52 lb.-ft. at 3800 rpm
Compression ratio ..XL .... 7.5 to 1
                  XLCH, XLH .. 9.0 to 1
Spark plugs (heat range for average use) .No. 4

Note: After break-in period, No. 5 plug is recommended for hard service—XLCH and XLH models.

The engine (serial) number is stamped on the left side of the engine crankcase. Always give this number when ordering parts or making an inquiry.

Specifications

Transmission

Type .... Constant mesh - foot shift
Speeds .... 4 forward

Number of Sprocket Teeth	1966 & Earlier XL-XLH 1967 XLH-XLCH (Optional)	1966 & Earlier XLCH 1967 XLH-XLCH (Standard)
Engine	34	34
Clutch	59	59
Transmission	21	20
Rear Wheel	51	51

Gear Ratios	1966 & Earlier XL-XLH 1967 XLH-XLCH (Optional)	1966 & Earlier XLCH 1967 XLH-XLCH (Standard)
First (Low) Gear	10.63 to 1	11.16 to 1
Second Gear	7.69 to 1	8.08 to 1
Third Gear	5.82 to 1	6.11 to 1
Fourth (High) Gear	4.21 to 1	4.42 to 1

Tire data

Tire size—
  XLCH, 1967 XLH .... Front 3.25/3.50 x 19
                                Rear   4.00 x 18
Tire size—1966 & earlier XL, XLH .. 3.50 x 18
Tire pressure—
  XLCH, 1966 & earlier XLH .. Front 14 lbs.
                                      Rear 18 lbs.
  1967 XLH .... Front 16 lbs.
                                      Rear 20 lbs.

Note: The tire inflation pressures given are based on a rider weighing approximately 150 lbs. or more. Increase tire pressure as follows: For each 50 lbs. of overload, increase pressure of rear tire 2 lbs., front tire 1 lb.

ALGONQUIN REGIONAL LIBRARY.
Parry Sound, Ontario